The
Use of
the Bible in
Theology/
Evangelical
Options

ROBERT K. JOHNSTON
Editor

Wipf and Stock Publishers
EUGENE, OREGON

Wipf and Stock Publishers
199 West 8th Avenue, Suite 3
Eugene, Oregon 97401

The Use of the Bible in Theology/Evangelical Options
Edited by Johnston, Robert K.
Copyright©1997 by Johnston, Robert K.
ISBN: 1-57910-097-X
Publication date 12/9/1997
Previously published by John Knox, 1997

to Anne
whose basic theological insights
serve as a constant reminder of
the need for a professional
theologian to remain humble

Acknowledgments

I wish to thank each of the essayists for taking time from their crowded schedules to reflect self-critically on their own approaches to the theological task. Thanks are due as well to two of my student assistants, Kent Egging and Noel Cisneros, for helping with the notes and bibliography. I am indebted to Marjorie Carlson, Anne Stevenson, and Cheryl Boydston for helping in the preparation of the manuscript. Finally, without Walter Sutton's early commitment of John Knox Press to the project, it would never have gotten off the ground.

Robert K. Johnston
North Park Theological Seminary

Foreword

In her book, *The Anatomy of Judgment*, M. J. L. Abercrombie bemoans the fact that among her medical students in London "scientific ways of thinking did not automatically result from learning the facts of science." When dissecting an animal, for example, students "often did not distinguish sufficiently sharply between what was there and what they had been taught 'ought' to be there." She found that the average medical graduate has a well-loaded memory, but "tends to lack curiosity and initiative; his powers of observation are relatively underdeveloped; his ability to arrange and interpret facts is poor; he lacks precision in the use of words."[1]

There is a danger that we who identify with the evangelical wing of the Christian church are in a comparable position to Abercrombie's medical students with regard to our understanding and explication of the Christian faith. It is this situation that the following essays address. Although the "facts of Scripture" are memorized and the truths of the "orthodox" faith affirmed, there is too often a lack of curiosity and initiative, an underdevelopment in our power of observation, an imprecision in the use of words, and an inability to arrange and interpret biblical, traditional, and cultural facts. That is to say, the danger is that those of us within the wider Christian church who are committed to Scripture as our ultimate authority—who are modern day evangelicals—lack the ability to discern clearly the "data" of the Christian faith and to translate it into authentic and consistent thought and action.

It is the need for more adequate judgment, for theological wisdom, that many evangelicals are recognizing as a pressing concern. How do we evangelicals interpret the authoritative Word? In doing theology, what is the role of the imagination? Reason? Tradition? The believing community? The Holy Spirit? The wider culture? How do we evangelicals use the Bible for faith and life? In what sense is theology necessarily constructive in its approach rather than merely descriptive?

Some have viewed evangelical theologians who ask such questions as "post-Evangelical pilgrims."[2] But such is not the case. A chief watershed for evangelicals is not the willingness (or lack thereof) to address matters of theological method and interpretation. Theology as a human enterprise has no other choice. (Perhaps a willingness to consider method does distinguish evangelicals from Fundamentalists, however.[3]) The watershed, rather, is one's continuing commitment to the Bible as the Christian church's ultimate authority. It is for this reason that the title for the collection of essays has been chosen: *The Use of the Bible in Theology/Evangelical Options.*

The genesis of this volume was the planning sessions of the Evangelical Theology Group of the American Academy of Religion, then chaired by Mark Lau Branson of InterVarsity Christian Fellowship. Wanting to explore the issue of evangelical theological hermeneutics, the group asked me to organize and lead a half-day discussion on the topic. The result was a consultation at the AAR annual meeting in New York in December 1982, at which Gabriel Fackre, James Packer, John Howard Yoder, and Clark Pinnock presented preliminary drafts of their papers in this collection and Donald Dayton and Paul Mickey offered responses. From that beginning the volume has grown in an effort to represent as wide a spectrum of the evangelical community as possible. A variety of traditions are included in what follows. Donald Bloesch and William Dyrness are Reformed; Donald Dayton, Wesleyan; Clark Pinnock, Baptist; Russell Spittler, Pentecostal; James Packer and Robert Webber, Anglican; John Yoder, Mennonite; David Wells and Gabriel Fackre, Congregational; and myself, Free Church.

It will be evident to readers of this volume that not only a wide diversity of backgrounds but also a plurality of methodologies prevails within evangelicalism. There is much present ferment. Yet there is also a singularity of authorizing norm. Such a theological position—at one and the same time open and defined—is only now beginning to be appreciated both within and outside the evangelical church. Yet its potential for creativity should not be minimized.

I am reminded of Igor Stravinsky's comments concerning his own composition of music:

> As for myself, I experience a sort of terror when, at the moment of setting to work and finding myself before the infinitude of possibilities that present themselves, I have the feeling that everything is permissible to me. . . . I shall overcome my terror and shall be reassured by the thought that I have the seven notes of the scale and its chromatic intervals at my disposal, that strong and weak accents are within my reach, and that in all of these I possess solid and concrete elements which offer me a field of experience just as vast as the upsetting and dizzy infinitude that had just frightened me. It is into this field that I shall sink my roots, fully convinced that combinations which have at their disposal twelve sounds in each octave and all possible rhythmic varieties promise me riches that all the activity of human genius will never exhaust. . . . I have no use for a theoretic freedom. Let me have something finite, definite. . . .[4]

The given of eighty-eight notes on the piano keyboard provided Stravinsky a context for creativity. Similarly, evangelical theologians have found in the sixty-six books of the Bible the limits within which to develop their Christian thought. The permutations and combinations are inexhaustible within the limits of a biblically authorized perspective. Here is both the defining and the liberating stance that characterizes American evangelical theology in the 1980s.

Contents

Happily, one need never claim to be doing theology well, only to be doing it rightly. For one does it in the communion of many saints, living and departed, who think better, pray better, and love better.

Geoffrey Wainwright, "Towards God," *Union Seminary Quarterly Review* 36, supplementary issue (1981), p. 21.

The Lord has more light and truth yet to break forth out of His Holy Word.

John Robinson

All Scripture is inspired by God and profitable for teaching, for reproof, for correction, and for training in righteousness, that the man of God may be complete, equipped for every good work.

2 Timothy 3:16–17

1   Introduction: Unity and Diversity in Evangelical Theology

ROBERT K. JOHNSTON
North Park Theological Seminary
Chicago, Illinois

Evangelicals are increasingly recognizing the need to ask methodological questions as they do theology. This is not a capitulation to modernity as a few continue to charge. Rather our growing hermeneutical concern is evidence of evangelicalism's continuing commitment to the lordship of Christ and the authority of Scripture. How can we better understand and explicate our faith? This is the rightful question evangelicals are beginning to address. It is not enough merely to exegete a text, although some traditionally have stopped here. Nor is it enough to repeat the theology of Luther, Calvin, or Warfield, although some continue to confuse Scofield and the Scriptures he annotated. Theology is neither simply "Bible" nor "tradition." What it is and how to do it, however, are more difficult to define.

Ninian Smart sticks close to the etymology of the word "theology" in his definition: "Doing theology, in the proper sense, is articulating a faith."[1] Granted, but how is this to be accomplished? In his book, *The Uses of Scripture in Recent Theology* (1975), David Kelsey provides a helpful starting point by demonstrating that Christian theology is always tied to the biblical text in some way.[2] This is true of all Christian theology, whether conservative or liberal. Kelsey, himself a liberal in theological orientation, chronicles how seven leading theologians have used the Bible in their theology. All see the Bible as in some sense authoritative, but each views it in a different light. For Warfield, the content is inspired; for Bartsch, it is distinctive. For Wright, Scripture's narrative shows God to be dynamic, while for Barth, it makes an agent (Jesus Christ) alive and present. For Thornton, Scripture's expressiveness is as image; for Tillich, it is as symbol; and for Bultmann, it is as myth. In each of the three final cases Scripture's expressiveness both gives the past its occurrence and occasions present reality. Kelsey comments, given the multiple use of Scripture to authorize a theological proposal, we must conclude that Scripture is only indirectly the authorizing agent. The real validation comes from the worshiping community. That is, Scripture's authority according to Kelsey must be viewed functionally as flowing from the body of believers. Scripture is what the church accepts as definitive for its faith and life.

Evangelical Theology's Unity

Such a proposal, however provocative, flies in the face of evangelicalism's commitment to the intrinsic authority of the Bible in all that it affirms. It is increasingly difficult to provide an inclusive definition of evangelicalism (Donald Dayton's article is helpful in pointing out the variety). Even Billy Graham has been quoted as saying, "Evangelicalism is a great mosaic God is building, but if you asked me to, I'd have a hard time giving you a definition of what it is today."[3] This is the same Graham about whom Martin Marty writes, evangelicals can be defined as "people who find Billy Graham or his viewpoints acceptable."[4]

Evangelicalism is "a river that doesn't have its banks very well defined," comments Robert Schuller.[5] Yet, although the banks might be ill-defined, the central theological channel can still be straightforwardly articulated. Evangelicals are those who identify with the orthodox faith of the Reformers in their answers to Christianity's two fundamental questions: (1) How is it possible for a sinner to be saved and to be reconciled to his or her Creator and God? (the answer: *solus Christus; sola gratia; sola fide*); (2) By what authority do I believe what I believe and teach what I teach? (The answer: *sola scriptura*).[6] Evangelicals, that is, have a personal faith in Jesus Christ as Lord and a commitment to the Bible as our sole and binding authority.

Evangelical theologians, thus, distinguish themselves from other theologians within the Christian community by accepting as axiomatic the Bible's inherent authority. Opinions abound concerning the role of tradition vis-à-vis Scripture. A variety of answers are given concerning the contribution of the theologian's context in his or her theological formulations. Some evangelicals stress the experiential dimensions of the Christian faith and see these as central to the theological enterprise. But within this diversity there is a centeredness. To use a phrase which became a benchmark for theology within my own denomination—the Evangelical Covenant Church—there is a commitment to ask the question: where is it written?

In the following collection of essays this biblical focus is clear. Gabriel Fackre writes, "Tradition is *ministerial* and Scripture is *magisterial*." Clark Pinnock similarly "would want to distinguish between a ministerial and a magisterial role for science in theology, just as for reason in theology." He goes on to define evangelicalism's theological center, saying, "Adherence to the Bible for me means acquiescence to all its teachings and a refusal to allow any rival to stand above it, whether tradition, reason, culture, science, or opinion." J. I. Packer argues for "the permanent binding force of all biblical teaching," and, to give a final example, John Yoder echoes this same sentiment, "The Bible will serve . . . as the total value frame in which priorities need to be determined."

Evangelical Theology's Diversity

Given evangelicalism's common theological center with regard to Scripture, it is surprising to some when evangelical theology's diversity in approach and perspective is highlighted. Some, in fact, confuse this plurality in method with Kelsey's functionalism, but this is to misunderstand the diversity's common underlying perspective. The collection of essays which follows, written by leading evangelical theologians, demonstrates convincingly the breadth of evangelicalism's umbrella. It is large in its stretch but not without its limits.

Thus, in the collection of essays J. I. Packer argues that the *"biblical texts must be understood in their human context"* while Donald Bloesch's christological hermeneutic emphasizes the need to go beyond the literal sense of the text to discern its larger significance. Theology must show forth Christ. Russell Spittler, on the other hand, argues for an exegetical theology. Only through a commitment to Scripture does he find validation for his tradition. For Clark Pinnock theology must be hermeneutical theology. The current tendency to relate theology to present-day issues is a "recipe for Scripture-twisting on a grand scale." Only what is revelation, i.e., only Scripture, can "be made a matter of theological truth."

David Wells argues for theology's twin tasks of "decoding" (of discovering what God has said in and through Scripture) and of "encoding" (of clothing that conceptuality in fabric native to our own age). William Dryness argues alternatively that to do theology properly "we must begin not with a doctrine of Scripture but with our life in the world." "Scripture will function much more like a musical score than a blueprint for our lives. A score gives guidance but it must always be played afresh." Here is a contextual hermeneutic that is two-directional.

For John Howard Yoder theology is an activity on behalf of the church. Its function is neither that of maintenance nor that of generalization, however. Theology is the church's servant through a missionary and aggressive "biblical realism." Theology protects against overly confident or overly relevant applications. It is meant to correct and renew the church.

For Robert Webber theology is an activity from out of the church's tradition. The standard for judging a theology's adequacy is not Scripture alone, for the thoughtful working out of much of theology took place in the centuries following the writing of Scripture. This is not to put church practice on a par with Scripture. It is only to recognize that the apostolic tradition did not fully emerge until the fourth and fifth centuries and, thus, it is the Church Fathers whom we must study if we are to theologize aright.

Finally, Gabriel Fackre argues for a "full-orbed approach" to theology. In this approach the world, the church, Scripture, and the gospel core all have their function.

From this survey which could be broadened still further to include evangelicals as diverse as Carl Henry (a philosophical rationalist) and Bernard Ramm (a Barthian), Paul Mickey (a process theologian), and James Olthius (a Dooyeweerdian), it should be apparent that there is no one evangelical theological methodology. Bloesch's christological focus can be contrasted with Spittler's exegetical theology. Packer's canonical interpretation provides something of a bridge, but it is still a third perspective on biblical interpretation. Wells' contextualization as application can be contrasted with Dyrness' contextualization as two-way dialogue between Scripture and world. And Dyrness in turn finds himself critiqued by Pinnock's hermeneutical theology. Yoder's theology for the church is rooted in present biblical realism; Dayton's, in a recovery of Wesleyan truth. Webber's church theology, on the other hand, is grounded in the developing dogma of the Fathers. Finally, Fackre would argue for an eclectic approach to the theological task, finding the gospel core to be theology's ultimate focus.

Just as evangelical social ethics spreads across a wide spectrum from Jerry Falwell to Mark Hatfield, from Jimmy Carter to Carl Henry, so evangelical theologians demonstrate a cross section of hermeneutical approaches. Those who interact with evangelical theologians will not encounter simply a conservative, theological monolith based in philosophical rationalism. Such a philosophical approach is but one of many options.

Evangelical Theology's Continuing Questions

Having recognized both the diversity and the commonality of evangelical theological hermeneutics—that is, both its freedom and its rootedness—it will be helpful to readers of this collection of essays if we return to ask with greater care concerning the nature of evangelical theology's diversity. What issues are surfacing? Where is the present ferment? Five questions can be isolated as being of particular current interest.

What Is the Role of Our Present Context in the Shaping of Our Theology?

Robert McAfee Brown, a mainline Presbyterian theologian, relates how he was brought up short by a Latin American colleague who asked him at a conference, "Why is it . . . that when you talk about *our* position you call it 'Latin American Theology,' but when you talk about *your* position you simply call it 'theology'?"[7] Such a question could rightfully be addressed to traditional evangelicalism. Most of us have assumed ours to be the normative position, "that we stand at the point where the true understanding of Christian faith is located, and that others indulge in interesting cultural or geographical deviants from our norm."[8] Writing in 1977, Harvie Conn of Westminster Theological Seminary bemoaned this "Evangelical failure of awareness of our cultural boundness." He spoke of a typical "Evangelical thinness of treatment" regarding our cultural rootedness.[9]

Yet, "the times, they are a-changing." Evangelicals are increasingly becoming involved in contextual theology. This is not without its debate, however. The growing difference within evangelicalism regarding contextualization is described helpfully by David Wells in his essay: "In the one understanding of contextualization, the revelatory trajectory moves only from authoritative Word into contemporary culture; in the other, the trajectory moves both from text to context and from context to text. . . ." Increasingly, evangelicals are opting for the second of these models—an "interactionist" approach, to use William Dyrness' terminology. Mission strategists and Third World evangelicals like Charles Kraft, Rene Padilla, and Harvie Conn are arguing strongly for a hermeneutical circulation.[10] Without capitulating to "humanistic patterns overlaid on the Scripture," theologians must reformulate Christian truth "in terms of new conceptual frameworks" and these new "conceptual frameworks themselves must be reformulated in terms of the Scripture."[11] Here is one approach to evangelical contextualization, a hermeneutical circulation.

Others, such as Clark Pinnock, are suspicious of such two-way conversation, believing Scripture's authority to be compromised in the process. David Wells similarly would argue for a contextualization in regards to application, but not with reference to one's basic understanding of doctrine. One might say that, for him, contextualization is what changes doctrine into theology. Doctrine, however, is pre-contextual.

Is a fully developed contextualization the opportunity to hear Scripture speak again with clarity and conviction, or is it the abdication of a commitment to biblical authority? If the danger is syncretism, on the one hand, the danger is a complacency, on the other hand, toward God's particular address. Harvie Conn writes:

> . . . the fear often is expressed that the "rather amorphous middle position termed 'evangelicalism,'" living between a left wing capitulation to ethnology-sociology and a right wing reaction to the same disciplines, "seems more ready to expend their time and energy in defense of older formulations of Christian truths than to grapple with the matter of reformulating these truths in terms of new conceptual frameworks." . . . the alternative fear . . .[is] that the growing interest in what some have labelled ethno-theology or "contextual theology" (as opposed to systematic theology) may be done without sufficient attention to a biblically critical analysis of the systems of anthropology and sociology and appropriated by the evangelical. . . .[12]

Common human experience and Christian fact must both be reflected on theologically. How these two "sources" for theological reflection are to be in co-relation so as to preserve the integrity of each remains the question.

What Role Can Tradition Play in Theological Formation?

In his inaugural lecture at Union Theological Seminary in New York (1980), Methodist Geoffrey Wainwright argued that any theology not substantially congruous with the Christian tradition was unprofitable to the church. He recalled that, in his first inaugural lecture at a seminary in Cameroon, he, an Englishman, had argued for the "Africanization of Christian worship." Now, he saw an opposite need as a newcomer to America—the "theologization of America." Wainwright pleaded, "We should be seeking to bring the churches and Christians of this country to a deeper awareness of the riches of the great Tradition."[13]

Increasing numbers in evangelical circles are agreeing with Wainwright. An important evidence of this fact was the Chicago Call, an appeal by forty-five evangelicals which was issued in May 1977. The Call read in part:

> We confess that we have often lost the fullness of our Christian heritage, too readily assuming that the Scriptures and the Spirit make us independent of the past. In so doing, we have become theologically shallow, spiritually weak, blind to the work of God in others and married to our cultures.[14]

The signers went on to argue:

> We dare not move beyond the biblical limits of the Gospel; but we cannot be fully evangelical without recognizing our need to learn from other times and movements concerning the whole meaning of that Gospel.[15]

For too long the evangelical church has operated from out of a theological parochialism, sometimes arrogant and always debilitating. Typically, evangelicals have viewed creeds and systems as of limited usefulness, valuable at best as road maps for the faith but unnecessary if you knew the way. Because it was possible for Christians (to say nothing of non-Christians) to misread Scripture, the church was right in developing a "mere Christianity" to aid readers.[16] However, in another sense there needed to be "no creed but the Bible." As long as it seemed that uniformity of biblical interpretation would prevail, Scripture seemed a sufficient guide.

Such an assessment is now receiving a challenging critique from within evangelicalism. At the extreme end of the evangelical spectrum are those like Michael O'Laughlin of the Evangelical Orthodox Church. He writes: "The Gospel cannot be fully comprehended outside of the timeless Church. . . . Standing within the tradition of the Church is necessary to properly interpret Scripture."[17] Others, like Robert Webber, also argue for the necessary role of tradition, even if their language is more moderate. Webber writes: "In the first place evangelicals should recognize that a doctrine of inerrancy is not a sufficient basis for authority. . . .evangelicals should recognize that the key to interpreting Scripture is the 'rule of faith.'"[18]

Not all agree with such assessments, however. Although understandable, "the longing for a tradition that will make sense out of our evangelical tower of Babel, the recoil from self-serving exegesis, and the dissatisfaction with the miserable and stultifying parochialism of much evangelicalism" should not cause us to opt for an authoritative creed (and an authoritative church resting behind the creed).[19] For which creed is to be chosen, and why? Or which Church Fathers are to be thought correct? Peter Abelard once illustrated the diversity of viewpoints among the early Fathers by citing one hundred and fifty examples in which they widely disagreed. Among the myriad of creeds and confessions that have been written, there simply is no univocal testimony.[20]

Can one really understand the "rule of faith" (standardized in the Apostles' Creed) as a "canon within the canon," or is all tradition rather (to use the words of James Dunn) a "*canon outside the canon*"?[21] How can tradition be used ministerially while Scripture remains magisterial? That is, can one place confidence in the positions of the Church Fathers, or Calvin, or Wesley, and still avoid placing tradition on the same level as Scripture? Such are the questions awaiting further discussion.

Are There Limits to the Critical Study of the Bible?

James Dunn, an English evangelical, in his article, "The Authority of Scripture According to Scripture," asserts there is evangelical unity regarding the Bible's inspiration and authority. "Where Evangelicals begin to disagree," he writes, "is over the implications and corollaries of these basic affirmations. . .

What does the assertion of the Bible's inspiration require us to affirm about the continuing authority of any particular word or passage of Scripture?" He asks where an evangelical "line of defense" should be pitched. Dunn argues that the line should not be drawn too restrictively, always allowing for the "intention" of the text. Otherwise, the authority of Scripture will prove to be "more abused than defended."[22]

It is clear to even the most casual observer that a commitment to biblical authority is not in itself a sufficient guarantee of biblical faithfulness. Adequate biblical interpretation is demanded. The Jehovah Witnesses are "Arian"; Victor Paul Wierwille's The Way International has a "dynamic monarchianism"; and Herbert W. Armstrong's Worldwide Church of God is binitarian. Yet all three are "inerrantists," as Robert Price points out. All hold to a strict, high view of Scripture.[23] What must be said is that some biblical interpretation is in error. But which? And by what criteria do you evaluate the various claims? Clark Pinnock centers the issue even more pointedly as he asks, "How is it that those who take a high view of the Scriptures are known to produce less by way of creative biblical interpretation than those who either bracket the question or treat the text as a human document?" Unfortunately, evangelicals have more often defended Scripture than expounded it. We have been preoccupied with its divine side and neglected its human dimension.

Fine and good. Many evangelicals have learned the lesson of the need to interpret. Over the last thirty-five years we have been challenged to engage in serious criticism and we have entered in. But are there critical limits? The following essays suggest two, though each is not without its evangelical skeptics. There is no uniform answer as of yet concerning the scope of the critical enterprise.

First, we must not set Scripture against Scripture in a way that closes off part of the canonical witness. Theologians like James Packer and Clark Pinnock are correct in arguing that the Bible must be read as a whole, coherent organism, for it is not only human words but also God's Word. Such an approach would reject any relativization of Old Testament Scripture. It would also reject those who would set Paul at irreconcilable odds with James or one of the Gospel writers. As Pinnock argues, "The doctrine of inspiration [authority?] implies belief in the coherence, if not tight uniformity, of Scripture and commits us to the quest for canonical wholeness." But where does diversity leave off and disunity begin with regard to interpretations? What qualifies as "coherence" remains the question. What constitutes contradiction?

Secondly, Scripture's intrinsic divine authority suggests the correlative qualification of human thought. For this reason *Sachkritik* ("content criticism") remains a problematic critical approach as does deconstructionism. Both set the interpreter's judgment over Scripture rather than understanding it as in the service of Scripture. Again a host of questions intrudes. Some evangelicals are asking: how can the historical character of biblical language be maintained if Scripture's intrinsic authority is asserted? Others, like James Dunn or Paul Jewett, see contradictions in the text that demand the arbitration of human reason. To qualify reason risks stultifying theology. Not to do so risks revelational abandonment. The interplay between human reason and divine revelation is complex; the limits to the critical study of Scripture are not easily defined.

Is There a Central Biblical Message or Schema That Can Control Our Theologizing?

Karl Barth, in his 1939 report to the readers of *The Christian Century* on "How My Mind Has Changed," wrote the following concerning his theological pilgrimage during the 1930s: "In these years I had to learn that Christian doctrine, if it is to merit its name and if it is to build up the Christian church in the world as she must needs be built up, has to be exclusively and conclusively the doctrine of Jesus Christ—of Jesus Christ as the living Word of God spoken to us men."[24] Thirteen years later Barth stated his position even more radically: "At the risk of more headshaking and displeasure I will at any rate venture to whisper one thing to you, namely, that I have become increasingly a Zinzendorfian to the extent that in the New Testament only the one central figure as such has begun to occupy me—or each and everything else only in the light and under the sign of this central figure."[25]

Barth is perhaps the best known contemporary theologian to develop a program of "christological concentration." But others, both evangelical and non-evangelical in orientation, have adopted similar methodologies. In his book, *Confessions of a Conservative Evangelical*, Jack Rogers makes clear both the distinction between two levels of approach to the Bible and his own preference: "The first level is the central saving message of the gospel. . . . Around that saving center lies a vast body of supporting material that is often complex, difficult to interpret, and subject to a variety of understandings."[26] Rogers, in emphasizing the first level, is consistent with his theological mentor, G. C. Berkouwer, who wrote: "Every word about the God-breathed character of Scripture is meaningless if Holy Scripture is not understood as the witness concerning Christ. . . . It is only regarding this centrality that it is legitimate to speak of the unity of Holy Scripture."[27] Such a christocentric model of interpretation also characterizes the approach of Donald Bloesch in this volume. He argues for the "need to go beyond authorial motivation to theological relation," i.e., to the Jesus Christ of sacred history who is our ultimate norm in faith and conduct.

A christocentric theological model is a means of both overcoming theological diversity and centering biblical teaching. Ecumenical dialogue becomes possible around the common confession, "Jesus Christ is Lord." So too does meaningful interaction with modern society. For a concentration on christology allows the theologian to escape becoming bound to a bygone world-view or a particular societal perspective. Even more importantly, a christocentrism allows one to concentrate on the Bible at its actual center (there is no "other foundation . . . than that which is laid, which is Jesus Christ" [1 Cor. 3:11].) In doing so, it helps preserve the theologian from indulging in false comfort to a world that knows neither "certitude, nor peace, nor help from pain."[28]

Yet there are questions which a christic approach must face.

Is the biblical text not itself a statement of truth, or is it only a pointer to some more central message? If it is a pointer, how does one avoid a subjectivism in the application of such a *sensus plenior* to Scripture? That is, what criterion for judgment is used in discovering Christ as the central message of each of the Bible's books? Why, for example, should we continue to spiritualize the Song of Songs? How is the authority of the text—of all the biblical text—maintained?

This question is particularly pressing with regard to the "antilegomena" (the "disputed books" of the canon).[29] Why should Jude be retained and the Didache rejected if a christological norm is imposed? And what of Esther? Bloesch argues that it is the Spirit acting within Scripture that gives us the theological significance of the biblical text, not what historical or literary criticism can tell us. But does the Spirit operate apart from the Word or even in addition to it? How can this move from Word to Spirit be carried out, so that there is neither friction nor reduction in the theological core? Such a question remains a pressing concern for evangelicals and non-evangelicals alike.

How Should the Role of the Spirit Be Understood in Theology?

The contributors to this volume tend to subsume the role of the Spirit under one of the other headings—Scripture, tradition, christology, and the present context. Representatively, Russell Spittler, the one Pentecostal contributor, develops his exegetical theology with only a concluding reference to the need to "link subjective piety with scientific (historic) objectivity." Spittler recognizes that "exegesis puts one in the vestibule of truth; the Holy Spirit opens the inner door." Nevertheless, objective biblical scholarship helpfully aided by tradition remains his focus, and the Holy Spirit is only indirectly and in conclusion mentioned as a contributor to evangelical theology.

Somewhat analogously, David Wells makes reference to Luther's delineation that the "three factors indispensable to the construction of 'right theology' are *oratio*, *meditatio*, and *tentatio*." *Oratio* (prayer) and *meditatio* (reflection on Scripture) are matters in which we engage. Thus, Wells discusses these in detail. *Tentatio*, however, is the work of God; it is "something which occurs to us and, for that reason," he concludes, "I wish to say little about it."

Donald Bloesch, on the other hand, gives the Holy Spirit a more explicit discussion, seeing the theologian's task as discovering not only "the intent of the author but also the way in which the Spirit uses this text to reveal the saving work of Jesus Christ." J. I. Packer argues similarly, as does Gabriel Fackre when he writes:

> Because there is an Author of this Book who works in, with, and under the authors of these books, neither source nor substance comes home until the truth of the affirmations met here convicts and converts. . . . Thus a double subjectivity is bound up with the soteric use of Scripture: God the subject by the power of the Holy Spirit present in the believer's subjectivity of encounter. When this happens . . . the doctrine of grace becomes a cry of exultation (below, pp. 217–218).

Fackre's comments are suggestive as they link theology to doxology—to praise of God given his presence among us.[30] Here is an area for further exploration by evangelical theologians.

But is this the extent of possible discussion concerning the role of the Holy Spirit in theological hermeneutics? Additional help comes from the German evangelical Helmut Thielicke. In his three-volume systematic theology, *The Evangelical Faith*, Thielicke begins with the work of the Holy Spirit.[31] It is the Spirit who grants accessibility to revelation affecting the miracle of divine self-disclosure, of participation in God's self-knowledge. Ontologically, God's being in himself takes precedence. But, noetically, we must begin with the actual encounter with God through his Spirit.

Both "modern" and "conservative" theologies are dismissed as Cartesian by Thielicke. That is, their focus on the human subject, whether as one who feels or as one who reasons, ends up subjecting the kerygma to an *outside criterion*. Christians must be pointed away from themselves and toward salvation history. They must be oriented to Christ by having his past actualized and made present to us. This is the work of the Holy Spirit, creating men and women anew, as they are incorporated into the salvation event. Such an approach does not ignore the human context, but sees it through the Spirit as the object of a retrospective glance.[32]

Where Spittler, Wells, Packer, Fackre, and Bloesch all moved from Word to Spirit in their hermeneutical discussions, Thielicke has instead written from the perspective of the Spirit. It is from out of one's real knowledge of God through the Spirit that propositions about God and God's Word must be formulated. But how this is to be done, that is, how Christian theology is to move from Spirit to Word without friction or reduction, is not fully resolved by Thielicke. Thielicke's personal truth is presentational; it is to be told in narrative form. In this sense Thielicke is similar to Fackre. What remains unclear is how Christian proclamation and doctrine are to flow out of and interpret this truth. The question remains: how should the role of the Spirit be understood as foundational for theology? Or can it be?

Concluding Remarks

Theology's sources are multiple as the above questions would indicate. John Wesley understood theology's resources to be Scripture, tradition, reason, and experience. In an earlier book I argued for these being Scripture, tradition, and world. I wrote, "Theology is the translation of Christian truth into contemporary idiom with an eye toward Biblical foundations, traditional formulations, and contemporary judgments."[33] In their book on *Protestant Christianity*, Claude Welch and John Dillenberger describe "the development of theology" as always being "a dual movement, an expression of the inner life of the community of faith as it acknowledges the presence of God in Jesus Christ, and at the same time a partial reflection of the contemporary world."[34] Donald Bloesch speaks of the need for a "catholic Evangelicalism," by which he means a theology that is grounded in the Word and open to the full range of Christian voices through the ages.[35]

Jack Rogers has argued in his survey of theology at the beginning of the 1980s:

> I am personally committed to the development of what I would call a *confessional centrist theology*. Such a theology would be evangelical in that it would be committed to the authority of Scripture as the model for theological judgments as well as the model for living a Christian life in faith. This theology would be committed to the centrality of Jesus Christ as the saving and transforming presence of God in human history. It would seek to remain in that central Christian tradition represented by the census among confessional statements of various Christian groups down through the ages. . . . It is important that a contemporary confessional centrist theology be open to the research data and the methods of analysis provided by the social and natural sciences.[36]

Such descriptions of theology's resources can be multiplied end-lessly. The questions remain: How are these various compo-nents of Christian thought to be combined? And what are their interrelationships?

In the following essays it is Gabriel Fackre's "full-orbed" the-ology that provides perhaps the most provocative description of theology's interrelationships. Whether or not one ultimately ac-cepts all the details of his description, he nevertheless shows what is at stake in seeking "to honor the contribution of a va-riety of constituencies. . . ." For Fackre, the *setting* which grants perspective to one's theology is the world. It is our cultural anal-ysis, contemporary experiences, and rational explorations that raise the formative questions and perceptions. Within this con-text the church, through its tradition, whether living or ancient, provides an invaluable *resource*. The church, moreover, focuses us inward, pointing us to the Bible—to Scripture and its narra-tive as our theological *source*.

The *substance* of the biblical record is the gospel story and its final *standard*, Jesus Christ himself, both as he speaks through his Spirit providing *illumination* and as he provides an objective norm against which to judge all truth in light of his full, histor-ical self-disclosure. Thus there is theologically, according to Fackre, a movement from the wider culture through the Chris-tian tradition to the biblical record with its definitive good news of Jesus Christ as revealed through his Spirit.

Such an ordering has consistency and force. Others will argue with it, desiring the role of tradition to be enhanced, or resisting a christocentric concentration within biblical interpretation, or desiring the Holy Spirit to provide our theological entry point. Whatever the delineation, however, the question remains: how are we to move reasonably between our present context, the widest possible Christian tradition, and an authoritative Scripture, while allowing the Spirit to witness definitively to Jesus Christ as savior and Lord? It is such a question that each of the following essays addresses. For it is just such a question that describes the challenge of the theological task for evangelicals today.

2   How I Use the Bible in Doing Theology

CLARK H. PINNOCK

McMaster Divinity College
Hamilton, Ontario, Canada

I

E. J. Carnell defined Protestant orthodoxy as *"that branch of Christendom which limits the ground of religious authority to the Bible."*[1] This major theological pre-understanding underlies my own approach to and use of the Bible. It means that the Bible is the one and only normative pole of theological information and that the claims of tradition or modernity possess no inner-theological relevance. I understand my task to be an explication of the deposit of faith in the Bible leading on to a serious attempt to communicate it in a relevant way to the people of my generation. The quest for relevance, important in itself, can never assume the influential role which only the Bible should have.

It is clear then why the question of biblical authority is so important to evangelicals: belief in the infallibility of the Scriptures is the pillar which supports our theology—without it the edifice would surely crumble. It is the realization of this, plus a sense that the Scripture principle is severely threatened in religious liberalism, which keeps the debate alive among us. Warfield could entertain in theory the possibility of Christianity existing without the Bible, but he would have been the first to stress its indispensability in practice.[2] I take Scripture to be, on what I think to be good and sufficient evidence, the prescriptive norm and paradigm tradition, the canon and rule of faith and practice. It is not enough to receive it as the occasion of an encounter with God (although it is) or as an invitation to join up with God's plan for human liberation (also true) or a host of other redefinitions of the nature of biblical authority. What it means to me to receive the Scriptures as the gift of God's Spirit to the church is that I subject myself, body, mind, and spirit, to whatsoever the Bible can be shown to teach or advise me according to its own intention. Mine is a stubborn creed when viewed from our age of theological permissiveness in that I am simply unprepared to back down from ascertained scriptural truth on the strength of any extra-biblical ground. Adherence to the Bible for me means acquiescence to all its teachings and a refusal to allow any rival to stand above it, whether tradition, reason, culture, science, or opinion. It leads me (some would say, compels me) to believe a string of truths regularly denied in circles which reject or reduce the Scripture principle: the reality of Satan; the existence of angels; the bodily resurrection and sacrificial atonement of Christ; the historical fall into sin; the deity as well as humanity of our Lord; the certainty of his coming again; and the dreadful judgment of the wicked.

Although my approach is identical to the basic stance of classical Protestants of the past, it is also marked by conscious awareness and opposition to the enormous ideational shift which has occurred in modern theology affecting this and all topics of theology. It is a shift in theological method from locating the basis of authority in the objective written Word of God to placing it in human reason and experience. It was done with the best of motives, a desire to make the gospel meaningful to the modern person but it resulted in a systematic revision of all Christian categories and, ironically, an almost total failure to reach the secular person for Christ. Indeed, the most obvious effect of this shift has been the reduction of the faith and the secularization of the churches. In the case of the doctrine of revelation and inspiration the shift meant that the Bible and its teachings came to be viewed as the product of human cultural experience, time conditioned and relative in authority, and certainly not a suitable cognitive guide to thinking persons today. The shift has created a great antithesis in the church between classical Christians who desire, as I do, to remain faithful to the faith once delivered and religious liberals by whatever name who seem intent on endlessly revising the message until it seems relevant to the modern person. I see no way to bridge this chasm. If we ever get beyond it I suspect it will be either from the demise of religious liberalism as it follows its course of self-destruction or from a failure of the evangelicals to grasp the present opportunity of leadership on account of their refusal to grow up to maturity in various areas. But at the present there is in place a great barrier reef, put there by religious liberalism in its zeal to "save" Christian beliefs, which stands as the great obstacle to unity of our time and as the reason why the doctrine of Scripture is certain to be debated in the foreseeable future.[3]

It is obvious that if the Bible is handled as a merely human document, then its claims may be accepted or rejected, its teachings may be in agreement or disagreement with each other, its subject may or may not be found relevant to our belief today. The advantage is that we are left free to follow our own light and opinion; the disadvantage, that we are left with no divine Word to guide us. The significance of the evangelical conviction in this context is that it stands as a granite boulder squarely in the path of liberal revision and therefore attracts a good deal of anger and contempt. It is a serious impediment to theological experimentation and by itself practically rules out most of the precious convictions liberals hold fast to: i.e., the validity of other religions, a purely functional christology, situational ethics, and the like. A high doctrine of Scripture and theological novelty do not go well together as everyone ought to be aware by now. *Sachkritik* is simply ruled out and this is all very frustrating to theological freethinkers. Therefore this concept of biblical authority is a weapons emplacement which must be destroyed first before the rest of Christian belief can be successfully breached. (Military imagery seems appropriate if we take a full measure of the seriousness of the present conflict.)

I am, of course, aware of a host of objections to my continuing to lean for support upon biblical infallibility. Wacker says it cannot do justice to the historical character of Scripture. Ruether claims she finds mistakes in the Bible. Dunn traces impossible contradictions. Ogden finds the true canon behind the canon. Critical scholarship is supposed to have proven the unscientific nature of belief in biblical authority. It is also held to be immoral and stultifying to restrict the mind in this way. Kelsey even charges that Warfield got his notion of authority from his mother's milk and not, as he thinks, from Jesus Christ and the Apostles. Psychologically one might say that it represents a childish wish for an oracular authority in order to make sense of the world; or that it jeopardizes the freedom of critical scholarship to play its needful role in theology; or that it forces theology to be just hermeneutical and never constructive; or that it cannot work because it is too optimistic about the classic text in terms of its unity and reliability and relevance; or that, inspired or not, the Scriptures still have to be interpreted by fallible persons whose agendas affect the work significantly and contaminate the source. It is quite obvious to me that unless conservative theologians pay more attention to explaining their methodological choice they will not be successful in gaining leadership in the higher levels of theological work whether their group is numerous or not. The future outlook is not clear. While it seems obvious that the revisionists are steadily surrendering their distinctively Christian identity and thus threatening their enterprise as a Christian one, it is not clear whether conservative theology is going to be able to rise to the occasion and give the answers which are called for. What a fine tragedy it would be if those with the most Christian and promising option proved unable to make good their case against many objections so that the shift away from classical faith continued despite their work and effort.

My first point registers the conviction that *the* primary hermeneutical principle arises from the decision how to approach the biblical text, whether to view it as I do as God's written Word or to see it in a reduced mode such as is common today. One's pre-understanding of the Bible either as God's infallible

Word or as merely human traditions from which both illuminating and distorting ideas come is critical to one's use of the Bible. I wish there were not a chasm between those who take it one way and those who take it the other but I fear that there is. I wish we could move beyond this "fundamentalist–modernist" conflict but I do not see how we can.

II

Having accepted the principle of biblical infallibility, the next point to emphasize is exegetical excellence. When I cite the Bible in support of some theological or ethical truth, it is essential that the citation be apt, intelligent, and discerning. I do not want to be sued by the Scriptures for exegetical malpractice. Satan, as Jesus discovered (Matt. 4:6), and false teachers, as Peter noticed (2 Peter 3:16), were quite prepared for and adept at twisting the Scriptures to serve their own ends, and no one is immune from doing the same thing. The fact that the very term "proof-texting" has such a bad ring to it is evidence of the frequent lack of exegetical excellence. It is troubling and disconcerting to look up the verses cited by orthodox theologians (but not just them) only to discover that the proof melts away under closer scrutiny of the meaning and context. Calvin's theology, on the other hand, is good theology because on the whole his exposition is careful and sound.

Evangelicals have no business feeling smug about their Scripture principle. We must stop pretending it is an easy matter to retrieve biblical answers to modern questions from the Bible. It sounds easy if you keep repeating the formula "infallible, infallible," but when you get down to work it is not so easy. What does the Bible teach about gender roles, about wealth and poverty, about violence, about capital punishment, about predestination? Is it not all too common to find people using the Bible as a weapon in their own particular cause quite irresponsibly? And when this happens do we not have to ask whether the Bible is highly regarded for its own sake or because it serves as a means of bathing our traditions in an aura of inerrancy? We ought to strive for exegetical excellence and ought not to suppose that it will always make us comfortable.

Lest the reader suppose that only classical authors can be faulted for Scripture-twisting, let me hasten to give an example of it in the most avant-garde liberal theology at the present time. Since Schleiermacher's day there has been a strong tendency to revise christology in the direction of a dynamic, functional model. A concerted effort has been made to understand Jesus as the embodiment of godliness rather than the incarnation of the eternal Son. In an effort to get the New Testament on the side of the liberal revisionists, exegetes are feverishly reworking their understanding of the old proof-texts for the true deity of Christ in order to undercut the metaphysical approach of the ancient creeds and of the vast majority of Christians. Until recently it was conceded that this revision could not claim the support at least of the fourth Gospel, though a fairly good case could be made for it elsewhere.[4] But now the final assault is being attempted even upon John's Gospel by J. A. T. Robinson who claims to be able to show that John's christology too goes no further than a revelational one.[5] Now we may understand why his early dating of John poses no threat to his radical theology as conservatives first thought it must. All I can say here is that such a hypothesis regarding the New Testament, which makes such nonsense of its soteriology (a man who merely reveals God cannot save us in the way the text says he can and does) and which goes against the *prima facie* sense of such texts as Philippians 2:6–9 and John 20:28, cannot long succeed whatever luminaries put their names to it.[6] It is perfectly clear to me at least that what motivates this "exegesis" is not scholarly objectivity but a desire for what is supposedly apologetic relevance. But with opponents of the high caliber of Dr. Robinson, the orthodox theologian has to keep on his or her exegetical toes.

Regarding this quest for exegetical excellence, I would admit that I have to take care to be more discriminating than evangelicals sometimes are. I have to take a close look at the text in its original context, observe its scope and direction, consider the question it may be answering, and the like. I must consider the strength of its affirmation, its place within cumulative biblical revelation, and its distinctive tone within the symphony of the scriptural choir. Appealing to the Bible for theological norms is a more difficult thing to do than many evangelicals are aware and I try to be cognizant of that myself. Not to accept these qualifications of exegesis is to run the risk of twisting the Bible in the name of conservative thought.

While we are on this subject, how is it that those who take a high view of the Scriptures are known to produce less by way of creative biblical interpretation than those who either bracket the question or treat the text as a human document? One might think that presupposing infallibility would stimulate relatively more productivity rather than less. It might be that the time of the conservatives is taken up in defending the Bible, not leaving them time to expound it. But that does not seem to be true, quite apart from the inelegance of such a situation in itself—the results in the area of methodology are not full and impressive enough to support this explanation. I suspect the answer is to be found in a less complimentary direction. I think that our preoccupation with the divine side of the Bible has resulted in our neglecting the human side of it and misled us into thinking that we have already grasped (and appropriated in our evangelical traditions) the revelational freight which it delivers. We have tended to opt out of critical study of the Bible and left it to others in a spirit of complacency as though the meaning of the Bible were exhausted already. If so, we are guilty of an impiety and will live to see the transfer of exegetical wealth from our side to the other.

III

In systematic theology we reach for the whole of the scriptural witness and try to comprehend it. Negatively this means that one is not free to leave anything out. Gordon Kaufman, even in his less radical days, could admit that God's wrath played no role in his theology of God, even though Jesus often spoke about it, because it falls foul of the reconstructed norm he has created by his own reading of the Bible. Wrath is no part of God's revelation in Christ as Dr. Kaufman sees it.[7]

Obviously I am not free to pick and choose between biblical doctrines as he is. I am not free to perform the theological reduction that marks the shift to humanity in religious liberalism. Nor am I at liberty to do what J. Christiaan Beker does when he reads Paul in a way that puts the Apostle at odds with much of the Pauline corpus and most of the rest of the New Testament.[8] It would not be true that I take this stance because I can easily see how to refute his actual argument. (Its weakness would perhaps lie in Galatians where the favored apocalyptic theme is marginal, endangering Beker's thesis. A proper refutation will have to be done by the New Testament scholars, not by theologians.) I simply presuppose its falsity on the grounds of my confidence in Scripture, the inspiration of which carries with it an assumption of its unity and coherence. Any hypothesis which postulates the self-contradictory character of the Bible is automatically suspect by the evangelical theologian. This frank admission of mine may lead scholars like Kümmel to conclude that objective scholarly work is excluded by such a presupposition belonging to theological orthodoxy.[9] It would interest me more to learn, however, just how scholarship which does *not* assume coherence in the Scriptures can credibly be called Christian scholarship.

Positively, the quest for the whole picture in the Bible means searching for the doctrinal models and keys which fit its complex locks and opening them up to the reader. Somewhat like scientific theories, dogmas are conceptual gestalts built up retroductively through imaginative attempts to render the biblical phenomena intelligible. The Bible itself is the "foot" which the doctrinal models must fit. As Montgomery puts it: "Science and theology form and test their respective theories in the same way; the scientific theorizer attempts objectively to formulate conceptual Gestalts (hypotheses, theories, laws) capable of rendering Nature intelligible, and the theologian endeavors to provide conceptual Gestalts (doctrines, dogmas) which will 'fit the facts' and properly reflect the norms of Holy Scripture."[10] The language of dogma may be different from the language of Scripture, but the message must be the same. The theologian must strive to duplicate the teachings of Scripture even if the latter is written in ordinary language and the theologian's own essays are written in a more academic mode. Both ways of speaking are valid, just as the different ways in which the meteorologist and the person in the street speak about the weather are valid.[11]

In appealing to the whole of Scripture I do not imagine either that the text is uniformly doctrinalist or that it assumes a simple unity of texture and emphasis. The Bible must be used circumspectly with a willingness to respect the kind of norm it is in every place. I try to have regard for the richness and diversity that it offers on all the major topics and not to force it into models dear to my church tradition. On the fall, the person of Christ, or the millennial reign, I seek to assemble the relevant data, not slighting any of it, and let my reflection partake in the inexhaustible richness of the text. This includes not forcing the analysis further than the data will allow. If the New Testament refuses to tell us how Jesus can be both human and divine at the same time (which it does), then I will have to live with that fact and look longingly at the questions I wish we could answer.

Reaching for the wholeness of Scripture is to read each text in the canonical context, not to see it as an atomic unit all alone but as a member of the divinely willed body of the canon such that the light of every part is shed on all the rest. The doctrine of inspiration implies belief in the coherence, if not tight uniformity, of Scripture and commits us to the quest for canonical wholeness. I am convinced that everything in Scripture is meant to be there and to have value. The challenge is to discover what truth and usefulness there is in it for us.

IV

In the quest for doctrinal models I also search for interrelationships between the concepts. The proper work of systematic theology is, after all, the search after coherence and intelligibility. I desire to understand not only the religious experience or the time-bound perspectives of the writers but also the system of truth deposited by the Spirit in this text. I want to go beyond analysis to synthesis, beyond an understanding of a concept like sin to an understanding of it in relation to the doctrine of Christ and his saving work. Theology, as Millard Erickson points out, is organic in character. The view one takes in one area will affect the interpretation at other points as well. One's view of the atonement will reflect one's understanding of the plight of humanity and what needs to be done to effect human salvation. If one's problem is ignorance, one needs to be informed; if it is fear, one needs to be assured; if it is guilt, one needs propitiation.[12] Just as the numerous strings of a piano have to be tuned in relation to each other, so the several truths of the Bible have to be viewed from many angles to determine the meaning of the whole. In doing so I am assuming that, whatever else the unity of the Bible may consist of (e.g., religious experience, overall perspective), it has a cognitive dimension to it which invites reflection on its truth claims.

How then does one find the system of truth which informs the Bible? While aware of the fact that one's denominational tradition provides it to us long before we seek it out, I contend that we ought to search the Scriptures for it. In the Bible there are, after all, generous clues as to the heart of its message. Luther turned to Romans to find the truth of God's plan of justifying sinners through the atonement of Christ. Here the Apostle Paul himself tells us what God is doing for us and saying to us. Luther read it as the heart of the gospel and the center of the Bible.[13] This is not the only clue and center even in the letters of Paul, not to speak of the New Testament at large, but it is a crucial dimension of it and gives the theologian a marvelous framework for displaying and exhibiting the message of the Bible in relation to the needs of people today. Because the Scriptures are richly textured and inexhaustible, it is important to leave the system loosely drawn in order to allow for new insights and changes of perspective which can always come. It should be seen as an interpretive hypothesis open to revision and useful for the task of proclamation. Given the variety of centers people seize upon (Luther, Calvin, Wesley, Barth), it is important that we be willing to explain and defend the center we have chosen. In particular it is essential to be able to show that the center was chosen not because of contemporary cultural concerns but on the basis of biblical substance. It is all right to be concerned about relevance, but one should not replace revelation with relevance.

The Bible itself places real limits on the systematic work we can do. We cannot go beyond the evidence. We have to respect the practical orientation of much of the text. We cannot invent new data or eliminate any. We have to learn to be content with what we have in exegesis too. We may even have to accept antinomies which offend the rational impulse.[14] Our curiosity must often go unsatisfied, and we must be willing to change our minds when the evidence mounts up against our treasured system and unseats it.

To be honest about this I would have to grant that the systematic framework we use is not ordinarily derived from a purely inductive examination of the Bible—it is given to us by the Christian tradition which we respect. We read the Bible as Baptists, or Anglicans, or Catholics, or Lutherans, and this fact influences what we read. It forcibly reminds us that the work of interpretation is not done by single individuals or even a single generation but by the catholic church over time. The system we receive is the product of the reflection on Scripture by countless believers for hundreds of years. As such it deserves respect, but being self-aware ought also to make us self-critical and open to correction. In my own teaching of theology I find it best to use, rather than a single textbook with a single point of view, a reader which presents several angles of interpretation on specifics and on the whole because it forces students confronting a plurality of systems to decide for themselves what the Scriptures say. My own hope is that the whole church would move toward a greater appropriation of its apostolicity, toward "the unity of the faith and of the knowledge of the Son of God, to mature manhood" (Eph. 4:13).

V

Now let me comment on how I relate to contemporary human concerns in my basically hermeneutical theology. Since I reject critical correlation in which one can critique the scriptural classic out of modern experience, and yet since I have to apply the text to the situation, whatever that situation is, how do I respond to challenges from the side of culture, reason, and tradition? Culture is a factor external to Scripture: how do I respond to the issues it continually throws up? Obviously it involves some swimming against the stream and a forfeiting of some of the liberty enjoyed by constructional theologians.

Modern theology is characterized by an acute awareness of the historicity of the interpreter and an equal passion to relate to what contemporary people bring to the text. It is as if the awareness of our time-bound condition has made us determined to conform theology to our situation rather than to protect it from possible corruption. I see the current tendency to relate theology to struggles of the present day, while commendable if it were to represent a desire to apply the Scriptures, to be a recipe for Scripture-twisting on a grand scale. The desire to be relevant and up-to-date has caused numerous theologians to secularize the gospel and suit it to the wishes of modern hearers (cf. 2 Tim. 4:3–4). The desire to be relevant has overcome the desire to be faithful to God's Word with the result that a great accommodation is taking place. Non-revelational factors are being permitted to take precedence over revelational norms. Bultmann's use of existential categories and Cobb's use of process thought cannot be explained in terms of biblical reflection but must be explained in terms of the influence of secular modernity. Our desire to be politically radical, or feminist, or gay, or religiously tolerant, or academically respectable—these are the factors moving much modern theology, not God's Word. And we must resist it as resolutely as the Reformers resisted the mistaken human opinions in Catholic theology at the time. Of course, I too am moved by all these pressures. I too would like to think that the Buddhist will be saved by faith apart from Jesus Christ and that the darker picture found in Romans might be overdrawn. But I cannot enjoy the luxury of such speculations when the Bible already indicates its mind on such matters.

The principle is that what is not revelation cannot be made a matter of theological truth. Only what is taught in Scripture is binding on the conscience. This was always our objection to earlier forms of Roman Catholicism—we must not add human traditions to the scriptural revelation as if they were binding on the church. We take the same line on the cults like the Mormons, Christian Science, and the Witnesses—it is unacceptable to allow the most revered writings or theories to occupy a place above the Scriptures. The same is true for the writings of Heidegger, Whitehead, Marx, and Freud. In them we find brilliant insights, but not the saving Word of God. From them we derive much useful analysis, but not written revelation. We take our stand against all those who infringe upon the authority of the Bible and the liberty of God's people by imposing on the church their own opinions as if they were final and enjoyed a status above God's Word. As Ramm put it, "The encroachment of the word of man upon the Word of God is a danger we should be constantly alert to, and with all our strength we should maintain the freedom of the Word of God from the word of man."[15] Fortunately the inexhaustible richness of Scripture ensures that our loyalty to it does not leave us without a relevant word to say to modern culture but actually unfailingly provides a compelling word to speak into the culture whatever that is.

Let me add that this does not mean that I ignore the influence of culture upon me as an interpreter. Obviously we are influenced by our place in history in a thousand respects. Yet this is the reason we must not succumb to it but must instead take measures to ensure that bias does not overcome God's truth. Precisely because we tend to be prejudiced (what people politely call "having a pre-understanding") we have to be self-critical and take action against the danger of Scripture-twisting. There is a hermeneutical circle, but it need not be a vicious one. What we need to do is to strive for such interpretation of the Bible which anyone reading the text can see even if he or she does not come with the opinions we hold ourselves. Perfect objectivity is not something we can achieve, but it is an ideal we can strive for by consciously opening ourselves to criticism and correction both by God, speaking through the text, and by the convictions of others.

VI

In relation to reason I have to strive to integrate independently arrived at convictions with Scripture in a biblically faithful manner. Reason may tell me, for example, that if God knows the future exhaustively, then every detail of it is fixed and certain and the freedom most humans believe they have (and which Scripture itself seems to say that we have) is an illusion. Biblical teaching about the divine foreknowledge appears to contradict biblical teaching about human freedom, and it is nigh unto impossible to see how the puzzle can be resolved rationally. The writers simply do not seem to feel that the two notions are mutually exclusive, but instead they place the two ideas in juxtaposition at every turn and seem indifferent to our intellectual dilemmas. This drives us back to a more precise definition of freedom, to speculations about time and timelessness, to problems of theodicy, to discussions about God's will(s), and the like. The whole issue has been debated practically nonstop for hundreds of years and resists a final word. The lesson we have to learn from this is not to reduce such questions to a simple solution which tampers with the scriptural data. We must not seize the sovereignty pole and block out the human freedom pole, or vice versa, which would violate the Bible's integrity. Theologies which have tended to do this have resulted in really unfortunate positions by way of implication and extension. The biblical balance is what we should strive to maintain in our theology too. The mark of a wise and sound theologian is to let the tensions which exist in the Bible stay there and to resist the temptation from reason to tamper with them. In this particular case, the metaphysical competence of our reason is humbled. I cannot tamper with the data as regards divine sovereignty and human freedom just because it would be easier if one were at liberty to do so.

As for the area of creation and science, has not reason compelled us to abandon the referential meaning of the biblical texts in Genesis and forced us to treat them in a theological and even mythological way? No, that is not the situation I find myself in. Science has surely forced me to re-examine aspects of the traditional exegesis of the text, but it has by no means had the effect of discrediting the source or forcing me existentially to reinterpret it. Science has raised new questions for the text to answer but by no means has it replaced the Scriptures as the authority. I would want to distinguish between a ministerial and a magisterial role for science in theology, just as for reason in theology. Just as we use insights from archaeology and linguistics to shed light on what the text says, so science sends us back to the Bible with new insights that need do no violence to the text but still illuminate it. Upon re-examining the biblical narratives in the light of these insights I find new ways of interpreting them which involve no immoral Scripture-twisting. The polemical characters of Genesis 1 and the symbolic nature of Genesis 2 and 3 are both close to the original intent of those texts and in agreement with certain of the scientific theories now widely entertained. At the same time, scientific thought in all these areas is far from unified or complete, and there is no particular urgency to reconcile every discrepancy at this time. When one finds Fred Hoyle announcing his conviction that evolution cannot have taken place on this planet from scratch in the time available, but must instead have been brought in from outer space, the Bible believer obviously is under no pressure to get into line with the evolutionists whose house itself appears to be in considerable disrepair. New light can arise from science and help us in our understanding, but nothing from that quarter need make us forsake the Scripture principle.

Another scientific objection occurs in the judgment of many against the mighty acts of God recorded in the gospel. It is often maintained that a scientific viewpoint presupposes a uniform continuum of cause and effect which would require us to reject the supernatural and magic. In part, this is a question of people's plausibility structures. Undoubtedly those with a materialist frame of reference do find it impossible to take seriously such a claim as Jesus' bodily resurrection. But, then again, not everybody has this frame of reference. Believers in the living God shape their expectations of the world in relation to this belief so that the question of credibility looks quite different. Besides, in the wider society it is by no means the case that most people accept the narrowly materialist reading. On the contrary, we see evidence of paranormal beliefs everywhere: in amulets; in astrology columns; in clairvoyance; in mediums; in the quest for healing. Obviously it is an exaggeration to say that the "modern person" can and cannot believe in this area, and it is quite presumptuous to legislate metaphysically what can and cannot happen. While it is true that the scientific method cannot easily handle the category of non-natural objects or events (like the Shroud of Turin), this fact does not say anything about the possibility of miracle. This lack of ability to address miracles may create a problem for apologetic strategy should we want to argue evidentially from miracles, but it really poses no great theological difficulty.[16]

Reason is a faculty of great usefulness to theology and exegesis. Occasionally it rises up to challenge Scripture and when it does we ought to put it in its place, its place being a supportive, ministerial, non-legislative one. But for the most part reason serves us well.

VII

In relation to tradition, is this not an extra-biblical factor which affects my use of Scripture and refutes the claim that it is the sole norm? Obviously tradition does color the way I read my Bible. When I, as a Baptist, or my sister, as a Catholic, reads the verse "this is my body," a flood of opinions pour out as to the meaning of that text. These traditions of ours provide contexts in which the search for its meaning has gone on and is going on.

In the case of all great classic literature like the Bible or Shakespeare, people have pored over it for centuries and placed various constructions and estimations upon the work. All of it together represents a rich comprehension of the original text which guides the new reader's own quest.

Tradition serves me in another way as well. When I confront heretical teachers who advance their novelties in the name of some lost-sight-of exegetical insight (and which of them does not?), the creeds of the church universal, though not infallible, both provide temporary respite by alerting me to the time-honored convictions of multitudes of believing persons before my time and make me pause before accepting innovations. Tradition has a way of buying time for me while a proper exegetical response is worked out. The burden of defending the faith is not one we have to carry alone but one which is shared by countless others living and dead. Looking back through the corridors of tradition makes me realize that there is no real danger that the truth of God faithfully witnessed to for millennia will change its shape and wither away.

The biblical faith is never found apart from tradition. It does not exist in pure essence free of historical forms and fallibilities. But the essence and the forms are not identical and must not be equated. The Bible represents within the flow of history the norm and criterion for determining what is permanent and what is changing, what is legitimate and what is not. Tradition never mirrors purely and perfectly the truth of the gospel, and it always needs to be monitored by God's Word. Tradition is a wonderful servant but a poor master. It serves the church in many ways. But it does not share the same plane with the Scripture. It can and should be placed beneath the Bible and corrected when necessary by the biblical message when it becomes corrupted or complacent. The marvel of God's Word is its demonstrated and proven power to speak with fresh power and to reform and renew the church and its theology. We humbly ask the Lord to do it again for us and for our time.[17]

3   In Quest of Canonical Interpretation

JAMES I. PACKER

Regent College
Vancouver, British Columbia, Canada

Having been asked for a personal statement on how I use the Bible in theologizing, I shall attempt one—though not without anxiety. Not that asking a theologian for such a statement strikes me as in any way improper. On the contrary, it is a supremely fitting thing to do, for one's answer to the request will at once show how seriously one takes one's trade, and that is something which the church needs, and has a right, to know. Furthermore, any theologizing that has integrity will reflect something of one's Christian identity, as that has been formed in experience, and making that identity explicit should therefore help others to understand and assess one's work. Paul's example in Acts 22, 24, and 26, Romans 7, Galatians 1–2, and Philippians 3 shows that it is no solecism for theologians to say where they come from experientially when that helps them to model or confirm what they want to get across. Professional theologians today hesitate to share their experience, fearing lest the pure objectivity and the transcendent reference point of their God-thoughts be thereby obscured; but this is a great pity, for when they define their role merely in ecclesiastical or academic terms, thus in effect hiding behind their official identity, it renders their theology at best enigmatic and at worst downright boring. For my part (so far as I understand myself), the theology that I "do" in my churchly and academic roles is a conscious confessional expression of my personal identity and spirituality *coram Deo*, and to be asked to identify that identity, as it relates to my handling of Scripture, is no hardship at all. Nonetheless, I find myself feeling some prickles of anxiety as I turn to the task.

Why so? Because anyone who voices certainties as a Christian in directly personal terms runs the risk of being misheard, as if to be saying: "Believe this, or do that, because it is what I believe and do, and my own experience has proven that it is right;" in other words, "take it from *me*, as if I were your God and your authority." It was, I think, Kierkegaard who observed that the greatest misfortune for any person is to have disciples, and anyone who talks in a personal way about one's convictions maximizes the risk of disciple-making. I have seen Christians in both academic and pastoral work attracting admirers who then progressively lose the power to distinguish between devotion to their human teacher and loyalty to their divine Lord, and I don't want anything of that kind to happen to me. That is why some folk who have asked to have me as their mentor and role model have received dusty answers. I am a pastoral theologian; my aim is to attach disciples to Jesus Christ my Lord, not to myself; and nobody is going to become a Packerite if I can help it. So I shrink somewhat from highlighting what I believe and do, as distinct from what God says ought to be believed and done.

Moreover, since God is infinitely good to all who truly seek him, I do not see how anyone's experience of grace or formation by grace can settle the truth of one confessional position as against another, and I don't want to look as if I think that the quality of my Christian experience or the strength of my Christian convictions should be decisive in persuading others to accept my views. The truth of theological assertions should be decided by asking whether they faithfully echo Scripture, not whether God has blessed folk who have held them. Certainly, one whose religious experience is lacking does well to inquire whether one knows enough as yet of God's truth about spiritual life, just as one who knows that truth sufficiently does well to take note of how God confirms it in experience. But it is Scripture as such, the written Word of God, that must finally identify

God's truth for us—Scripture, and in the last analysis nothing else.

Hence, then, my anxiety. I fear lest by the very act of making a personal statement I risk both obscuring an emphasis which is basic both to my own Christian identity and to the message I seek to spread and sounding insufferably egocentric in the bargain. But that risk is unavoidable. All I can do about it is ask my readers in charity to believe that my goal is to celebrate God rather than to project Packer; and that I only talk about Packer because I was asked to; and that I would have felt freer and happier altogether if the title of this symposium could have been, "How *the Bible uses me* when I do theology." (That title would have meshed directly with my experience of the Bible during the forty years since my conversion. How often in modern contexts has my heart echoed the protest of John Rogers, the Reformation martyr, against the alleged inertness of the biblical text: "No, no, the Bible is alive!"). Enough, now, of preliminary remarks. I move into my assignment forthwith.

My Perception of the Bible

The first thing to say is that I perceive the sixty-six books of the Protestant canon to be the Word of God given in and through human words. Canonical Scripture is divine testimony and instruction in the form of human testimony and instruction. Let me explain.

By "God" I mean the pervasive personal presence, distinct from me and prior to me, who is the source and support of my existence; who through Scripture makes me realize that he has towards me the nature and name of love—holy, lordly, costly, fatherly, redeeming love; who addresses me, really though indirectly, in all that Scripture shows of his relationship to human beings in history, and especially in the recorded utterances of his Son, Jesus Christ; and who is daily drawing me towards a face-to-face encounter and consummated communion with him beyond this life, by virtue of "the redemption which is in Christ Jesus" (Rom. 3:24). For academic purposes you may call this my model of God, to be set alongside other models, deistic, pantheistic, panentheistic, or whatever. But it is no mere notion; this is my non-negotiable awareness of the One whom I worship, an awareness that has been relatively clear and steady since I experienced a full-scale pietistic conversion from religious formalism to the living Christ at age eighteen.

By "Word of God" I mean God's own self-declaration and message about the way of godliness—worship, obedience, and fellowship in God's family—that Jesus Christ made known to the world. Some evangelicals use "Word of God" to mean the text of Scripture as such, known to be God's communication but viewed as still uninterpreted. I use the phrase as the Reformers did, to signify not just the text in its God-givenness but also the God-given message that it contains. This is in line with the way that in Scripture itself "Word of God" means God's message conveyed by God's messenger, whether orally or in writing. The narrower usage really involves a false abstraction, since no one ever has or is entitled to have a clear certainty that Scripture is from God when that person has no inkling of its message. I doubt whether any latter-day evangelicals ever deserved to be called bibliolaters, worshipers of the written Word of the Lord rather than the living Lord of the World. But if any did, it was this narrow usage that betrayed them by leading them to focus on the book itself as a sacred object, unrelated to the God of whom it speaks.

Many since Kant have doubted whether God, who gave us language, actually uses language to communicate with us—whether, that is, God's "speaking" to people is a cognitive event for them as my speaking to you would be, or whether this "speaking" is a metaphor for some non-cognitive way in which we are made aware of his presence. Here, however, the incarnation is surely decisive. Rabbi Jesus used language (Aramaic, to be exact) in order to teach. But Rabbi Jesus was God come in the flesh. So the principle that God uses language to tell us things is at once established; and the claim that Scripture is a further case in point—a claim, be it said, that is irremoveably embedded at foundation level in Jesus' teaching about his Messiahship and God's righteousness[1]—presents no new conceptual problem.

By "canon" I mean the body of teaching that God gave to be a rule of faith and life for his church. God created the canon by inspiring the books that make it up and by causing the church to recognize their canonical character. The gaps and uncertainties that appear when we try to reconstruct this process need not detain us now. Suffice it to say that I read the historical evidence both as showing that this was how the early church understood the canon (Jesus' Bible) in Jesus' own day and as confirming rather than calling in question the authenticity of our entire New Testament. (Scholars will agree that this is a possible and even natural way of reading that evidence, even if it cannot be established as the absolutely necessary way.) Then, theologically, I see the attestation of the Protestant canon by the Holy Spirit growing stronger year by year as more and more Bible readers have the sixty-six books authenticated to them in actual experience. (The problem of the eccentric Tridentine canon, which contains seventy-eight books, cannot be dealt with here.) We have to realize that only one theological question about the canon faces us, namely whether any evidence compels us to challenge its historic bounds. Once we grasp this, it becomes clear how we can accept with rational confidence the canon which the church hands down to us, even though many questions about the origin, circulation, and stages of acceptance of the various books remain unanswered.

Knowing how a belief began never, of course, proves it true, and not all convictions for which the Holy Spirit is invoked stand the test of examination; nonetheless, the following facts may be of interest. C. S. Lewis wrote of a motorcycle ride in 1931 to Whipsnade Zoo, a ride at the start of which he did not believe that Jesus Christ was the Son of God and at the end of which he found he did. Similarly, in 1944 I went to a Bible study at which a vision from the book of Revelation (I forget which one) was expounded, and whereas at the start I did not believe that all the Bible (which I had been assiduously reading since my conversion six weeks before) is God's trustworthy instruction, at the end, slightly to my surprise, I found myself unable to doubt that indeed it is. Nor have I ever been able to doubt this since, any more than I have been able to doubt the reality of the biblical Christ whom I honor as my Savior, Lord, and God. When, years later, I found Calvin declaring that every Christian experiences the inward witness of the Holy Spirit to the divine authority of Scripture,[2] I rejoiced to think that, without ever having heard a word on this subject, I had long known exactly what Calvin was talking about—as by God's mercy I still do.

My Practice of Theology

The next thing to say is that, as the believer, theologian, and preacher that I am, I read Scripture in the way followed before me by Chrysostom (regularly), Augustine (fitfully), and all Western professional exegetes since Colet, Luther, and Calvin— that is, I approach the books as human documents produced by people of like passions with myself. I read these books as units of responsive, didactic, celebratory, doxological witness to the living God. Those who wrote them, being believers, theologians, and preachers themselves, were seeking to make God and godliness known to their original envisaged audience, and the first question to be asked about each book has to do with what its writer saw it as saying and showing about God himself. But when I have seen this, my next task is to let the book's message universalize itself in my mind as God's own teaching or *doctrine* (to use the word that Calvin loved) now addressed to humankind in general and to me in particular within the frame of reality created by the death, resurrection, and present dominion of Jesus Christ.

That last phrase is important, for it determines my way of applying Old Testament material. I see the Old Testament in its totality laying a permanent foundation for faith by its disclosure of God's moral character, sovereign rule, redemptive purpose, and covenant faithfulness and by its exhibiting of the positive dispositions of faith, praise, and obedience contrasted with the negative dispositions of mistrust and rebellion. But on this foundation it sets a temporary superstructure of cultic apparatus for mediating covenant communion with God; and this apparatus the New Testament replaces with the new and better covenant (that is, the better version of God's one gracious covenant) which is founded on better promises and maintained by the sacrifice and intercession of Jesus Christ, the better and greater high priest. This amounts to saying that I think the Old Testament should be read through the hermeneutical spectacles that Paul (Romans and Galatians), Luke (Gospel and Acts), Matthew, and the writer to the Hebrews provide. The typology of the New Testament teaches me to transpose everything in the Old Testament about typical provisions and promises (i.e., cultic prescriptions, expectations of this-worldly enrichment, and imperialist eschatological visions) into the new key, which we might call the key of fulfilllment and which was established by the New Testament revelation of the corresponding antitypes—spiritual redemption through Christ, the heavenly Jerusalem, and the world to come. Reading Old Testament books in the light of this principle, which was long ago expressed in the jingle "the New is in the Old concealed, the Old is in the New revealed," I find in their teaching about God and godliness a significance which a Jewish colleague would miss.

My way of reading Scripture involves five distinct convictions about theological method. That one's method must be a *posteriori* and biblically determined is for me a truth of first importance. These five convictions together fix the method to be followed when one faces problems of faith and practice and seeks to grow in the knowledge of God. This method, as will be seen, is kergymatic in content, systematic in character, and normative in purpose. The analytical and descriptive techniques of historical, philosophical, phenomenological, political, and sociological theology have their interest and use as both sources and sieves of material for kerygmatic reflection, but only as one follows the kerygmatic method can one be said to be theologizing; any God-talk that falls short of this is no more than a contribution to the history of ideas. It is now the kerygmatic method that I describe as I detail my five convictions.

First conviction: by entering into the expressed mind of the inspired writers I do in fact apprehend God's own mind. What Scripture says, God says. In the writers' witness to God and communication about him God witnesses to himself and communicates personally with the hearer or reader. When they announce the mighty works of God in creation, providence, and grace, God is in effect setting before us fragments of his own autobiography. The identity of what the writers say about God with God's own message about himself is the truth that has historically been indicated and safeguarded by calling the biblical books *inspired*. Inspiration makes it possible to achieve a theology which, to use the old terms, is *ektypal* in relation to God's own thoughts as *archetypal*; a theology which, in other words, literally thinks God's thoughts after him. Such a theology is my goal. But such theology is essentially biblical interpretation; and biblical interpretation must begin with correct exegesis, lest by misunderstanding biblical authors I misrepresent God; and correct exegesis is exegesis that is right *historically*. So I am grateful for the deepened insight in the West over the past two hundred years as to what historical understanding involves. I appreciate the critical awareness of differences between the present and the past, with techniques for determining those differences in particular cases, that the new historical sensibility has brought, and I welcome the refining of historical exegesis in Western churches that has resulted. For understanding of God can grow only as we better understand—understand, that is, with greater historical accuracy—what the biblical writers meant by what they said about him.

Second conviction: since all sixty-six books come ultimately from the mind of our self-revealing God, they should be read not just as separate items (though obviously one must start by doing that), but also as parts of a whole. They must be appreciated not only in their particular individuality of genre and style, but also as a coherent, internally connected organism of teaching. This, after all (and here I throw down the gauntlet to some of my academic peers), is what examination shows them to be. It is fashionable these days for Scripture scholars to look for substantive differences of conviction between biblical writers, but this is in my view an inquiry as shallow and stultifying as it is unfruitful. Much more significant is the truly amazing unity of viewpoint, doctrine, and vision that this heterogeneous library of occasional writings, put together by more than forty writers over more than a millennium, displays.[3] The old way of stating the principle that the internal coherence of Scripture should be a heuristic maxim for interpreters was to require that *the analogy of Scripture* be observed.[4] This is the requirement which the twentieth Anglican Article enforces when it says that the church may not "so expound one place of Scripture, that it be repugnant to another." The modern way of expressing the point is to require that interpretation be *canonical*, each passage being interpreted kerygmatically and normatively as part of the whole body of God's revealed instruction. Accepting this requirement, I infer from it the way in which theology should seek to be *systematic*: not by trying to go behind or beyond what the texts affirm (the common caricature of systematic theology), but by making clear the links between items in the whole compendium of biblical thought.

Third conviction: biblical teaching, like the law of the land, must be applied to the living of our lives. So, as in legal interpretation, the interpreter has a twofold task. First, one must discern the universal truths and principles that particular texts exhibit in their particularized application to particular people in particular circumstances. Second, one must reapply those same truths and principles to us in our circumstances. Therefore one must look not only *at* but also *along* the Bible, just as one looks along a ray of light to see the things that it strikes and shows up. Biblical teaching, received as instruction from God, must be brought to bear on the world and life in general and on our own lives in particular. Interpreted Scripture must be allowed to interpret its interpreters; those who in procedural terms stand over it to find out its meaning and bearing must recognize that in spiritual terms they stand under it to be judged, corrected, led, and fed by it. Interpretation has to be *imperative*, *self-involving*, and thus (to use an abused word) *existential* in style. The divinely authoritative claim on our compliance which biblical teaching makes, must not be muffled. My ears—and yours, too—must always be open to the Bible's summons (God's, really) to what Bultmannites call *decision*, what most Anglo-Saxons call *commitment*, and what the Bible itself calls *repentance, faith, worship, obedience,* and *endurance*.

Here the Holy Spirit's ministry is decisive. Commentaries will tell us what each writer's words *meant* as an utterance spoken into that immediate historical situation, but only the Spirit who gave them can show us, by using them to search us, what they *mean* as they bear on us today. Luther's famous observation that a theologian is made by prayer, meditation, and spiritual conflict (*oratio, meditatio, tentatio*) reflects his awareness of the way in which the Spirit does this.

Fourth conviction: The basic form of obedient theology is applicatory interpretation of Scripture in the manner described, reading the books as God's witness to his saving grace in Christ and God's call to sinners to believe and respond. Such theology is of necessity a form of preaching, just as true preaching is of necessity an exercise in the theological interpretation of Scripture. The technical disciplines taught in universities and seminaries—technical dogmatics, ethics, spirituality, apologetics, missiology, historical theology, and so forth—find their value as they lead to richer biblical interpretation. Dogmatics are for the sake of Scripture study, not vice versa, and so with all technical branches of theology. (By "technical" I mean using terms and forms of analysis that are developed within the discipline for its own furtherance.) Academically and professionally, my job description as a theologian may be to develop and teach one of these technical disciplines, but in terms of the theologian's calling and churchly identity my main task is and always will be the interpreting of Scripture.

Fifth conviction: I must be ready to give account of my interpretative encounters with Scripture not just to my human and academic peers but to God himself, who will one day require this of every theologian and of me among them. This is to say that I must follow my method *responsibly* as one who must answer for what I do.

To sum up this section, I can schematize my use of the Bible in theologizing as follows. I make use of the Bible (1) in personal devotion, (2) in preaching and pastoral ministry, (3) in academic theological work. Use (3) underlies use (2) and is fed by use (1). I approach the Bible in all three connections as the communication of *doctrina* from God; as the instrument of Jesus Christ's personal authority over Christians (which is part of what I mean in calling it *canonical*); as the criterion of truth and error regarding God and godliness; as wisdom for the ordering of life and food for spiritual growth; and, thus, as the mystery—that is, the transcendent supernatural reality—whereby encounter and fellowship with the Father and the Son become realities of experience. I attempt theological exegesis and exposition in the way and for the ends already described, depending on and expecting light and help from the Holy Spirit. I see ethics, spirituality, catechetics, preaching, and all pastoral counsel as needing to be informed and regulated by theological interpretation of Scripture, and I do not expect to see any good practical Christianity where this discipline is neglected. If you ask me for models of my kind of Bible-based theologizing, I would name John Calvin and the Puritan, John Owen.

The mention of Calvin, that most ecumenical of writers, prompts one last question: how, in seeking a canonical interpretation of Scripture, do I relate to church tradition? The answer is that, like Calvin, I theologize in constant dialogue with the whole Christian heritage of study, proclamation, and belief insofar as I can acquaint myself with it. Theology is a cooperative enterprise, and the fellowship of its practitioners has a historical as well as a contemporary dimension. In essence, tradition means neither *theologoumena* ecclesiastically imposed nor superstitions ecclesiastically sanctioned (the common Protestant stereotype), but the sum of attempts down through the ages to expound and apply biblical teaching on specific subjects. It should be appreciated as such and, finally, be evaluated by the

Bible which it aims to echo and bring down to earth. (The old Roman Catholic idea, now generally abandoned, that tradition supplements Scripture can be safely dismissed as a freak.)

In tradition, enlightenment from God's Spirit and blindness due to sin coexist and coalesce, often strangely, so that treating tradition as infallibly right or as inevitably wrong is a mistake in either case. Dismissing tradition as representing only the worldliness of the church reflects unbelief in the Spirit's work since Pentecost as the church's teacher; embracing the dogma of faultless tradition reflects a lapse into ecclesiastical perfectionism. In seeking to profit from tradition I oppose the deifying of it no less than the devaluing of it. The worth of tradition as a help in our own interpreting of Scripture depends on its being constantly exposed to the judgment of Scripture. Its relation to us is ministerial, not magisterial, and we must keep it so.

My Method Applied: A Case Study

Nobody theologizes aimlessly; as in all one's mental life, one thinks for a purpose and to a point—though agendas are sometimes hidden! My agenda is no secret, however. My concerns, biblically directed I trust, are churchly. Like my convictions, they reflect Luther rather than Erasmus; I seek to advance learning not for its own sake but for the good of souls.[5] My goal is theology that will guide and sustain evangelism and nurture, pastoral care and spiritual renewal.[6] I draw heavily on Calvin and the English Puritans, for I find in them great theological and interpretative resources for the task. I contend for biblical authority—that is, the permanent binding force of all biblical teaching—because this much-challenged facet of Christ's Christianity is basic to the theology I build and to the Christian life to which that theology leads.[7] I contend for biblical inerrancy because acknowledgment of Scripture as totally true and trustworthy is integral to biblical authority as I understand it.[8] On these various themes I have written a good deal. In the tangle of history and polemics that has marked my treatment of them it has doubtless been easy to miss what I was after, and any who have in fact failed to see it should not be blamed too harshly. They would in any case be to some extent victims of the habitual failure to probe motivation (what the Germans call one's theological intentions), which seems to me to be a chronic weakness of English-speaking scholarship. But if there is to be genuine understanding, the question of motivation (what's it all in aid of?) needs to be asked, and it seems to me that the motivation that has produced my published work has really been clear all along.

My goal is not adequately expressed by saying that I am to uphold an evangelical conservatism of generically Reformed or specifically Angelican or neo-Puritan or interdenominational-pietist type, though I have been both applauded and booed on occasion for doing all these things, and I hope under God to continue to do them. But if I know myself I am first and foremost a theological exegete. My constant purpose was and is to adumbrate on every subject I handle a genuinely canonical interpretation of Scripture—a view that in its coherence embraces and expresses the thrust of all the biblical passages and units of thought that bear on my theme—a total, integrated view built out of biblical material in such a way that, if the writers of the various books knew what I had made of what they taught, they would nod their heads and say that I had got them right. I have been asked in the present essay to illustrate my use of the Bible, and that means showing how I work my way towards the canonical interpretations which are the goal of my theological endeavor. I shall now attempt to do this, taking as my paradigm case a theme that I have not mentioned so far, the much-debated question of what is currently called role relationships between the sexes.[9]

This is a many-sided question. It arises in connection with (1) church order (may women function as elders? sole pastors? bishops?); (2) family ethics (what kind and measure of subordination, if any, of wives to husbands is biblically required?); (3) socio-political ideals for the modern world (does Scripture imply that privileges, opportunities, rights, and rewards should everywhere be equal, irrespective of sex?); and (4) pastoral nurture of men and women to fulfill their God-given vocations in relation to each other. As secular society everywhere is split on these matters, so is the church generally and the evangelical sector of it specifically. For Christians the basic question is whether the undisputed spiritual equality of the sexes before God and in Christ sanctions equality of function, i.e., carries God's permission to share and exchange all non-biological roles in home, church, and community; or, whether God has ordained a hierarchical pattern whereby in some or all of these spheres men are to lead and certain roles are not for women. The main biblical evidence is (1) the stories of the creation (Gen. 1:26–27 with 5:1–2; 2:18–25) and the fall (3:16–20); (2) Jesus' respect for women, whom he consistently treated as men's equals (Luke 8:1–3; 10:38–42; 11:27–28; 13:10–17; 21:1–4; Mark 5:22–42; John 4:7–38; 8:3–11; 12:1–8); (3) references to women ministering in the apostolic church by prophesying, leading in prayer, teaching, practicing Samaritanship both informally and as widows and deacons, and laboring in the gospel with Apostles (Acts 2:17–21; 9:36–42; 18:24–26; 21:9; Rom. 16:1–15; 1 Cor. 11:2–16; Phil. 4:2–3; 1 Tim. 3:11; 5:1–16; Titus 2:3); and (4) the seemingly mixed signals of Paul's assertion of equality in Christ (Gal. 3:28) alongside both his asymmetrical teaching on the duties of husbands and wives (Eph. 5:21–33; Col. 3:18–19) and his real, if problematical, restrictions on what women may do in church as compared with men (1 Cor. 11:2–16; 14:34–36; 1 Tim. 2:11–15).

This material raises many interpretative difficulties, which makes this an excellent case study of what seeking a canonical interpretation of biblical testimony on any subject involves. I offer now, not an attempted resolution of all the problems (!) but an applied statement of relevant hermeneutical principles, which will establish limits within which, here and in all cases, canonical interpretation lies. Evangelicals have not always noted the complexity of the hermeneutical task; indeed, sometimes they have let themselves speak as if everything immediately becomes plain and obvious for believers in biblical inerrancy, to such an extent that uncertainties about interpretation never arise for them. Granted, reverent Bible readers regularly see in texts practical lessons which are really there, and which doctrinaire students miss. Nonetheless, inerrancy is a concept that demands hermeneutical qualification, for what is true and trustworthy is precisely the text's meaning, and this only correct interpretative procedures will yield. Moreover, while the central biblical message of new life through Christ is expressed so fully and clearly that one who runs may read and understand (which is what Reformation theology meant by the *clarity* and *perspicuity* of Scripture), there remain many secondary matters on which certainty of interpretation is hard if not impossible to come by. The present exercise will, I think, make that clear. Here, now, are the hermeneutical principles that I propose to illustrate from the role relationship debate.

(1) *Biblical teaching is coherent and self-consistent*: for, as I said above, with whatever variety of literary form and personal style from writer to writer and with whatever additions and amendments as redemptive history progressed, it all proceeds from one source; namely, the mind of God the Holy Spirit. Any adequate hermeneutical hypothesis on this or any topic, therefore, will have to show the internal harmony of all relevant biblical material. No hypothesis positing either the inconsistency of one biblical teacher with another or a biblical teacher's self-contradiction (as when Paul Jewett diagnosed self-contradiction in what his apostolic namesake said about Christian women[10]) can be right.

(2) *Biblical moral instruction corresponds to human nature*: for it stands in a maker's-handbook relation to us, showing the natural, God-planned, and therefore fulfilling and satisfying way for us creatures to behave. Half-way houses, therefore, must be deemed faulty when they approve women ruling men in secular affairs (because Scripture nowhere forbids it and sometimes exemplifies it) but not in the church or home (because Scripture requires male leadership in both), or when they approve women ruling in today's church (because Paul's restriction on this seems to be culturally determined) but not in the family (because biblical teaching on this seems to be transcultural and timeless). I say this not because of any particular failures or arbitrarinesses

of argument, real though these may be, but because these views overlook the fact that in his enactments about role relationship, whatever they are, God is legislating for the fulfillment of human nature as it was created in its two forms, male-masculine and female-feminine. You can hold that a woman is so made that she enters into her sexual identity and so finds a particular fulfillment by giving cooperative support to a male leader, or that she is not; you can hold that a man is so made that he enters into his sexual identity and so finds a particular fulfillment by taking responsibility for a female helper, or that he is not; and you can argue across the board for whichever view of Bible teaching on role relationships fits in with your idea. But what you cannot do is argue that *both* views are true at the same time in different spheres. Human nature is either one thing or the other, and only across-the-board arguments are in place here.

(3) *Biblical narratives must be evaluated by biblical norms*: for it is not safe to infer that because God caused an event to be recorded in Scripture he approved it and means us to approve it too. As it does not follow that Paul approved of baptism for the dead because he mentions the Corinthians' practice of it (1 Cor. 15:29), so it does not follow that every action of a believing woman that Scripture records is there as a model; we must evaluate those actions by normative teaching before we can be sure. Nor can it be argued (for instance) that God, when cursing Eve after the fall and describing to her how it was now going to be ("your husband . . . shall rule over you" [Gen. 3:16]), was thereby prescribing that thus it evermore ought to be, even in the realm of redemption. Normative teaching from elsewhere must settle whether that is so or not.

(4) *Biblical texts must be understood in their human context*: for otherwise we shall fail to read their real point out of them and instead read into them points they are not making at all. Only through contextual study can exegesis be achieved and eisegesis be eliminated. That Scripture interprets Scripture is a profound truth, but lifting biblical statements out of context to fit them into mosaics of texts culled from elsewhere is a corner-cutting operation (beloved, alas, of a certain type of "Bible teacher")

which that profound truth cannot be invoked to justify. We must know the literary genre, historical and cultural background, immediate situation and occasion, and intended function of each passage before we can be confident that we have properly understood it. When, for instance, Paul tells Corinthian women to be silent in church (1 Cor. 14:34) and then, maybe eight years later, tells Timothy that he requires women not to teach but to be quiet (1 Tim. 2:11), is he making exactly the same point? Contextual study of each passage is needed to determine that.

But when we look we find that the context and intended function of Paul's restrictive statements about women is less clear. What abuses or questions prompted them? Had some particular women disgraced themselves in a way that Paul was determined to clamp down on? Or did he bring in this teaching because it was part of a universal congregational order, modelled on the synagogue, which he believed that God intended for all churches at all times in the way that the unchanging gospel was intended for all churches at all times? In 1 Timothy 2:13–14 he justifies the silence rule as appropriate because of the order of creation and the sequence of events in the fall; but was he imposing this rule to be law forever, or simply as a rule of prudence which experience had shown to be expedient *pro tempore* in the churches for which he was caring? If we knew those things, we should at once know a great deal more. We should know, for instance, whether in these passages he is talking about all women or only wives (the Greek word which he uses, *gunē*, regularly means both and is the only regular Greek word for both, so that linguistically this ambiguity is unresolvable). We should also know whether in 1 Timothy 2:12 he is forbidding women to teach men or to teach anybody in the public assembly (the Greek allows both renderings) and whether he would regard the completing of the canon and its availability in print to all Christians today (so that teachers need never say "take it from me," but always "take it from Scripture") as so changing the situation that his ban on women teaching no longer applies. We should know too whether the silence rule of 1 Corinthians 14:34

means that, after all, women must not lead in prayer nor prophesy publicly, as 11:4–10 seemed to allow them to do, or only that women must take no part in judging prophets, which is the theme of the immediate context, 14:29–33. But the pieces of information which alone could give us certainty on these points are lacking, and in their absence no guess as to what is probably meant can be thought of as anything like a certainty. This leads to the next point.

(5) *Certainties must be distinguished from possibilities*: for only certainties can command universal assent and obedience. In the present field of discussion the only points of certainty seem to be these: (a) both creation and redemption establish the equality of men and women before God, as both image bearers and children of God through Christ (Gen. 1:26–27; Gal. 3:26–29); (b) within this equality the man (or at least the husband) is irreversibly "the head" of the woman (or at least his wife), i.e., is of higher rank in some real sense (though the exact sense is disputed—causal priority only? or leadership claim too?—(1 Cor. 11:3; Eph. 5:23); (c) Christian partners are to model in their marriage the redeeming love-responsive love relationship of Christ and the church (Eph. 5:21–33). Beyond this, everything—all that was mentioned in the last paragraph, and just how Paul would have expounded his key words about women's roles, "be subject," "respect" (Eph. 5:21–24, 33; Col. 3:18; cf. Peter's "obey," 1 Peter 3:5), and "submissiveness," "have authority over" (1 Tim. 2:11–12)—is a matter of rival possibilities, on none of which may we forget the real uncertainty of our own opinion, whatever it is, or deny to others the right to hold a different view. It is the way of evangelicals to expect absolute certainty from Scripture on everything and to admire firm stances on secondary and disputed matters as signs of moral courage. But in some areas such expectations are not warranted by the evidence, and such stances reveal only a mind insufficiently trained to distinguish certainties from uncertain possibilities. Among those areas this is one.

(6) *What is explicitly forbidden must be distinguished from what, though unfitting, is not forbidden*: for action that is undesirable,

because unfitting, is not necessarily sin. That which is unfitting by reason of God's work should not be equated with that which is unlawful by reason of God's command: the two categories are distinct. Should it appear from Scripture that woman was not fitted by creation to fulfill leadership roles in relation to man, that would not *ipso facto* make it sin for a woman to be President or Prime Minister or general manager or chairman, or to have a male secretary, or even (if one does not judge Paul's silence rule to forbid this) to be a missionary church-planter or a sole pastor or a bishop. It could still be argued that these roles impose strain on womanly nature; that they are not what women are made for; that they show a certain lack of respect for God's work of creation; that in fulfilling them a woman is likely to treat men maternally, which will impose undue strain on masculine nature; and that the woman's womanly dignity and worth are to some extent at risk while she does these jobs; but it could not be maintained that she and those who gave her her role have sinned by disobeying God's command. The facts of creation in this as in other matters do not of themselves constitute a command, only an indication of what is fitting; and the various forms of ethical unwisdom and indignity which do not transgress explicit commands cannot be categorized as sin.

(7) *The horizons of text and student must mesh*: for only so can God's teaching in the text deliver us from the intellectual idolatry which absolutizes the axioms of contemporary culture. The "meshing" or "fusing" of horizons is a picture, taken from H.-G. Gadamer, of how the inspired text, which we question in order to find its meaning and relevance, questions, criticizes, challenges and changes us in the process.[11] Some who today raise the proper question, whether there are not culturally relative elements in Paul's teaching about role relationships (all the material has to be thought through from this standpoint), seem to proceed improperly in doing so; for in effect they take current secular views about the sexes as fixed points, and work to bring Scripture into line with them—an agenda that at a stroke turns the study of sacred theology into a venture in secular ideology. We need grace both to believe, as our forebears did, that we

really do not know our own nature, any more than we know God's nature, till taught by Scripture and to apply this truth to our own sexual nature in particular. The biblical word of God, which lives and abides forever, must be set free to relativize all the absolutes, avowed and presuppositional, of our post–Christian, neo-pagan culture and to lead us into truth about ourselves as our Maker has revealed it—truth which, be it said, we only fully know and perceive as truth in the process of actually obeying it.

I take the discussion of role relationships no further. Suffice it to have illustrated from this one case some, at least, of the procedural principles which I try to observe when on any subject at all I seek a canonical interpretation of Scripture—the goal at which, in my view, all theologians ought centrally to aim and to which the study of theological ideas should be viewed as a means. The greatest of the Church Fathers saw the matter so; Luther, Calvin, and Owen did the same; Karl Barth, in a slightly odd manner determined by his epistemological preoccupation and his eccentric sort of christocentricity, took essentially the same road; I follow in their train, as best I can.

There are, of course, many other principles of importance in the quest for canonical theological interpreation of Scripture— for instance, the continuity of God's work in Old and New Testament times and the biblical typology that is based on it; the trinitarian identity of the God of the Old Testament; the theomorphism of humanity which makes possible and meaningful the so-called anthropomorphism of biblical language about God; the nature of redemption as a restoring of fallen creation and so a fulfilling of God's original purpose for the world; the real overlap of the age to come (that world, heaven) with the present age (this world, earth) through the ministry of Christ prolonged by the Holy Spirit—but none of these can be discussed here. Other tasks, too, besides interpreting Scripture face theologians, tasks both intramural (dealing with the church) and extramural (dialoguing with the world)—tasks of phenomenological analysis of theologies past and present and of apologetics, philosophical, evangelistic, and defensive—but these cannot be spoken of here either. I end here by repeating my conviction that the canonical interpretation of Scripture is the theologian's main job and by adding to it my further conviction that only those who give themselves to this task first and foremost will ever be fit to interpret anything else on God's behalf.

4   Scripture and the Theological Enterprise: View from a Big Canoe

RUSSELL P. SPITTLER

Fuller Theological Seminary
Pasadena, California

> **Mis · sour · i**[1] (mi zoor′ ē) *n.* [<Algonquian, lit., people of the big canoes]. **1.** *pl.*-**ris, ri** any member of a tribe of Indians . . . **from Missouri** [Colloq.] not easily convinced; skeptical until shown definite proof . . .
>
> -Excerpted from *Webster's New World Dictionary* (1970 edition)

As in medicine, theology names a whole field by one of its parts. Also as in medicine, the term "theology" has at least three distinct levels of meaning. (1) Broadly, the word designates a profession comparable to law or accounting. (2) More narrowly the term describes a systematic written presentation of religious truth for a particular group and within a specific era. (3) In its most limited sense "theology proper" (as it is sometimes called) consists of ideas about God's nature and work—often the very first topic for a treatise on systematic theology.

"Theology" Among Pentecostals

These nuances of the word "theology" enjoy no uniform acceptance within the Pentecostal family of churches.[1] Indeed the term acquires, in some quarters there, a pejorative flavor, so persistent among Pentecostals is a characteristic mistrust of the formal academic enterprise. Pentecostal clergy will more naturally describe themselves as "in the ministry" than "in theology." The exploration of "theology proper," a ready activity in Pentecostal schools, more often than not will be done with the aid of systematic theologies bearing the names of authors who pre-dated the Pentecostal movement—Charles G. Finney, Charles Hodge, W. G. T. Shedd, A. H. Strong, R. A. Torrey.

But there have been a few Pentecostal efforts at publishing systematic theologies, though not very successful ones if customary academic canons are applied. The earlier ones already showed the relation of Scripture to theology in Pentecostal practice: such works were simple, uncritical explanations of biblical teaching for recent converts and for new but untrained ministers. Scriptural references interlaced expository paragraphs as documentation for biblical ideas described. Engagement with contemporary exegetical or theological literature was rare.

The exemplar of Pentecostal systematic theologies was authored by Myer Pearlman, an early Pentecostal writer who flourished in the 1930s and 1940s and who, as a Jewish youth, had studied Hebrew in the synagogue. In use continuously for nearly a half century, *Knowing the Doctrines of the Bible* is subtly competent in its conception though simple in language.[2] It has been translated into Spanish and several other languages, and the volume finds wide use by Pentecostal missionaries in the task of training national ministers for evangelism. Within the Pentecostal movement no volume has rivaled the influence of Myer Pearlman's doctrinal handbook.

In other words, the most widely used "systematic theology" in the Assemblies of God—if use of the term applied to that book be permitted—has an instrumental, missionary function. Biblical understanding is held to be subordinate to and necessary for the preaching of the gospel. So far as any published "systematic theology" is concerned, a self-conscious effort to frame religious truth for the Pentecostal tradition within its own time and space—something even remotely comparable to Donald Gelpi's work for Roman Catholic charismatics, not to mention Karl Barth's magisterial *Church Dogmatics* for the Reformed tradition—there simply *is* no such Pentecostal theology.[3] Even the *interest* to produce such a work has barely surfaced.[4]

Hence in the Pentecostal tradition doctrine appears more readily than theology. And doctrine is viewed as assumed and given (or received), not really subject to elaboration or helped by periodic restatement. When two major classical Pentecostal bodies in the past dozen years established graduate theological schools, both avoided the term "theological seminary." The Assemblies of God Graduate School in Springfield, Missouri, was established in 1972. The Church of God School of Theology in Cleveland, Tennessee, began in 1975. That no similar limitation beset the Charles H. Mason Theological Seminary, established in 1970 by the Church of God in Christ (largest of the dominantly Black classical Pentecostal bodies), can be attributed to the circumstances of its origin as part of Atlanta's Interdenominational Theological Center—a cluster of schools accredited by the Association of Theological Schools.

Formative Churchly Influences

Interestingly enough, not "theology proper" but a statement on Scripture appears as the first item in the formal doctrinal statement of the Assemblies of God (AG). Here is the language of the opening point in the Statement of Fundamental Truths as it read when, as a late teenager in the early 1950s, I first began the study of theology:

> 1. The Scriptures Inspired.
> The Bible is the inspired Word of God, a revelation from God to man, the infallible rule of faith and conduct, and is superior to conscience and reason, but not contrary to reason. 2 Tim. 3:16, 17: 1 Pet. 2:2.

The statement accords with the faith of most conservative Protestants: it reflects a fairly traditional Reformation outlook. I include it here not only to show the character of a revision made in the early 1960s (discussed below) but also to report the earliest influence—so far as theological statements are concerned—in my own theological formation. It was under this Statement, under all sixteen items of the Statement, that I was ordained in 1961 as a minister of the AG. I continue to serve gratefully as a member of the clergy of that body.

Later in 1961, the "Statement of Fundamental Truths" underwent its only major revision since it was framed originally in 1916. And not very major, at that. Following World War II, Pentecostals developed a thriving friendship with the emerging "New Evangelicals"—a welcome recast of souring pre-war Fundamentalism—in which strong roles were played by persons like Harold Ockenga and Billy Graham and by institutions like *Christianity Today*, Fuller Theological Seminary, and the National Association of Evangelicals (NAE).[5]

It was not long till the Assemblies of God became the largest member church in the NAE. Not surprisingly, Thomas F. Zimmerman, head of the AG from 1957 to date, in 1960 became the elected president of the NAE. And in the next year the AG doctrinal statement was changed.[6]

Here is a fascinating chapter in the history of evolving doctrinal statements. It was, I think, exactly this warming courtship of the Pentecostals and the evangelicals—I haven't decided who was courting whom—that led to what might be called the evangelicalization of the AG doctrinal statement.[7] In 1916 when the Statement was drafted, no one had thought to include statements about Jesus which were assumed by all: his virgin birth, sinless life, substitutionary atonement, bodily resurrection, and exaltation to God's right hand. (Informed readers will recognize the echoes of *The Fundamentals*.) No matter: a wholly new point, "The Deity of the Lord Jesus Christ," would be added. Not to suggest any major alteration to the structure of the Statement, two points in the then-existing Statement (#5, Baptism in Water; #6, The Lord's Supper) were grouped as one in the 1961 Statement (#6, "The Ordinances of the Church: a. Baptism in Water; b. Holy Communion"), thus preserving the overall total of sixteen points.[8]

But more. The phrase in vogue at the time within evangelical discussions regarding the doctrine of Scripture was the term "verbal inspiration." The 1961 changes made to the Statement of Fundamental Truths yielded the following revised form of the point quoted earlier:

> 1. The Scriptures Inspired
> The Scriptures, both the Old and New Testaments, are verbally inspired of God and are the revelation of God to man, the infallible, authoritative rule of faith and conduct (2 Tim. 3:15–17; 1 Thess. 2:13; 2 Pet. 1:21).

That is the way the Statement now reads. I especially lament the loss of the earlier line, ". . . superior to conscience and reason, but not contrary to reason." But there have been still other developments.

As a theological slogan, "verbal inspiration" of the 1950s seems to have been displaced by "inerrancy" since the 1970s. Some years before Harold Lindsell triggered *The Battle for the Bible* in 1976[9] by arguing that inerrancy is the hallmark of evangelicalism, the AG published in 1970 an official position paper bearing the title "the Inerrancy of the Scriptures."[10] While this "position paper" (and others since issued) does not hold the constitutional status of the Statement of Fundamental Truths approved by the AG's highest body, the biennial General Council in session (typically four to nine thousand voters), the paper does bear the approval of the (roughly two hundred man—no women) General and Executive Presbyteries all of whom are elected by General Council membership.

Thus the formal church statements under which I work, and to which I commit, express a major feature of my own approach to theological work: I believe that the Bible (Protestant canon) is the Word of God in written form, and that it may properly be described as authoritative, infallible, verbally inspired, and inerrant in what it teaches. Those adjectives I have arranged in descending order of appropriateness. Were I to write my own doctrine of Scripture, I would emphasize qualities of potency, effectuality, and sufficiency.

The question of "errors" in Scripture is a volatile one and not one I can treat very fully here. All too easily among professional users of Scripture—ecclesiastics and academics—the phenomena actually present on a page of biblical text cannot or will not be discussed without a prior salute to one or another of the prevailing reductionist shibboleths about the Bible. Some of my former pastors, all of whom were not schooled men, side-stepped my early, honest questions about the biblical text. At a crucial age I was left wondering if no answers *given* meant no answers *possible*. Some fellow members of ministerial credential committees reviewing young candidates for the Pentecostal ministry, sought (to my embarrassment) not how these youths thought of the biblical text but whether the incriminating sibilant could be heard when the speech of the clergy applicants got to be a creedal shibboleth. Such theological hopscotching is no mere handicraft of conservatives. Some of my very freed-up university teachers could not be led to allow the possibility of miracle and interruption in natural law. For them—indeed for us all—it is all too easy to conclude truth from habit. It requires, in the end, a grand work of the Holy Spirit to dredge from the clogged channels of our minds the waste quietly expelled for decades into the flowing stream by those very shore establishments whose useful products have made us what we are. Such dredging the Apostle Paul called the renewal of the mind (Rom. 12:2).

So I cannot speak of "errors" until I reach agreement with my discussants about the ground rules. Meanwhile, one clue to the future discussion. Among my books sits an inexpensive red-letter edition of the King James Version of the Bible. For use in Christian work at a women's reform school in Elgin, Illinois, while we were Wheaton students in the late 1950s, my wife and I bought up a dozen or so of them at the bargain price of $1.65 each.

I now know why those Bibles were so cheap. If you were sitting nearby, I could show you p. 95 in the New Testament of this Bible. There appears Acts 7:18–19, Stephen's words about Pharaoh, "another king . . . which knew not Joseph. The same dealt subtilly with our kindred, and evil entreated our fathers. . . ." But the pronoun in the phrase "our fathers" as printed in this Bible is spelled—rather *mis*spelled!—"ou*t* fathers."

An "error"? "Merely a misprint," one will say. All right, call it what you will. But acknowledge that here is one specific, particular Bible—"The Bible," after all, only exists as various Bibles here and there—in whose printed text there is *something* awry. You may say it's easily explained. And I will say it is indeed, and there are many similar explicable irregularities in three millennia of the copying and recopying of thousands of biblical manuscripts. It is not the precision of philology but the politics of rhetoric that controls the choice of terms to describe such phenomena in the biblical text. I deplore such pollution in the environment of Christian discourse.

I am not among those who, for anterior philosophical reasons, will conclude from such alleged "errors" that the Bible cannot be taken seriously as having any warranted religious authority. Neither am I among those who insist that the adjective "inerrant" is not only the best but also the watershed qualifier for evangelical orthodoxy.

As for the current intra-evangelical debate about Scripture, I will say only that inerrancy with the needed footnotes weighs in about the same as naked infallibility,[11] or so it seems to me.

The Impact of Schools

Not only my church but also my schools have shaped my style of theologizing and my stance toward Scripture. My first schooling after high school (where, half-way through, I switched to a vocational high school to follow a life-long interest in electronics) consisted of three years in a then unaccredited, three-year Bible Institute operated by churches of the AG in the Southeast.[12] To this day, considering the impact of my several schools, it would be the last whose influence I would surrender. A lot of what is today called spiritual formation happened there, though we didn't call it that. There I experienced Pentecostal community and formed values my readers will readily detect.

The Bible Institute I attended had an arrangement in those days (early 1950s) with Florida Southern College, an accredited Methodist school in the same city, permitting transfer of its three years straight across in order to complete an accredited baccalaureate for a fourth year's work. The major impact of Florida Southern upon me was the experience of its magnificent Frank Lloyd Wright architecture. (Sitting one day in the library of his design, I saw and then heard a student unwittingly stride directly into a deck-to-ceiling glass panel. The next day, at the offending place, a sticker reading "Give to the United Fund" appeared at a prudent altitude.) Since nearly all of my Bible Institute work was in religion and I needed general education subjects for graduation, I hold a baccalaureate in religion from a college at which I did not take a single course in the field.

But at Wheaton College (Illinois) Graduate School scales fell from my eyes: I discovered *history*.[13] Earlier, in the Bible Institute, we had ticked off the biblical books in canonical order. Today, Matthew, twenty-eight chapters; key verse, Matthew 28:19; date, sixth decade; author, the tax collector; outline, such and such. "For our next class session, please read the Gospel of Mark," and so on.

But at Wheaton, I discovered that Scripture had not dropped from heaven as a sacred meteor that arrived intact. I learned (and should have known much earlier) that the books of the Bible grew from the soil of fervent Christian activity in a real though long-ago world, that literature is a centrifugal spin-off of history. I didn't yet see all the implications of that insight, but it was like being born again, again. More later about its methodological significance.

What happened, in fact, exemplifies the perspicacity of Professor Grant Wacker's analysis of what he calls "The Texture of Pentecostal Faith." Following Mircea Eliade and some others, Professor Wacker shows that "the distinctive theological ideas pentecostals lived for and fought about invariably reflected one of the central features of folk religion: ahistoricism."[14] I had discovered historicalness, and I would never be the same again.

Enough time was spent at Wheaton taking courses beyond

the M.A. to allow, within a year, completion of the seminary degree (B.D. in my day) at Gordon Divinity School (now Gordon Conwell Theological Seminary, north of Boston). The year there (1957/8) was demanding though fragmentary: I was scrambling for those "requireds" which now and again interfere with one's education. But there I learned that the church, too, had a history.

My first years of teaching were in the (AG) Central Bible Institute (now of course, Central Bible College) in Springfield, Missouri. Invigorating encounter with the students and a few graduate courses at Concordia Seminary in St. Louis (in the pre-Seminex days) confirmed an inclination to teach. After four years of teaching my family and I were off to Cambridge, Massachusetts, for doctoral work in New Testament.

For this essay, a word about the choice of field for graduate study is relevant. A generalist at heart and a newborn historian, I would have settled for a broad program in religion and a thesis somewhere in modern American intellectual religious history. But I had no major in history and few courses of relevance. As I assayed my rather narrow and repetitive background, it looked as if I were best qualified in the field of New Testament. So there I applied, and there I was accepted, actually graduating in 1971.

It is still true at Harvard that one speaks, not of the field of "New Testament," but of "Christian Origins." History again. Interest flourished in the environment out of which the New Testament emerged, and that led to a high interest in background studies. My first graduate seminar dealt with the book of First Enoch. I studied with professors who served on the international team editing the Dead Sea Scrolls—Frank Cross and John Strugnell (who also was my thesis mentor). We used to say we didn't need to go to Europe to study. Rather, Europe came to us: Helmut Koester and Dieter Georgi (German), Krister Stendahl (Swede), John Strugnell and Arthur Darby Nock (Britishers), and, as a visiting professor, Gilles Quispel (Dutch). The Israeli archaeologist, Nachman Avigad, was also a visiting professor and one of my doctoral examiners.

There were no required courses at Harvard, and I benefited mostly from the lectures (and sometimes, example) mainly of

Krister Stendahl in New Testament and Richard R. Niebuhr in Theology. My thesis consisted of an introduction, translation, and notes for the Testament of Job, a minor Jewish work about as long as the New Testament book of Romans and written in Greek in the first century B.C. or A.D. This curious document has the daughters of Job speaking in the language of the angels (*Test. Job* 48–50), so its appeal to a classical Pentecostal is understandable.

Once or twice my Harvard teachers lightly groused about my choice of research outside the text of the New Testament. They worried about conservatives who "evaded critical issues" by working in various Hellenistic exotica. I suppose they were justified. In my studies till then I had encountered no real sympathetic introduction to the use of the modern critical methodology. And in the end I have never been able to give myself, body and soul, to the approach as if it were the sole avenue of truth. To what extent I have absorbed the method should carefully be described, and I shall come to that.

My point in these pages has been that, so far as I can tell, my church and its teaching on Scripture have been the primary influences in my approach to theology. Though some of my fellow church folk may wonder that it could be so, I must affirm that it is my belief in the authority of Scripture which led me to the schools I attended, to the beliefs I cherish, to the ministry of teaching I enjoy, to the theological method I apply. From my commitment to the formative, first item in the AG Statement of Fundamental Truths, all else flows—even the risk of being thought to mispronounce the later points. The Word of God is indeed a two-edged sword and, as Paul said, "We cannot do anything against the truth" (2 Cor. 13:8).

A Theological Sample

The effect of my churchly and academic influences has been to make me primarily an exegete. I understand myself to be a student of and a listener to the Word of God. It is enough if, reading carefully, I can hear the word of Him whose voice I know. I used to tell my students that my hair was not the right color to be a systematic theologian. Now the emerging gray gives little hope—long since abandoned anyway—that I would function as a systematician. I am an exegete en route, not enthroned.

What follows therefore is a sample piece of my style of "theology." You'd have to call it exegetical theology, I suppose. I propose to present at some length an interpretation—an exegesis—of 1 Corinthians 11:2–16. That will be followed by an analysis of the character of the exegesis against my background just sketched. The result should fulfill the purpose of this paper—an account of how one Pentecostal uses Scripture in the theological enterprise.[15]

Custom-breaking at Corinth: 1 Corinthians 11:2–16

Surely, more is known about the church at Corinth than about any other New Testament assembly of Christians. Besides the two letters of Paul addressed to the Christians at Corinth along with the full account in Acts 18 of the origin of the church, both Romans 1:18–32 and 1 Thessalonians 5:19–22 reflect probable composition of those letters at Corinth as well. Corinthian congregational fission reappears at the end of the first century in First Clement 45–47, and the catalogue of New Testament Apocrypha includes Third Corinthians, the "Apocalypse of Paul," and even a modern and useless apocryphon called the "Epistle of Kallikrates." Moreover, the site of Corinth has undergone excavation for over a century. The archaeological reports rival, in shelf space occupied, the *Oxford English Dictionary*.

Here is a Pauline church which also knew the oratory of Apollos, the medical skill of Luke, the preaching of Peter (perhaps), the timidity of Timothy, the hospitality of Priscilla and Aquila, the municipal office of Erastus, the conversions of Stephanas and Sosthenes, the ministry of Phoebe—to say nothing of other named Christians whose lives touched Corinth in untold ways: Silas, Titius Justus, Crispus, Gaius, as well the traveling trio of Stephanas, Fortunatus, and Achaicus.

So far as the biblical record recounts, the Apostle spent more time at Corinth—eighteen months—than anywhere else, except at Ephesus. The church at Corinth, despite the Apostle's tutelage, fell into behaviors that would depress, if not destroy, any modern pastor. Among the disorders clear from a reading of First Corinthians are congregational disunity, ministerial favoritism, sexual laxity, incest, litigiousness, overdone marital asceticism, spiritual elitism, pneumatic individualism, sacramental and charismatic abuse, theological heresy, even unfilled financial pledges.

Context

First Corinthians arose when the concerned founder-pastor wrote in response to reports about (1 Cor. 1:11; 5:1; 11:18) and queries from (7:1, 25; 8:1; 12:1; 16:1, 12: all verses where the Apostle uses the phrase "now concerning" to bring up a new subject) a charismatic Christian community approaching crisis. It does well for the interpretation of the letter to accept Professor F. F. Bruce's guess that the arrival of Corinthian friends with additional news and a letter from Corinth led the Apostle, who had already written 1—4, to the specific interests addressed in 1 Corinthians 5—16.[16]

One of those interests lay in the effort of some of the women at Corinth to discontinue use of the veil—the subject of 1 Corinthians 11:2—16. But it aids the interpretation of the passage to recognize that 11:2—14:39 as a whole deals with aspects of community worship: use of the veil in female prayer or prophecy (11:2–16); proper conduct at the Lord's Supper (11:17–34); spiritual gifts (12—14).

Surprisingly, neither the issue of headcovering here (11:2–16) nor the treatment of resurrection (Chap. 15) are introduced by the recurring phrase "now concerning." It appears the Apostle wanted to address a practice at Corinth not among those about which the Corinthians had inquired. So he used a strategy of commendation: "I commend you because you *remember me in everything* and *maintain the traditions even as I have delivered them to you.*" The italicized phrases, as the commentators suggest, may well have been taken directly from the letter brought from the Corinthians to Paul (7:1). But these quoted words will be bent back upon the Corinthians.

That "commend" is the strong word in the sentence is argued, too, from its reappearance at 11:17 where Paul takes up the next topic—misuse of the Lord's Supper. "But in the following instructions I *do not commend* you. . . ."

The flow of thought seems clear; the Corinthians should imitate Paul's example of living in the service of God and others, even at the forfeiture of personal rights (10:31—11:1). Speaking of imitation, claimed regard for the traditions of Paul is breached by the behavior of some at Corinth who disregard his characteristic teachings (11:2–16). Nor does their sacramental frivolity warrant praise for loyalty (11:17–34). And these are but samples: "About the other things I will give directions when I come" (11:34b)—one of the truly astonishing lines in First Corinthians.

No unanimity flourishes among interpreters as to exactly what practice here draws the Apostle's attention. Despite English translations the actual word "veil," in fact, nowhere occurs in the underlying Greek of the passage even though it is within the Apostle's vocabulary (2 Cor. 3:12–18). Most commonly conceived is female use of an oriental veil when praying or prophesying. But it could be (as the NIV notes) a preference among some Corinthian women for short hair, contrary to the customary long hair for women. Since Greek used the words here translated "man" and "woman" also for "husband" and "wife," neither is it clear whether Paul limits his language to women as females or as wives. Finally, even if a veil is assumed, it cannot be determined which of several types known from Hellenistic art may be in view.

Fortunately, the major point of the passage does not vary with these cultural details: the Corinthians should not so readily disregard customary liturgical dress, if indeed, as they claimed, they "maintain the traditions" gotten from Paul.[17]

Structure and Interpretation

I find in 1 Corinthians 11:2–16 a series of six arguments listed by the Apostle in his effort to quell a trend toward the eradication of difference in dress at corporate worship. Certain Corinthians, it appears, sought to bring to social visibility a theological anthropology which anticipated the eschatological elimination of sexual difference. Paul himself was wont to teach that there is "neither male nor female" in Christ (Gal. 3:28). Some of his disciples at Corinth (likely the "Christ party") viewed themselves as endowed with a special insight—the conviction that their experience of the Spirit thrust them into identification with the risen Lord in heaven. As a result, the future was absorbed into the present—furnishing theological motivation to act as if the eschaton had arrived. Hence, no need for distinguishing women from men. No need to have, especially so at corporate worship, any head-wise distinction in dress between men and women.

The same underlying theology, often called incipient gnosticism, explains Corinthian immorality (viewing fornication as immoral attests ignorance of the freeing power of insight), asceticism (mundane behavior should reflect the ethic of the eschaton), denial of the resurrection (lofty spiritual experience is itself the resurrection, which is thus "already past"—cf. 2 Tim. 2:18), and virtually all Corinthian deviations.

To oppose the effort Paul mounts six arguments which seem more significant in their cumulative effect than convincing in their logical compulsion. Here are the arguments.

(1) *Creation* (11:3–6). A natural order exists, the Apostle affirms, in which "the head of every man is Christ, the head of a woman is her husband, and the head of Christ is God." The order given does not follow a top-down (or bottom-up) hierarchy. But husband, wife (I think the Apostle here views men and women in their usual social roles), and Christ all have their respective "head"—which has more the quality of "source" than of "supervisor" though both meanings are possible. Even "source" implies, in the end, some degree of control. Though the legitimacy of the distinction is contested, administrative subordination need not—and in many daily social contracts does not—imply essential inferiority.

The Apostle seems to say here that there is a certain social taxonomy wherein each has a role. If the argument seems not overwhelmingly convincing, that introduces a feature of this section: the reader who follows along down the list of arguments increasingly gets the feeling Paul is not making his point well.

(2) *Scripture* (11:7–9, 11–12). Genesis 1:27 and 2:20–23, familiar to the Rabbi of Tarsus, lie in the background of 11:7–9. A rabbinic hermeneutic concludes the social priority of the husband from the temporal precedence of Adam. Yet in 11:11–12 Paul urges, by an ingenious reversal, the mutuality expected from his comments in 1 Cor. 7 and more characteristic of the Apostle's own domestic design.

(3) *Angels* (11:10). This is a difficult passage. At least since Tertullian it has been explained in the light of Genesis 6:1–4 as a caution against presenting sexual temptation, by inappropriate dress, to angels.

More recently, several commentators have suggested a different interpretation in view of ideas about angels expressed in the Dead Sea Scrolls. There, the sectarian militants are cheered in the War Scroll (1QM vii.6; xii.4; xix.1) by the assurance that the angels will fight on their side in the final apocalyptic war. In the community guidelines (1QSa ii.3b–10), maimed or scarred persons are excluded from the high-level councils of the sect because they may offend the angels, perfect creatures of God, who also attend the councils. Hence, Paul may here be urging proper communal behavior so as not to offend, by social impropriety, the angels before whom Christian lives unfold.

(4) *Propriety* (11:13). The Apostle invites their own estimate: can it be right "for a woman to pray to God with her head uncovered?" This ad hoc appeal blends into the next argument where, however, the ground shifts.

(5) *Nature* (11:14–15). The appeal to the natural order raises unsolvable queries about physiological differences between men and women regarding the average length and rate of growth of hair. The statement is not intended to give scientific precision, but it restates the argument from propriety, this time appealing to things as they are—"nature." Once again the logic may ap-

pear less than compelling—exactly so, which leads to the next, last, and by far, most decisive argument.

(6) *Tradition* (11:16). "If any one is disposed to be contentious, we recognize no other practice, nor do the churches of God." This statement flatly ends the discussion. It is really no argument at all, just an announced refusal to attend to any arguments.

My sense is that Paul, at the outset of this literary unit, was uneasy about his grounds on which to discourage the custom-breaking going on at Corinth. That led to a rapid-fire array of arguments, those just listed, some looking rather farfetched, which separately or together do not overwhelmingly make the point. So in the end he stops mounting arguments and simply declares, to put it baldly, "This is the way we do things around here."

The word translated "practice" (or custom) echoes the "traditions" of 11:2 and 11:17. The only other Pauline occurrence of the term speaks of former idolators who were "hitherto accustomed to idols" (8:7). The only other use of the term elsewhere in the New Testament is quite illustrative: the Jews had a *custom* of releasing one prisoner at Passover (John 18:39). In view in all cases is a habitual group behavior.

Thus the passage opens shrewdly by commending the Corinthians for their own claimed recollection of and adherence to Paul's traditions. It closes on the same note—an appeal to custom whose characteristic Corinthian fracture leads on in the next verse (11:17) to another example of custom-breaking (misuse of the Lord's Supper).

Reference to existing practice in the churches surfaces elsewhere in First Corinthians. The phrase "in (all) the churches" occurs twice in 1 Corinthians 14:33–34 where Paul appeals to churchly custom in support of balancing charismatic ardor and liturgical order. His regular practice as an apostle yields the counsel of contentment with whatever life the Lord assigns: "This is my rule in all the churches" (7:17). Paul writes that when Timothy returns to Corinth "he will remind you of my ways in Christ, as I teach them everywhere in every church"

(4:17; author's translation). Reference to a concordance will show Paul to be no stranger to tradition and custom as a guideline for church behavior.[18]

Application

Tradition, Scripture teaches, is a proper source of religious authority. I conclude that from 1 Corinthians 11:16. As a theological statement that sentence is explosive but true, for the Bible teaches it.

A helpful context for issues of religious authority is given in James Packer's book *"Fundamentalism" and the Word of God.*[19] The first question in matters religious (maybe the second: the first queries are always epistemological) is: What constitutes ultimate religious authority? Upon answers to that query are built the major world religions—minor ones too, down to the last storefront cult.

Three common responses are given, as Professor Packer shows: Scripture; tradition; and reason. Biblical authority is the hallmark of the Protestant Reformation. The priority and superiority of churchly teaching—tradition—marks specially the Roman Catholic heritage. The modern era has witnessed a toppling of any external authority, Bible or Pope, and the elevation of human reason as the ultimate religious authority. Theological liberalism thus emerged in the church, a movement honoring neither Protestant nor Catholic boundaries. Of course, a little of each—Scripture, tradition, reason—affects the others. But the generalizations apply.

Given my own commitments to the primacy of Scripture over tradition or reason, you can imagine my surprise, as a cautious and, hopefully, careful exegete, to discover *in the Scripture* that tradition has authority. I expressed that surprise once when addressing a group of Navy chaplains who represented the three major faiths. Remarked a Catholic priest in subsequent discussion, "You should not be too surprised; many of us who are Roman Catholic priests are also rediscovering the Bible and its authority."

Some of Jesus' hardest words were directed at religious leaders who had higher regard for traditions than for the Word of God (Matt. 15:6, e.g.). That is the peril of tradition, its penchant to displace the Word of God. Yet this same Jesus displayed a critical loyalty toward his own heritage by never leaving the synagogue.

How far is tradition valid? It is valid, on an evangelical understanding, only where it does not violate the teaching of Scripture. Conclusions for personal and church behavior are far-reaching. If tradition may specify limits to community action within biblical norms, then tolerance should emerge among Christian groups whose group customs—say, the weekly day of worship—may oppose each other and yet lie within biblical standards. If tradition is valid, some practices biblically permissible—the use of wine, to pick an example sure to be contested—would be relinquished voluntarily by "enlightened" members of a Christian group in which a custom exists that out-bibles the Bible. (No one should worry that sects are usually lopsidedly excessive; in the overall growth of the church those excesses are often quick repairs to damage caused by accumulated neglect.)

If tradition is valid, the really major issue surrounds the role of tradition in the formation of Scripture itself. Endlessly debated in ecumenical dialogues, tradition impacts Scripture at the point of its canonical margins. Frankly, I am surprised at the eclipse of canon within contemporary intra-evangelical debate over Scripture. Banners of "inerrant" or "infallible," descriptions of Scripture as verbally inspired, plenarily inspired, or just plain "inspired," even denials or critiques of any of those qualifiers—all are statements about the *nature* of Scripture; left untreated is the *extent* of Scripture.

"All scripture," sure enough, "is inspired by God and profitable for teaching, for reproof, for correction, and for training in righteousness" (2 Tim. 3:16). The question is: which books are to be so regarded? The most conservative dating of New Testament writings would leave other New Testament books yet to be written if Paul writes these words in the mid-60s. Even if a second-century dating is assigned to First Timothy, exegetical outcomes would note that the "Scripture" here mentioned was that familiar to Timothy as a child—surely the Old Testament, but not certainly all thirty-nine books as we know the Old Testament.

I am not much helped to hear James Packer say that "the Church no more gave us the New Testament canon than Sir Isaac Newton gave us the force of gravity."[20] "Inspired" is the language of faith, the testimony of a believer. The extent of the canon is a matter of historical evidence, which so far yields a date of A.D. 367 (in the thirty-ninth Easter letter of Athanasius of Alexandria) as the earliest possible date by which *any affirmation at all* could be applied to a sixty-six book Bible. That means, among other things, that not only the apostolic church described in Acts but also the church of the second and third centuries knew of no "Bible" *precisely* ("infallibly" or "inerrantly"!) corresponding to ours. And if we value exactitude in discussions about the Bible, we had better speak exactly of a sixty-six book canon.

As an outcome I am driven to value the role of tradition on the human side of the formation of the Bible. By that I mean that I now recognize that, however inspired the texts of Scripture are, they got that way from an external, historical viewpoint in the lap of the church. I am guided by the suggestion of the Old Princeton theologian, B. B. Warfield, to the effect that if we had a right doctrine of providence, we should not need a theory of inspiration. What some call the role of tradition in the formation of the Bible I prefer to describe as the gracious gift of God in sovereign control of human affairs so as to result in the Bible—the Word of God written. Neither the human nor the divine aspect of the Written Word, as with the living Word, Jesus himself, may be neglected in any full appreciation of the Word of God among us.

Analysis of the Theological Sample

Contemplation of the mix of Pentecostal heritage, evangelical training, and the graduate school context of my own work leads to the several generalizations about the use of Scripture in theology among contemporary classical Pentecostals. It is important to observe that these comments do not ncessarily apply to charismatic scholars who, though they may share with Pentecostals certain values of spiritual evidence, emerge for the most part from mainstream Protestant backgrounds where there is generally a more positive evaluation of the academic enterprise. And I must state also that I speak for myself only and not in any official or representative sense.

(1) Most characteristic of the use of Scripture in the Pentecostal heritage is a simple, natural, and revered, though often ahistorical, use of the words of Scripture both in the nourishment of personal piety and in setting a mandate for evangelism as the chief agenda for the church.[21] I speak primarily of the use of Scripture among lay persons, but Pentecostal clergy for the most part are lay people who quit their jobs. They reflect a lay level of biblical education. Though educational interests are rising among Pentecostals and something of an indiscriminate stampede is on for a doctorate of any quality, my own church's constitutional documents are typical. Twice therein occurs the statement, "Any certain extent of academic education shall never be a requirement for credentials. . . ."[22] While there is always more to learn for any student of Scripture, however brilliant or trained, I am not at all prepared to say that such simple pietistic use of Scripture is defective; it is not so much wrong as limited.

(2) Discovery of the historical character of revelation together with deepening skills in exegesis, which is merely the historical treatment of texts, yields an exciting rediscovery of the worth, the relevance, and the majesty of Scripture. Advances in lexicography and archaeology have put us in a place to know more about the ancient world than it knew about itself. As an exegete I know no higher moment than the dawn of truth rising from the meticulous application of linguistic and other historical study. The outcomes of exegesis have virtually changed my life and fashioned my thought and values. Were it required of me to surrender my past training, my abilities to work in the Greek text of the New Testament would be the last to go.

(3) I have no illusion that unaided history is ultimate, any more than is uninformed piety. Exegesis puts one into the vestibule of truth; the Holy Spirit opens the inner door. For this reason I find myself as a Christian teacher, primarily concerned to link subjective piety with scientific (historic) objectivity. History and piety form the foci of the ellipse embracing Christian inquiry. I must ask historical (and therefore linguistic, archaeological) questions, not acting as if the Scripture was sent to me alone or to my tradition only. But I must also ask a utilitarian, pietistic question: how does God speak to me and to my communities (family, school, local church, denomination) through this text?

The interest of the university lies in history (legitimate). The interest of the Bible school lies in piety (also legitimate). The invitation to Christian scholarship consists in the balanced blend of both. The university may neglect piety. The Bible school may slight history. I shall have both. As a workplace for that quest, I could ask for no better environment than a graduate school committed to freedom and excellence (those twin virtues of the university) yet giving place to piety through the limited pluralism of a clear-voiced evangelicalism.[23]

(4) I am quite prepared to confess unresolved tensions in the methodological mix of history and piety. Historical method in New Testament exegesis means the use of the historical-critical method. I have reached a formulaic conclusion: the historical-critical method, when applied to Scripture, is both legitimate and necessary, but inadequate.

It is legitimate, because history is the sphere of God's dealings with the world and the stage of revelation. It is necessary, but not for Christian seniors in the rest home nor for Sunday School children who sing rather than read their theology. Rather, it is necessary in order to milk from Scripture the revealed truth it provides.

But it is inadequate, because—and here my Pentecostal heritage shows—the end of biblical study cannot consist alone in historical dates or tentative judgments about complicated and conjectured literary origins. The end of biblical study consists rather in enhanced faith, hope, and love for both the individual and the community. The historical-critical method is inadequate, in other words, because it does not address piety.[24]

(5) The theological sample provided earlier demonstrates these values. That the text comes from First Corinthians does not only reflect the predictable interests of a Pentecostal. That book of the Apostle also enjoys comparatively few critical (that is, historical) uncertainties. Its Pauline authorship is these days not seriously doubted; its date of composition is more clearly determined than perhaps any other book of the New Testament; the origin of the church is recounted in Acts; the geographic site of Corinth is known and excavated; the integrity of the text is not widely challenged; text-critical uncertainties are few. These comfortable conclusions of the consensus in critical assessment of First Corinthians no doubt played a large role in attracting me to that text.

I have made no comparable major study of any one of the Gospels not merely because of the limits of time and the demands of administration. The outcomes of critical inquiry into the Gospels have reached far less unanimity, and in truth I am not well-equipped to manage the conclusion that this or that saying of Jesus in the Gospels was rather a contrivance of the early church. Let me be clear: without the extensive personal study in the Gospels to the level I would require of myself before offering a studied opinion, I am prepared to allow that early Christians spoke in the Lord's name under the impulse of the Holy Spirit, just as happens in certain instances today among charismatic communities. But I do not find piety well served by such historical inconclusiveness and therefore I gravitate to where the certainties are higher. After all, love (piety), not knowledge (history), counts most in the end (1 Cor. 8:1b).

Or so it appears to one member of the Springfield, Missouri, tribe . . . one not easily convinced . . . one of the "people of the big canoes."[25]

5 A Christological Hermeneutic: Crisis and Conflict in Hermeneutics

DONALD G. BLOESCH

University of Dubuque Theological Seminary
Dubuque, Iowa

The discipline of biblical hermeneutics, which deals with the principles governing the interpretation of Scripture, is presently in crisis. For some time it has been obvious in the academic world that the scriptural texts cannot simply be taken at face value but presuppose a thought world that is alien to our own. In an attempt to bring some degree of coherence to the interpretation of Scripture, scholars have appealed to current philosophies or sociologies of knowledge. Their aim has been to come to an understanding of what is essential and what is peripheral in the Bible, but too often in the process they have lost contact with the biblical message. It is fashionable among both theologians and biblical scholars today to contend that there is no one biblical view or message but instead a plurality of viewpoints that stand at considerable variance with one another as well as with the modern world-view.

There are a number of academically viable options today concerning biblical interpretation, some of which I shall consider in this essay. These options represent competing theologies embracing the whole of the theological spectrum.

First, there is the hermeneutic of Protestant scholastic orthodoxy, which allows for grammatical-historical exegesis, the kind that deals with the linguistic history of the text but is loathe to give due recognition to the cultural or historical conditioning of the perspective of the author of the text. Scripture is said to have one primary author, the Holy Spirit, with the prophets and Apostles as the secondary authors. For this reason Scripture is believed to contain an underlying theological and philosophical unity. It is therefore proper to speak of a uniquely biblical life- and world-view. Every text, it is supposed, can be harmonized not only with the whole of Scripture but also with the findings of secular history and natural science. The meaning of most texts is thought to be obvious even to an unbeliever. The end result of such a treatment of Scripture is a coherent, systematic theological system, presumably reflecting the very mind of God. This approach has been represented in Reformed circles by the so-called Princeton School of Theology associated with Charles Hodge, A. A. Hodge, and Benjamin Warfield.

In this perspective, hermeneutics is considered a scientific dis- cipline abiding by the rules that govern other disciplines of knowledge. Scripture, it is said, yields its meaning to a system- atic, inductive analysis and does not necessarily presuppose a faith commitment to be understood. Some proponents of the old orthodoxy (such as Gordon Clark and Carl Henry) favor a metaphysical-deductive over an empirical-inductive approach, seeking to deduce the concrete meanings of Scripture from first principles given in Scripture.

A second basic approach to biblical studies is historicism in which Scripture is treated in the same way as any worthy liter- ature of a given cultural tradition. The tools of higher criticism are applied to Scripture to find out what the author intended to say in that particular historical-cultural context. Higher criti- cism includes an analysis of the literary genre of the text, its historical background, the history of the oral tradition behind the text, and the cultural and psychological factors at work on the author and editor (or editors) of the text. With its appeal to the so-called historical-critical method for gaining an insight into the meaning of the text, this approach is to be associated with the liberal theology stemming from the Enlightenment.

Historicism is based on the view that the historicity of a phe- nomenon affords the means of comprehending its essence and reality (H. Martin Rumscheidt). It is assumed that meaning is to be found only in the historical web of things. The aim is the historical reconstruction of the text, in other words, seeing the text in its historical and cultural context (*Sitz im Leben*). Historical research, it is supposed, can procure for us the meaning of the Word of God.

Ernst Troeltsch articulated the basic principles of historicism, but this general approach has been conspicuous in J. S. Semler, David Friedrich Strauss, Ferdinand Christian Baur, Adolf von Harnack, and, in our day, Willi Marxsen and Krister Stendahl. A historicist bent was apparent in Rudolf Bultmann and Gerhard Ebeling, especially in their earlier years, though other quite different influences were also at work on them.

It was out of this perspective that the quest for the historical Jesus emerged, since it was believed that only by ascertaining by historical science what Jesus really believed in terms of his own culture and historical period can we find a sure foundation for faith. Albert Schweitzer broke with historicism when he discovered that the historical Jesus indisputably subscribed to an apocalyptic vision of the kingdom of God. Finding this incredible to the modern mind, he sought a new anchor for faith in the mystical Christ.

A third option in hermeneutics is the existentialist one, popularized by Rudolf Bultmann, Ernst Fuchs, Gerhard Ebeling, and Fritz Buri, among others. This approach does not deny the role of historical research but considers it incapable of giving us the significance of the salvific events for human existence. It can tell us much about the thought-world and language of the authors, but it cannot communicate to us the interiority of their faith. Demonstrating an affinity with the Romanticist tradition of Schleiermacher and Dilthey, these men seek to uncover the seminal experience or creative insight of the authors of the texts in question, the experience that was objectified in words. Only by sharing this same kind of experience or entering into the same type of vision do we rightly understand the meaning of the text. Drawing upon both Hegel and Heidegger, these scholars affirm that real knowledge is self-knowledge and that the role of the text is to aid us in self-understanding.

In existentialist hermeneutics history is dissolved into the historicity of existence. The Word becomes formative power rather than informative statement. The message of faith becomes the breakthrough into freedom. Jesus is seen as a witness to faith or the historical occasion for faith rather than the object of faith. It is contended that we should come to Scripture with the presuppositions of existentialist anthropology so that the creative questions of our time can be answered.

In contradistinction to the above approaches I propose a christological hermeneutic by which we seek to move beyond historical criticism to the christological, as opposed to the existential, significance of the text. The text's christological meaning can in fact be shown to carry tremendous import for human existence. I believe that I am here being true to the intent of the scriptural authors themselves and even more to the Spirit who guided them, since they frequently made an effort to relate their revelatory insights to the future acts of cosmic deliverance wrought by the God of Israel (in the case of the Old Testament)[1] or to God's self-revelation in Jesus Christ (in the case of the New Testament). This approach, which is associated with Karl Barth, Jacques Ellul, and Wilhelm Vischer, among others, and which also has certain affinities with the confessional stances of Gerhard von Rad and Brevard Childs, seeks to supplement the historical-critical method by theological exegesis in which the innermost intentions of the author are related to the center and culmination of sacred history mirrored in the Bible, namely, the advent of Jesus Christ. It is believed that the fragmentary insights of both Old and New Testament writers are fulfilled in God's dramatic incursion into human history which we see in the incarnation and atoning sacrifice of Jesus Christ, in his life, death, and resurrection.

Here the aim is to come to Scripture without any overt presuppositions or at least holding these presuppositions in abeyance so that we can hear God's Word anew speaking to us in and through the written text. According to this view, the Word of God is not procured by historical-grammatical examination of the text, nor by historical-critical research, nor by existential analysis, but is instead received in a commitment of faith.

This position has much in common with historical orthodoxy, but one major difference is that it welcomes a historical investigation of the text. Such investigation, however, can only throw light on the cultural and literary background of the text; it does not give us its divinely intended meaning. Another difference is that we seek to understand the text not simply in relation to other texts but in relation to the Christ revelation. Some of the theologians of the older orthodoxy would agree, but others would say that what the Bible tells us about creation, for example, can be adequately understood on its own apart from a reference to the incarnation. With the theology of the Reformation and Protestant orthodoxy, I hold that we should begin by ascertaining the literal sense of the text—what was in the mind of the author—and we can do this only by seeing the passage in question in its immediate context. But then we should press on to discern its christological significance—how it relates to the message of the cross of Jesus Christ.

In opposition to liberalism, I believe that the text should be seen not simply against its immediate historical environment but also against the background of Eternity. To do this, we need to go beyond authorial motivation to theological relation. Moreover, it is neither the faith of Jesus (as in Ebeling) nor the Christ of faith (as in Bultmann and Tillich) but the Jesus Christ of sacred history that is our ultimate norm in faith and conduct.

According to this approach, God reveals himself fully and definitively only in one time and place, viz., in the life history of Jesus Christ. The Bible is the primary witness to this event or series of events. This revelation was anticipated in the Old Testament and remembered and proclaimed in the New Testament. The testimony of the biblical authors was directed to this event by the inspiration of the Holy Spirit. Yet this relationship is not always obvious and must be brought home to us and clarified by the illumination of the Spirit of God in the history of the church.

The Word of God is neither the text nor the psychological disposition of the author behind the text but is instead its salvific significance seen in the light of the cross of Christ. The criterion is not the original intention of the author as such but the intention of the Holy Spirit. This can be found to some degree by comparing the author's meaning to the meaning of the whole; yet even here the dogmatic norm, the very divine word itself, can elude us.

Although in the mystery of God's grace his Word is assuredly present in Scripture, it is nonetheless veiled to those who are perishing (2 Cor. 3:14–16; 4:1–6). It is not always obvious even to the people of faith, and this is why it must be sought in Scripture. This Word finally must be given by God alone and not until this bestowal of divine grace can we really hear or know.

It is not only what the Spirit revealed to the original author but what he reveals to us in the here and now that is the Word of God. Yet what he teaches us now does not contradict what he taught then. Indeed, it stands in an unbroken continuity with what has gone before. A can never come to mean B or C, but it can come to signify $A+$ or $A++$.

This is to say, a text can have more than one meaning in the sense that it can be used by the Holy Spirit in different ways. Certainly in his prediction of the birth of the child Immanuel in Isaiah 7, the prophet did not consciously have in mind the virgin birth of Jesus Christ; yet this text points to and is fulfilled in the virgin birth as this is attested in Matthew 1:23. The text had both an immediate reference and an eschatological significance, but the latter was, for the most part, still hidden at the time of Isaiah. The many texts about false prophets and antichrists in the New Testament have been used by the Spirit to refer to various adversaries of the faith in all ages of the church. The meaning of the text is thereby not annulled but expanded.

Under the influence of the philosopher Gadamer, the new hermeneutic today is concerned to merge the horizons of the text and of contemporary humanity. But this fusion of horizons can take place not by a poetic divination into the language of the text, nor by a mystical identification with the preconceptual experience of the author of the text, but by the breaking in of the Word of God from the Beyond into our limited horizons and the remolding of them, in some cases even the overthrowing of them. I have in mind not only the horizons of the exegete but also those of the original authors who may have only faintly grasped what the Spirit was teaching them to see (cf. 1 Peter 1:10–12). We should remember that some prophecies in the Bible were corrected or reinterpreted by further illuminations of the Spirit in later biblical history. To insist on a literal fulfillment of all the Old Testament prophecies, as dispensationalists do, is to contradict the New Testament assertion that the church is the New Israel and that at least some of these prophecies have their fulfillment in the church of Jesus Christ.

The christological hermeneutic that I propose is in accord with the deepest insights of both Luther and Calvin. Both Reformers saw Christ as the ground and center of Scripture. Both sought to relate the Old Testament, as well as the New, to the person and work of Christ. Their position, which was basically reaffirmed by Barth and Vischer, was that the hidden Christ is in the Old Testament and the manifest Christ in the New Testament.

Luther likened Christ to the "star and kernel" of Scripture, describing him as "the center part of the circle" about which everything else revolves. On one occasion he compared certain texts to "hard nuts" which resisted cracking and confessed that he had to throw these texts against the rock (Christ) so that they would yield their "delicious kernel."

The orthodox followers of Luther and Calvin did not always retain this christological focus, although most of them remained fairly close to their heritage. Philosophical speculation was the source of some of the deviations. Among Lutherans there was a drift toward natural theology in which the existence of God and the moral law were treated apart from the special revelation of God in Jesus Christ.[2] In Reformed circles, there was both a fascination with natural theology and a concentration on the eternal decrees of God. Reprobation was located in the secret will of God, which stood at variance with his revealed will in Christ. Jesus Christ was reduced to an instrument in carrying out this decree rather than being the author and finisher of our salvation (Heb. 5:9; 12:2). Scripture was used to support the idea of a God of absolute power, thereby obscuring the biblical conception of a God of infinite love whose power was manifest in his suffering and humiliation in Jesus Christ.

Christological exegesis, when applied to the Old Testament, often takes the form of typological exegesis in which the acts of God in Old Testament history as well as the prophecies of his servants are seen to have their fulfillment in Jesus Christ. Such an approach was already discernible in the New Testament where, for example, the manna given to the children of Israel in the wilderness was regarded as a type of the bread of life (John 6:31, 32, 49–50, 58). Typological exegesis differs from allegorical and anagogical exegesis in that it is controlled by the analogy of faith, which views the events and discourses of the Old Testament in indissoluble relation to Jesus Christ, to the mystery of his incarnation and the miracle of his saving work (cf. Acts 26:22; 1 Peter 1:10–12).

There are other hermeneutical options which cannot be covered in a brief essay of this kind, but at least two should be mentioned here. The liberationist hermeneutic draws upon Scripture to support the current struggle of the dispossessed for justice and liberty. In this view there can be no meaning apart from praxis, and liberationist theologians endeavor to show that the theology of the Old Testament prophets was articulated in response to economic and political upheavals.

Process theology tries to draw upon Scripture to undergird the modern world-view, which admits of only one reality, a world process in evolution. The language of Scripture is that of poetry and myth, but it needs to be given theoretical content if it is to have relevance for the "man come of age." It is held that the intuitive experiences of the prophets and Apostles, though not their limited understandings of God and the world, can be reconciled with similar experiences of geniuses and prophets of all religions throughout history.

In the case of both these hermeneutical approaches Scripture is no longer normative in any basic sense. Instead it is reduced to an aid in understanding either the unfolding cosmic drama (as with process thought) or the class struggle of history (as with liberation theology).

An Exposition of Some Key Texts

In this section I intend to illustrate the christological hermeneutic by showing how it bears on scriptural exposition. My aim is not to give an exegesis of the texts in question but simply to show the kind of approach I would use in discovering the meaning of Scripture.

(1) The curse of the serpent in Genesis 3:14–15 must be understood first of all as belonging to the saga that purports to describe events in the primal history of humankind. Saga as a literary genre refers to the total historical recollection of a particular people, a recollection expressed in poetic form. It pertains not to history as a firsthand description or recording of actual events (*Historie*) but to history in the sense of the phenomenal life of humankind in the world (*Geschichte*). The narrator, whom biblical scholarship generally identifies as the Yahwist, is concerned to show that through sin both the lower and higher creation carry a divine curse. Drawing upon an aetiological myth supposedly explaining both why snakes crawl rather than walk as other animals do and why, as it was thought, they eat dust, the author sees in the serpent a representation of pre-human evil, though very probably he does not have in mind the devil of later Hebraic speculation.

The church through the ages has discerned in these verses a proto-evangelium, a primitive form of the gospel. From my perspective the Fathers of the church were basically correct, even though it is unlikely that the narrator had in mind the victory of the future Messiah of Israel over the demonic powers of darkness. Yet our task is to discover not only the intent of the author but also the way in which the Spirit uses this text to reveal the saving work of Jesus Christ. First of all, we seek to ascertain how the meaning of the serpent evolved in Hebraic history and how the serpent was regarded in the New Testament. Isaiah associated the serpent with Leviathan, the sinister monster of the sea, whose destruction will take place on the eschatological day of the Lord (Isa. 27:1; cf. Ps. 74:14). In Revelation 20:2 the serpent is expressly identified with the dragon, Satan and the devil, who is thrown into the Abyss by an angel from heaven. Thus it is in basic accord with the wider perspective of biblical faith to see in the serpent a primal symbol of the demonic adversary of God and humanity.

The enmity between the seed of the woman and the seed of the serpent becomes apparent in the ongoing struggle between the devil and the human race. The prophecy in verse 15 that the seed of the woman shall bruise the head of the serpent can be held to be fulfilled in the overthrow of the devil by Jesus Christ, through his atoning death and glorious resurrection from the grave. This victory is carried forward in the obedience of Christians to the gospel of Jesus Christ (cf. Rom. 16:20).

(2) In Genesis 4:1–16 we are introduced to a related saga describing one of the most dreaded consequences of sin—murder—which goes back to the very beginnings of humankind. Historical criticism tells us that Cain was considered the embodiment or ancestor of the Kenites who, though they worshiped Yahweh, were never included in the covenant community nor were they heirs of the promised land. The curse that fell on Cain is considered by some commentators to be a curse that fell on the Kenites.

Some liberal scholars find the significance of this story in the tension between farmers (represented by Cain) and seminomads (represented by Abel). But this is a sociological or cultural-historical explanation of this ancient tale and certainly does not do justice to the theological concerns of the Yahwist.

Theologically considered, the story has two points of significance. First, the fact that the Lord accepted Abel's sacrifice over

Cain's is not to be attributed to any higher intrinsic goodness on the part of Abel. At the same time, this may have been the Spirit's way of showing that a blood sacrifice was necessary as an expression of true faith, and therefore Abel's sacrifice was honored by God (cf. Heb. 11:4). Or it may underscore the truth that the sacrifices we offer to God are acceptable only on the basis of grace, not human merit. The saga itself does not indicate any reason other than God's good pleasure for the preference of Abel over Cain, though the wider Old Testament context gives priority to blood sacrifice as a means of countering the effects of sin. In the New Testament perspective only the blood of Christ cleanses from sin (1 John 1:7). Abel can be considered a Christ figure, since he offered the sacrifice pleasing to God. New Testament faith regards him as the first martyr (Matt. 23:35), and the epistle to the Hebrews likens his death to the death of Christ (Heb. 12:24).

The second significant point of this saga concerns the sign that was placed on Cain to protect him from robbers and marauders. This sign is to be regarded as a type of the sign of the cross, as Wilhelm Vischer rightly points out,[3] for the cross signifies that Christ died for the whole world, for both the Cains and the Abels. Those who choose the pathway of sin, as did Cain, are still protected by the grace of God, despite the fact that they do not deserve this.

But the deepest christological significance of this story is that God's grace covers the sins of all people, for we are all Cains in the sight of God before whom we are all guilty of the murder of his Son. Yet despite our sin and guilt, we are accepted by God because his Son has borne the penalty of our sin in our place. The sign of the cross fulfills and renews the deepest symbolism in the sign of Cain. The sign placed on Cain points to the gospel of the justification of the ungodly.

Unlike fundamentalist scholars whose primary concern is the historical veracity of this story rather than its christological significance, I am not troubled that the author employs a poetic narrative to convey deeper truth. Scholars who adhere to a more conservative persuasion are bent on explaining how Cain found a wife in a land where, so it is recorded, other people dwelt. They are intrigued by the question: how can this be if Cain was one of the three sons of the original first couple? I would be willing to entertain the possibility that both Cain and Abel were historical figures in one of the tribal ancestries of ancient mid-eastern culture, but the intention of the author is not to convey factual information on the first murder but instead to show how murder is endemic to sin and how grace is available even to the worst of sinners.[4]

In relating this saga to the contemporary situation we can immediately see its christological relevance for such social issues as capital punishment and for such enduring psychic realities as the inner torment and rootlessness that sin fosters. It is interesting to speculate on what the Spirit of God would have us preach today on the basis of this passage, but because God's Word is always concrete and specific, in an essay such as this we cannot judge absolutely what God's Word might be in the existential situation of a particular congregation.

(3) Isaiah 35 is a prophetic depiction of the return of the exiles from Babylonia to Palestine. Scholars are uncertain as to its precise dating, but most agree that together with 34:1–17 it probably belonged originally to chapters 40–66 and is therefore exilic rather than pre-exilic. At any rate, it was not the product of the hand of Isaiah of Jerusalem, though some might wish to contend that the reference is to the return of the people of the Northern Kingdom to their homeland from Assyria.

Whatever the case, the context indicates that the author, who stands in the so-called Isaiah tradition, is envisaging a return of the chosen people of God to the land of Israel. The desert in verse 1 refers very probably to the wilderness area in the vicinity of the Dead Sea. The prophecy is eschatological in the sense that Isaiah is foretelling the ransoming of the people of Zion who are now in captivity.

From the perspective of the New Testament we see this prophecy fulfilled in the advent of Jesus Christ. He is the "holy way," and through him we enter into the glories of Zion. God in Christ has opened to us a "new and living way" (Heb. 10:20). Jesus Christ is "the way, and the truth, and the life" (John 14:6). The "haunt of jackals" in Isaiah 35:7 now becomes the habitation of demons as Christians make their pilgrimage through the valley of the shadow of death (Ps. 23:4). The vision of the lame leaping like a hart and the tongue of the dumb singing for joy seems to prefigure the healing ministry of our Lord. Jesus' ministry is also anticipated in Isaiah 29:18–19. It seems, moreover, that Jesus had in mind these very Isaiah passages in his announcement of his mission (Luke 7:21–22).

To hear the Word that God wishes us to hear in this passage for today, we can surmise that the return of the ransomed of the Lord to Zion could refer to the gathering of the elect into the covenant community of faith. Or it might also be a portrayal of the journey of believers, living in the exile of a fallen world, to the New Jerusalem, their final destination. The New Jerusalem is depicted as coming down out of heaven at the second coming of Christ (Rev. 21:2, 10). The waters breaking forth in the wilderness could well be a type of the living water, the outpouring of the Spirit of Christ at Pentecost (cf. John 3:5; 4:10–15).

When this passage is applied to the religious and cultural situation today, we can perhaps hear a call to endurance and hope as we travel the holy way to the New Jerusalem, to the heavenly Mount Zion. This passage will have a different impact and significance for persecuted Christians behind the Iron Curtain and in the impoverished nations of the Third World than it has for affluent Christians in the West. Here again, we cannot presume to know what God will disclose through his Word to people today, but we can prepare ourselves to hear what he has to say to us as individuals and to our churches in our own cultural contexts. The one conclusion that we can safely draw is that God's Word in this Isaiah passage will be a word of hope and comfort, for its deepest intimations are fulfilled in the coming of Jesus Christ who personifies and embodies the light that shines in the darkness (John 1:5). Indeed, it is possible to use this passage for a sermon on the Gospel itself.

(4) The prophecy in Joel 2:28-32 is incontestably a messianic one concerning the restoration of Israel and the coming day of the Lord. Joel undoubtedly did not consciously have in mind the coming of Jesus Christ, but his predictions about the sun turning to darkness and the moon to blood are associated in the New Testament with the glorious advent of Christ (Mark 13:24; Luke 21:25; Rev. 6:12). His prediction in vss. 28 and 29 about the sons and daughters of Israel prophesying and the old men dreaming dreams are regarded by the Apostle Peter as being fulfilled on the day of Pentecost (Acts 2:17-21). Joel envisaged a restoration of an earthly temporal kingdom, but in the light of the New Testament we see his prophecies concerning the restoration of the people of God being fulfilled in the inbreaking of the spiritual kingdom of Christ. Fundamentalists generally believe that the present kingdom of Israel is foretold in these ancient Old Testament prophecies, but this is to apply to these verses a dispensational as opposed to a christological hermeneutic.

When we read this passage in the light of the situation today, our eyes are opened to the amazing inroads of the church of Christ in the Third World nations, which may indicate a new Pentecost, a sign of the last times. Joel himself distinguishes between the early rain and the latter rain (2:23; cf. Hos. 6:3; James 5:7-8), and it could be said that the early rain occurred at the first Pentecost while the latter rain is now or will soon be descending upon us. This is a common Pentecostal interpretation of Joel, and it may have some validity. It should be remembered that in biblical usage the Day of the Lord can refer to both the coming of Jesus Christ and the judgment of God upon the nations at the end of time.

The Apostles of the New Testament felt free on many occasions to expand the prophecies of the Old Testament on the basis of the new light that was given to them. For Peter, on the day of Pentecost, *all flesh* included all nations (Acts 2:17). For Joel, on the other hand, *all flesh* (2:28) meant the Jews only.

As we try to relate this passage to the current situation, we are first reminded of the day of Pentecost, the second stage of the Parousia (according to K. Barth) when Jesus Christ came to dwell within his people by his Spirit and empower them for his service. But we are also called to contemplate on the renewal of Pentecost in our time as a sign of the coming again of Christ in power and glory to set up his kingdom that shall have no end. The signs and portents in the heavens can rightly be associated with both advents of Christ, and in every generation we should look for signs of the day when he will reveal his power and glory to all nations.

This passage might also be used by the Spirit in our time to extend the privilege of the public preaching of the gospel to women, since Joel says that both sons and daughters, both men-servants and maidservants will prophesy. In some situations God's Word may be that women should keep silent in the public services of worship (1 cor. 14:34) but in others that they should preach and prophesy.

(5) As we move on to the New Testament, we find ourselves in a qualitatively different situation, for the Apostles were eye- and earwitnesses of God's self-revelation in Jesus Christ, the revelation that fulfilled the partial revelations of the divine mercy in Israel's history. Yet the sad fact is that even New Testament passages are often interpreted without any real reference to the saving work of Christ on the cross.

Turning to the beatitudes, we can understand how easy it is to interpret these sayings of Jesus in such a way that an ethical style of life takes precedence over God's work of reconciliation and redemption in Jesus Christ as the Son of Man. To ethicize Jesus' teachings is to make Jesus into a sagacious teacher, a spiritual master, the greatest of the prophets, but this is not yet to acknowledge him as the divine Savior who rescues us from sin.

The beatitude as recorded in Matthew 5:9 reads: "Blessed are the peacemakers, for they shall be called sons of God." In exegeting this passage I would first concentrate on grammatical-historical criticism, contrasting the meaning of *makarios* (blessed) with *eudaimōn* (fortunate or happy). I would also explore the meanings of the Hebrew *shalôm* and the Greek *eirēnē* in an attempt to show that the pursuit of peace in the biblical perspective entails more than a spiritual or inner peace. It means to restore right relationships between people and between fallen humanity and the living God.

I would then move on to what is commonly called higher criticism and try to ascertain whether the beatitudes were spoken on a single occasion or whether they represent teachings of Jesus delivered on various occasions. I would also delve into the differences between the versions of the beatitudes in Matthew and Luke. Did the theological outlook or psychological disposition of the two authors color their perceptions of these sayings? Is this why Matthew's emphasis tends to be more spiritual and Luke's more social?

Now we are ready for a genuine theological treatment of the text in which we view it in the light of the wider message of Jesus and, even more, of the apostolic witness concerning the significance of his life, death, and resurrection. When we relate this text to Jesus' understanding of the kingdom of God, we see that the beatitudes represent guidelines for the style of life that is to characterize those who live in the new age of the kingdom. The way of the cross is the way of nonviolence, the way of suffering love, even nonresistance, whereas the way of the world is governed by the lusts of the flesh and the use of the sword.

When we proceed to relate this text to the apostolic testimony concerning the significance of the life, death, and resurrection of Jesus, we begin to see its christological import. The New Testament makes clear that there can never be peace in the world until people are in union with the Prince of Peace, Jesus Christ, a union effected by the Holy Spirit and realized in the decision of faith. The key to real peace is the preaching of the gospel of regeneration by which the spirit of peace is imparted to those who believe. The cross of Christ signifies not only the way *of* peace but the way *to* peace, for it is only as we grasp the meaning of the cross that we are enabled to die to the passions of the flesh and live and walk in the way of righteousness.

To be a peacemaker is a privilege granted by the free mercy

of God, not a meritorious work entitling us to special rights in his kingdom. Our peacemaking is the evidence but not the ground of our adoption into the family of God, which rests solely on his grace.

But we are obliged to say something more. It is Jesus Christ who by his atoning death and vicarious love reconciles a fallen human race to the God of infinite holiness and mercy. He alone is the perfect peacemaker, and therefore he alone is perfectly blessed. It is he who has torn down the walls that separate sinners from one another and from the holy God. We are all brought closer together by the shedding of his blood on the cross. "For he is himself our peace," declares Paul. "Gentiles and Jews, he has made the two one, and in his own body of flesh and blood has broken down the enmity which stood like a dividing wall between them" (Eph. 2:14–15; NEB).

To be at peace with our Maker as well as with ourselves is to know that our sins are covered by the righteousness of Christ. To know love in its supreme radicality is to experience the forgiveness of sins available to us through the death of Christ on the cross. It is only when we have this kind of peace that we can be peacemakers in the church and in secular society. To be a peacemaker is not only to walk in the steps of Christ, to be a reconciler where discord reigns, but it is also to direct people to Jesus Christ who alone imparts the peace that passes all understanding (Phil. 4:7). Our deeds of peacemaking will therefore be understood as signs and parables of the passion and victory of Jesus Christ. By paying the penalty for sin he made peace between God and sinful humankind. By putting sin to death in our own lives through the power of the cross of Christ we can be instruments of Christ's peace in the world.

(6) The parabolic statement of the binding of the strong man in Mark 3:27 affords another opportunity to see Jesus Christ as the hidden and sometimes the explicit meaning of the scriptural text. In its immediate context it is clear that Jesus is referring to the overthrow of Satan by himself. It is Jesus who binds the

strong man and plunders his house. A parallel image is the casting down of Satan to the earth (cf. Luke 10:18; Rev. 12:9).

The idea of the binding of the evil powers should be viewed in the context of the eschatological message of the kingdom (cf. Isa. 24:21–23; Rev. 20:1–3). This binding is already noticeable in Jesus' ministry of exorcism, but it becomes a cosmic reality when he dethrones the principalities and powers through his atoning death on the cross and his victorious resurrection from the grave (Col. 2:15). The New Testament pictures Jesus as leading a host of captives into the heavenly paradise by his resurrection from the dead (Eph. 4:8–10; cf. Ps. 68:18). The binding of Satan does not mean the destruction of the demonic force, but it does mean that his power is now significantly curtailed, since he is unable to block the advancement of the gospel in the world. He is like a barking dog that is chained (Augustine). He is able to inspire fear and thereby cause disruption in the world, but actually his real power has been taken from him. His "Titanic" scheme to gain mastery over the world has been irrevocably shattered, though he can still keep the world in confusion. By the gift of the Spirit we now come to realize that the power of the devil resides primarily in his ability to deceive. Only God has the power to cast into hell (Matt. 10:28), and Satan is an unwilling instrument in the hands of a holy God who uses evil to overthrow evil.

To affirm the christological meaning of the binding of the strong man entails a belief in a personal demonic adversary of God and humanity, called in the Bible Satan, Leviathan, Beelzebul, and the devil. While acknowledging that much of the depiction of the devil and his activity in the New Testament is in the form of myth or picture language, we cannot deny the supernatural reality which is the focus of the myth. We deny the presuppositions of historical positivism in which the life of humanity is portrayed as a closed system of historical causation. We must be willing to learn what historical and literary criticism can tell us about the construction of the text and the psychology of the author, but it is Scripture itself or rather the Spirit acting within Scripture that gives us the theological significance of the text.

When we deal with the question of the contemporary relevance of this particular text, we are reminded that the church continues its warfare against the principalities and powers. These powers have been dethroned, the dragon has been mortally wounded, but in his death throes he can be even more dangerous than before. Yet in the knowledge that his days are numbered, that his real power has been taken from him, we can, on the basis of this text, take heart that the church cannot be defeated in its mission to bring the whole world into subjection to Jesus Christ. Insofar as people continue to live according to the lie that the devil promulgates, they still need to be delivered. Exorcism should be part of the ministry of the church today. But we should bear in mind that it is the power of the gospel itself that frees people in bondage to the forces of darkness. It is not any special ritual of exorcism, though this may be appropriate in certain instances, but the preaching of the gospel itself that brings to a lost and helpless world the fruits of Christ's cross and resurrection victory.

(7) A text that has lent itself to much controversy in recent years regarding the role of women in ministry is 1 Corinthians 14:33-34: "As in all the congregations of the saints, women should remain silent in the churches. They are not allowed to speak, but must be in submission, as the Law says" (NIV). A comparable injunction is found in 1 Timothy 2:11-12, though the Pauline authorship of that particular epistle is questioned by many scholars, including some conservatives.[5] What is perplexing about 1 Corinthians 14:34 is that in the same epistle Paul acknowledges the right of women to pray and prophesy publicly in the assembly of the congregation (11:5, 13). Some critical scholars have concluded that these verses are an insertion of a later writer and reflect a hardening of attitudes on this question in the Christian community. I believe, on the contrary, that Paul's remarks are best understood in the light of a particular

problem in the Corinthian church of this time, namely, women glossolalists who were causing disturbances in the worship of the congregation. As Moffatt suggests, it may well be that, as Paul was trying to bring to a close this particular portion of his letter, new reports came to him of further commotion caused by overzealous charismatics who happened to be mainly women. He then felt constrained to curb this growing anarchy in worship by issuing an injunction forbidding women to preach publicly and to be subordinate, probably to their husbands and perhaps also to the elders or pastors.

Yet, that Paul was not making this an unconditional or universal command is obvious from the fact that in other epistles he speaks highly of Priscilla and Phoebe both of whom carried on an active teaching ministry. In Romans 16:2 Paul urges the entire Christian community in Rome to be at the disposal of Phoebe "in whatever she may require from you." In the same epistle he asks Roman Christians to greet "Andronicus and Junia, my kinsmen, and my fellow prisoners, who are of note among the apostles" (Rom. 16:7 KJV). (It is becoming more widely accepted in scholarly circles that Junia was a woman, not a man as suggested by the "Junias" used in most translations.)

Yet we still do not grasp the christological significance of our text until we view it in the light of Galatians 3:26–29 where the essential equality of the male and female members of the body of Christ is affirmed. Sexual differences are not annulled, but they are relativized by faith in Christ, for in Christ all are "sons of God" (Gal. 3:26).

Further illumination is given to the Corinthian text when it is related to Ephesians 2:14–22 where Christ is pictured as breaking down the walls that divide Christians from one another by abolishing "the law of commandments and ordinances" (vs. 15). The promise of woman's call to ministry in Acts 2:17–18 will also figure in a fuller theological exposition of this passage.

What our text seems to tell us is that in some situations women should keep silent in the church and let men assume control. In other situations, however, there may be a real place for women in the preaching and teaching ministry of the church. The barriers to women's ordination are sociological more than theological.

We should also say something about the principle of subordination. This is not overthrown in the Pauline epistles but given a new meaning or thrust. This principle, too, must be interpreted christologically, as Paul does in Ephesians 5:21–33. Just as Christ gave himself for the church, so the husband must give himself to the wife. His headship is realized in service. Her subordination is realized in her respect for and loving assistance to her husband; together they work out a common vocation under the cross.

Both men and women in ministry are called to practice subordination to one another and to the congregation which has called them. Subordination, indeed, is the law of the kingdom of God, but it must now be understood not as servile submission to authority but as service in fellowship. This is how Paul understood the team ministry of Priscilla and Aquila (note that in Rom. 16:3 he places Priscilla first); this is also how he conceived of his own ministry in relation to Lydia, Phoebe, and Priscilla.

The law of subordination is based on God's gracious condescension to a sinful humanity in the person of his Son Jesus Christ. It is also anchored in the subordination that Jesus practiced in relation to his disciples. It was he who washed their feet and not vice versa. It was he who suffered and died for them, not vice versa. He realized his headship in the role of a servant, and we are called to do likewise. His exaltation was manifest precisely in his humiliation, and this is true for his disciples in every age and race.

Word and Spirit

It can legitimately be asked whether I am operating with a canon within the canon. This is not the case if it means interpreting the whole from the vantage point of select books in the New Testament (in the manner of Käsemann). It is the case if it implies understanding the whole of Scripture in the light of the gospel of Jesus Christ, but this gospel is either explicit or implicit in every part of Scripture. I here concur with Luther who contended that every scriptural text can be law or gospel depending on how we relate it to Jesus Christ.

The gospel of the cross is indeed the hidden and not so hidden meaning of all the Scriptures, but this gospel cannot be extracted from Scripture as something apart from or independent of its context. Forsyth has cogently observed:

> The Word is not in the Bible as a treasure hid in a field so that you can dig out the jewel and leave the soil. It grows from it like a tree. It breathes from it like a sweet savour. It streams up from it like an exhalation. It rises like the soul going to glory from its sacred dust. The Word of God is not to be dissected from the Bible, but to be distilled.[6]

Because the gospel is basically a mystery of which we are stewards (1 Cor. 4:1), we can point to it but we cannot possess it. Our formulations cannot be identified with the gospel itself, but they should be regarded as a sign and witness of the gospel. They *become* the gospel when God unites his Word with our broken words by his Spirit. This is not mysticism, for I insist that meaning shines through mystery. Though our understandings are always partial, they are nonetheless valid for they have their basis in the illumination of the Holy Spirit.

The gospel as the transcendent Word of God will appear somewhat different to the church in every age, since the Spirit always has a fresh message for the churches. It is the same message, but it is revealed in a new way. For Augustine, at least in one stage of his ministry, the principal theme of the gospel seemed to be the vision of God (cf. Matt. 5:8; 1 Cor. 13:12). Luther perceived the essence of the Word to be justification by faith alone. For Calvin it was the life of regeneration based on the remission of sins gained for us by the death and resurrection of Christ. In the theology of Karl Barth, it was the theme of reconciliation and redemption revealed and enacted in Jesus Christ. For the Pietists it was personal conversion through total surrender to the will of God. For Ritschl and the liberal theologians who followed him, it was the proclamation of the kingdom of God. For us today, it might well be the call to obedience and perseverance amid growing persecution. This call is always grounded in the perfect obedience of Jesus Christ, which makes our partial obedience possible.

Historical research can be used to discover the literary background and cultural context of the passage in question, but it cannot procure for us the meaning of the Word of God. What historical criticism can give us concerning the events of sacred history mirrored in the Bible is a knowledge of probability, not certainty. It can throw light upon the *Sitz im Leben* of the text, but it cannot lay hold of its theological and spiritual significance. Does this mean that we should then move from a historical to an existential understanding of the text? In one sense this can be affirmed if it implies that we must now discover what the text means for us personally. On the other hand, we dare not tread this path if it signifies that our goal is simply to arrive at a new awareness of human existence in the light of the text. Against existentialist theology, I contend that what the text conveys to us is not simply a new self-understanding but *information* about the will and purpose of God, *knowledge* of the plan of salvation.

The revelatory meaning of the text cannot be procured by any technique, including that of existential analysis. It can only be conveyed by the action of the Spirit upon the text and within our hearts. The key to the mystery of the meaning of the text lies not in a poetic divination into the language of the text but in the gift of divine illumination. We must pray as Solomon did for an "understanding heart" (1 Kings 3:9–12; NKJ). We must ask the Spirit to teach us the mystery of his law (Ps. 119:18, 130). We must pray that the eyes of our hearts might be enlightened so that we can understand the meaning of our hope in Jesus Christ (Eph. 1:18).

What I am advocating is not a pneumatic or devotional exegesis in which we simply read meanings into the text under the inspiration of the Spirit. Instead, we are called to discover the intent of the text by comparing it to other texts and relating it to the meaning of the whole—the proclamation of "the law of the Spirit of life in Christ Jesus" (Rom. 8:2). We rely ultimately upon the guidance of the Spirit in this task, but this does not lead us to substitute feeling for reason. On the contrary, we seek to use our reason in the service of the Word.

Christological hermeneutics presupposes that Scripture was written within a community of faith. We cannot really grasp the various nuances of meaning that a text carries unless we stand in this community, unless we share in this faith. Our criterion is not the consensus of the community, but the Spirit of God working both within the text and within the community enabling us to understand—dimly but truly (cf. 1 Cor. 13:12). Our partial understandings will always be in continuity (though not necessarily in total agreement) with the basic understanding of the prophets and sages of the church throughout history.

It behooves us to avoid the perils of both subjectivism and objectivism. We should neither seek a higher spiritual meaning divorced from the text nor rely on the common sense meaning of the text available even to the "natural man." The Word of God is not self-evident in Scripture; it must be sought, but it must be sought in Scripture, not beyond it.

It is important to distinguish carefully between the culturally conditioned form of Scripture and its divine content. We should take pains to avoid both a fusion of form and content (as in the older orthodoxy) and a separation of form and content (as in liberalism). Our task is to penetrate through the form to the divine content, but this is not possible apart from a special divine illumination.

The challenge today is to regain confidence that the living Word of God will manifest himself in and through his written Word. It is not whether we have the right tools to dig out the Word of God in Scripture but whether the Spirit of God is ready to act to reveal his Word to the searching heart. No amount of exegetical dexterity or theological acumen can give us the revelatory meaning of the scriptural text. This is a gift bestowed only on the basis of faith in Jesus Christ, and a simple believer may find this meaning before a hermeneutical expert. This is not to deny that those who are educated in biblical studies and at the same time enlightened by the Spirit are able to understand the cultural and theological ramifications of the revelation of the Word of God far better than those who are illiterate in these areas. What I am saying, however, is that we cannot take pride in our ability to master the text, for its revelatory impact is available to us only when the text masters us. The revelation of the Word of God is a matter of the free decision of God, not a matter of bringing to the Bible the right kind of pre-understanding or the latest findings in form and redaction criticism. God is still sovereign even in the science of biblical interpretation, and both liberal and conservative exegetes need to acknowledge this anew.

6 The Use of the Bible in Theology

JOHN HOWARD YODER

University of Notre Dame
South Bend, Indiana

To ask how the Bible functions in theology is like asking how the ground floor functions in a house: there are several possible right answers, and any one of them looks a little silly when spelled out. The self-evident answer is holistically that it is the ground floor. In terms of traffic patterns, you can say that you have to go through the ground floor to get to the stairs which would lead to the other floors. In terms of architecture, you can say that it carries the weight of the upper stories. In terms of frequentation, you can say that the rooms there tend to be used by more people and to be more public. Any one of those answers is true, and any one of them is less than simply to say that the ground floor is the ground floor.

The utility of any specific answer to this question depends then on the particular sub-questions which the one putting the question has in mind. Is the person asking about traffic patterns or about the weight of the building or about the channeling of pipes and wires or about rental values per square foot? Most of the questions which might be interesting from one perspective will be uninteresting from another. How then are we to proceed? My first concern is to elaborate on the obviousness of our situation, in ways that do not immediately promise to decide any controverted question.

How Do People Theologize in a Believing Community?

Theology has a catechetical function. This will naturally be the first function encountered by a seeker or believer new to the faith community. Here it is appropriate that formulations of what we believe will need to be developed, which select from a much wider heritage those particular elements that one needs to know first. Priorities are established among the various things which older Christians know, or which the community at large knows and which are all good to know, by lifting out the minimal number of things which a new believer needs to know first. This must be done in the light of the total biblical heritage.

The Bible itself does not sort out any such minimal statement for us. It does record, sometimes explicitly, as in the account of the encounter between Philip and the Ethiopian, but more often implicitly, some wordings of baptismal confessions, but such a confession is less than a catechism. Some scholars suggest that the book of Matthew was developed to serve as a catechism in some early Syrian community, but that is to use the term "catechism" in a broader sense.

The decision about what to teach first will not only be based in the traditional materials, mainly the biblical resources from the early church's experience. It will not only seek to annunciate this primitive gospel. It will also need to take account of the prophetic and evangelistic clash with the particular world of unbelief from which that specific seeker or convert has come. The church must be open to recognize some priority denunciations or renunciations as a necessary part of Christian decision in any particular world. In Psalm 24:3–7 we have an example of such theological affirmation and negation. Two items are named which describe a generally pure character; one is ethical, and one says that the person has not served idols. There are thus both behavioral and conceptual components in the definition proffered. The renunciation of idolatry in 24:6 is an integral part of the definition, a specimen of denunciation which applies if the surrounding culture is idolatrous. One recalls that Jesus said in

Luke 14 that readiness to bear a cross is a prerequisite for following him.

The theological ministry of the catechete deals then with the criteria of appropriateness in selection and accent. The Bible will serve both as the first but not the exclusive source of the affirmations to be made and as the total value frame in which priorities need to be determined. Yet at two points the Bible is clearly not sufficient or self-expositing. It can replace neither the contemporary charisma of the teacher who makes that selection in a given circumstance nor the substance of the encounter with the world in which the particular catechumen has been nurtured and to which the corrective and informative impact of the message must be directed.

Persons who grow up within the believing community may never need catechism. They are surrounded with another kind of theology which might simply be characterized as *Christian culture*. There are the stories of faith told from one generation to the next. There is the language of worship and the several languages and styles of preaching. There is the way in which ethical deliberation draws upon the heritage of the believing community for illumination and adjudication. With this variety of communication going on, most of it nonprofessional and unsystematic, the child of a believing family grows up knowing a certain corpus of theological notions, understood more contextually than conceptually, their definitions more supposed than spelled out. This, too, is theology. The Bible constitutes its ground floor, but again its total composition will be determined by processes of selection and exchange which the Bible undergoes rather than directs. It will include considerable language originating later than that of the canon. More of it will come from hymns, sermons, and children's stories than directly from the text of Scripture.

The Bible is at the center of a larger field of teachings and testimonies from which the catechist will select what needs to be learned first. But precisely since catechesis is correlated with the particular unbelief from which a particular catechumen comes, the Bible itself does not do the selecting. The process of selection will be largely but not finally predisposed by the intrinsic lines of accent within the biblical material. With regard to the formation of awareness provided by the ongoing familial life of the body of Christ in nurture and worship, the Bible is at the center of a much larger body of materials. But if the life of that community is vital and in continuing connection with its own epoch, there will always be more to their stories and phrases, testimonies, lessons, and praises than a simple repetition from Scripture itself. Thus, an appropriate image would be the trunk of a tree supporting and nourishing branches which reach out to the leaves which interact with the atmosphere (and which need to be replaced once a year, without which the twigs would not grow, without which the trunk would die).

So if we ask how Scripture functions for these first two kinds of theology, the answer by definition cannot and should not be rigorous. It describes the relation of leaves and branches both to the atmosphere and to the trunk.

Theology has a corrective function. Beyond and within these more simply given kinds of communication, there are others carried on by fewer people in much more special circumstances. Sometimes we need to speak a word of correction to ourselves in our own community. Then we call it "renewal." Sometimes we address to others arguments about our differences. Then we call it "polemics" (if the argument is strong) or "irenics" (if it is gentle). What defines this new category is the existence of differences of conviction. Two or more persons differ as to what they hold it should mean to confess the faith. Such differences are always implicitly theological and sometime explicitly so; i.e., they have implicit or explicit rootage in how concepts are defined, how language is used, and how conclusions are explained.

It is at this point of difference that there arises a more specific function for Scripture than we have dealt with hitherto. When people differ, they either can or cannot appeal to some common authority which they recognize as above them both. If they cannot, then any further argument must be inchoate, impressionistic, and without final logical force. If, on the other hand, there is some common court of appeal or superior criterion, then the continuing dialogue about their difference can hold some promise of change which may be called "education," "repentance," "reconciliation," or "training," depending on the perspective in which we want to look at it.

In the specific Christian case, that ultimate court of appeal in the corrective use of theology is the revelation of God in Jesus Christ. To go back one step further we should of course say the ultimate court of appeal is God *in se*, since the functional meaning of the word "God" is such ultimacy. But apart from revelation in Christ we would not know which God or what kind of God we are talking about. Therefore, that last hypothetical degree of ultimate reaching back does not need further attention.

Obviously the label "Christ" as designating a revelatory authority is not simple but instead designates a semantic field. At the center there is the historic reality of Jesus. Surrounding that reality and mediating it to us, there is a circle of immediate interpretations by qualified witnesses who spoke about him in reliable Aramaic and Greek reports. Some of those reports were immediate testimonies about the life and work of Jesus. Others were less immediate in that they talked about the difference he made to them in terms of hope or atonement or initiation into community. The deposit of such testimonies is our New Testament.

Equally indispensable but one notch further out is the circle of assumptions and prerequisites, cultural backgrounds, and definitions of terms within which the primary testimonies have to be interpreted in order to know what those first testimonies meant. A dominant component of that context was the Hebrew heritage of which the Old Testament is our primary document. Another element of it is the contemporary *Zeitgeschichte* which is accessible to us only through the very fallible and fuzzy tools of literary and archaeological history, aided but also called into question by the ancillary disciplines of linguistics, literary analysis, anthropology, etc.

This way of schematically subdividing the kinds of theological discourse has intentionally left aside one of them. That one is the sense in which we are also talking "theology" when we talk to unbelievers. An unbeliever by definition is someone with whom we do not share an ultimate court of appeal, although we may very well share common penultimate criteria. With most of our unbelieving neighbors we agree to try to talk sense according to the laws of grammar and logic. With some of them we agree to try to argue according to the rules of rational debate. With most of them we get along most of the time assuming verifiable common readings on such matters as the price of eggs and the sovereignty of the United States of America. But on the matter concerning which they are unbelievers, those common criteria do not reach to convince or to condemn. Or, if they do, it is because through some special gift of providence some penultimate value is raised to a higher level of redemptive power. It may for instance be that some deed of loving service will touch a neighbor at a point of common humanity to communicate what argument could not. It will usually not be a biblical appeal. I thus conclude, within the oversimplification which is excusable for this kind of capsule argument, that apologetics or evangelism should not be thought of as constituting a distinctive mode of theological discourse for which we would need a specific definition of the place of the Bible.

How Did the New Testament Church Theologize?

The New Testament records indicate the presence in the early communities of a particular functionary known as the teacher (*didaskalos*). Which of the above functions are we to think of this person as exercising: a catechetical one, or a corrective one? Perhaps there was still something else which was done under that heading. The teacher's function is unique among those to which we find reference in the apostolic writings in the fact that it is specifically described in the epistle of James as a risky function which not many should seek to discharge. This is quite different from the general Pauline pattern which encourages everybody to seek all the gifts (1 Cor. 14:5, all speak in tongues, all prophesy; 1 Timothy 3:1, it is fine to want to be bishop).

The reason for this caution, we are told, is that the tongue is "an unruly member." Our subjective individualism makes us think of "tongue" as the individual's capacity for speech and of the "unruliness" then as a tendency to speak impulsively, unkindly, or carelessly. One must doubt whether James was so modern. The "tongue" in any Aryan language means the language, the phenomenon of language, and the social reality of communication. Language is unruly in that playing around with words or trying to be consistent in our use of words or dealing with issues by defining terms is a constant source of contestation and confusion. Here is James' caution. So it is, too, that Timothy can at the same time be invited to "follow the pattern of the sound words" which he had received from Paul (2 Tim. 1:13) and be warned against "disputing about words, which does no good, but only ruins the hearers" (2 Tim. 2:14). The teacher is then someone charged with care about verbal formulations, who must serve in the awareness that such instruments of the faith are at the same time both indispensable and misleading. It is with language as it is with the rudder of a ship, the bit in the horse's mouth, or the flame igniting a forest: there is a multiplier effect whereby any mistake in balance or aim produces greater damage through the leverage of language.

What does this have to do with how the Bible functions in theology? First of all, the Apostle warns that the Bible itself is the victim of that flexibility and leverage. Canonical scripture used by communities to shape their identity has that characteristic of being subject to manipulation in order to support whatever the later interpreters of the tradition want to have ratified. There is a sense in which the objectivity of the scriptural text in its unchanging wording can be appealed to as a corrective against the most highly fanciful flights of redefinition, but it would be part of the naïveté against which the Apostle warns us if we were to take that objectivity as a guarantee. It is rather the risk of abuse to which canonical texts are subject that calls upon the teacher to be more restrained than the poets and prophets in the interpretations which he or she allows people to commend to one another. The wording of the Bible is not an empowering ratification giving the theologian a special advantage in the knowledge of truths qualitatively different from the truths other people can know. The Bible is, rather, the victim of the corrosive and distorting effect of the leverage of language, and the theologian is its defender.

Everyone ought to read the Bible, and all ought to be free to interpret it soberly in relevance to their own situations. What we need the *didaskalos* for is to defend the historical objectivity of what the text said in the first place against the leverage of overly confident or "relevant" applications. Already in the early church this was a task that called for linguistic sophistication. One needed to know how discerningly to control the tongue. Today it is far clearer how such discernment can and must use the tools of linguistic science. The ancient concept of a "simple sense" of Scripture to be played off against the "fuller sense" and the allegorical sense of the text is obviously oversimple, but the concern which it represented is still appropriate. There are forms of articulation which are fruitlessly speculative, destructively relativizing, or unwholesomely accommodating. The task of the *didaskalos* is to defend the difference between the organic fidelity of our interpretation now and the meaning of the message then as well as to oppose other "adaptations" or "applications" which rather constitute betrayal.

The fact that people are tempted to abuse Scripture by calling upon it to support whatever they believe is one of the reasons it is inappropriate most of the time to think that the primary theological debate is about whether the biblical text is authoritative or not. Too many people are affirming its authority by claiming its support for interpretations which a more adequate hermeneutic will reject. The theologian's task is more often to defend the text against a wrong claim to its authority rather than to affirm in some timeless and case-free way that it has authority.

How Does the Bible Function Authoritatively?

Thus far it has been sufficient to look "phenomenologically" and then "biblically" at how a believing community will be seen thinking. There is no need to theorize about *why* the Bible has authority when one finds oneself living in a community in which that authority is presupposed and which is constantly being renewed through the simple experience of its operation. The "apologetic" notion that the appropriateness of that authority's being operative should be dependent upon our being able somehow to explain it in terms exterior to itself does not arise in the ordinary life of the believing community. In making this observation I am not expressing any interest in debating a systematic position of "presuppositionalism." That is also an apologetic stance. It is much more simply, descriptively the case that Christians gather around the words of the Word and that its message bears fruit in the ways described above without needing constantly to be pulled up by the roots in order to see why it should be working that way.

It is unavoidable, nonetheless, that within the process of reading this story acceptingly there should be in particular cases some selectivity as to which of the texts are found most central. This is true of the theologian serving the readers of a particular culture and class. When a culture is preoccupied by fear of the dark powers which rule the world, one will find especially the message of release from that fear. When a society is preoccupied with death, one will hear the message of resurrection and eternal life. When a society is anomic, it will be open to be illuminated by the Torah. There is no reason that in all times and places such initial priorities should not dictate a kind of "canon within the canon." It will be the responsibility of the theological discipline both to exercise this selectivity reasonably and to criticize it. The ultimate canon within the canon must in the end, however, be the person of Jesus and, in a broader sense, the narration of the saving acts of God. This follows from the fact that the Bible as a whole corpus of literature is narrative in its framework, although some of its fragments are not. That framework itself dictates the priority of the historical quality over levels of interpretation which would be less historical by being more abstract (ontology, systematic dogma) or individualistic.

As Paul Minear indicated long ago, we are most likely to learn from a text something which will constitute genuine learning if we attend to the points at which what a text seems to be saying is not something we already know or have under our control. This is true for any kind of human understanding, whether it be applied to the phenomena of physical or biological nature or to a piece of literature. Even more must it be the case for the Christian Scriptures, of which we confess that they testify to us of uniquely revelatory intervention. As the expository ministry of Minear did not cease to illustrate, the points at which we will most likely learn will therefore not be those already previously reduced to rational system but the odd, forgotten, or systemically erratic blocks within the literature.

One very fitting example from my own work is the "exousiology" of the Pauline writings. It can hardly be doubted that the handful of texts in the Pauline corpus which refer to "principalities and powers, thrones, angels . . ." represent in the minds of the Apostle and his disciples a coherent segment of a larger coherent cosmology. The work of Christ has an impact upon that cosmos. Christian interpretation since medieval times has assumed that this was repeating something about "angels" which we already knew and has therefore paid little further attention to those texts. Scholastic Protestantism gave them still less attention. Liberal Protestantism consciously excised them from its practical canon, knowing that they describe something which we already know cannot be; namely, a world of familiar spirits behind the causation of events. As a result, a major segment of Paul's understanding of the universe and of redemption has been made inoperative.

A series of Reformed theologians—Berkhof, Caird, Morrison, Markus Barth, and others—have revitalized our awareness of the relevance of this material. When I drew from them in a secondary synthesis in one chapter of my *Politics of Jesus*, there were those who felt it to be an inappropriate expression of my Mennonite bias, even though all of the sources I used, both the scriptural and the systematic theologians, were consistently in the Reformed tradition. But my present concern is not that my reading was Reformed, but that it was new yet old. The text was always there, but a new age opened our eyes to read it. This has been happening throughout the centuries, at least since St. Francis if not since Augustine. Scriptural orientation sharpens the ability to discern the signs of the times, but it is just as true that temporal orientation sharpens our ability to discern the signs in Scripture. This is a concrete case, in our age, of the fulfillment of the promise of which the puritan John Robinson has spoken: "The Lord has yet more light and truth to break forth. . . ."

It is most lively and productive to think of one body of literature, the Bible, representing in any time and place the testimony of the narrative stretching from Abraham to the Apostles, which can be juxtaposed to any other age by its Psalms being sung again, its letters being read again, its stories and parables being retold. Then in the juxtaposition of those stories with our stories there leaps the spark of the Spirit, illuminating parallels and contrasts, to give us the grace to see our age in God's light and God's truth in our words. This picture of how it works is more representative of the experienced facts but also more rigorous than the classical scholastic vision of an unchanging body of timeless propositions needing to be twisted to fit a new age by the special skills of rationalistic linguists.

Accepting the Bible's Own Shape as Defining "Theology": Toward a "Biblical Realism"

In the context described above, "theology" is not an end in itself, as it seems to be in some literary and academic contexts. The vocation of teacher is a ministry to the body, just as are the vocations of deacon and elder. The construction of a system is not valuable in its own right; we need to know to what end consistency or completeness is valued. The translation of older affirmations of faith into a new language is only worthwhile when we clearly identify the limits of faithfulness which keep that reformulation from selling out to the assumptions of the new language. The Bible itself can be a safeguard against theology as a system becoming idolatrous or an end unto itself, since the Bible itself is not what we would call theological in its style.

It speaks about God faithfully in pastoral, ministerial, and argumentative contexts, not in systematic or historical or expository ways. We still need to do theology as well in those ways, but the Bible will help to remind us to keep those operations both subordinate to the larger imperatives of the life of the body and relativized by their greater subservience to the demands of one's respective host culture. If we take the biblical authors as role models for theological discourse, they can protect us against overvaluing the didactic and the systematic modes.

The Bible is not simply a document of churchmanship with pastoral preoccupations. The particular kind of church of which it is the testimony is a missionary, aggressive, and subversive movement. We misunderstand even the practical/pastoral thrust of the Bible whenever we compare or equate it with the pastoral concerns of an established religion—with the maintenance of the life of parish and clan in a society where there are no longer any challenges being addressed to the powers that be, no longer any new believers coming in across the boundaries of nation and culture, and no longer any new threatening issues needing to be wrestled with on the missionary frontier. Pastoral care in the established church and in the minority missionary movement are two quite distinct operations. Scholastic theology tends to abstract out of that awareness; the Bible sustains it. "Biblical realism" is a tendency—hardly a school—which tries to make more of the Bible as a formal model.

We are accustomed to considering as "theological" those forms of expression that seek abstraction and generality. The Bible itself was not written that way. I do not argue that the reflexes of abstraction and generalization have no function at all, but we need to be more honest about their derivative quality and about the normalness of narrative or hortatory genres as good theology. The scandal of particularity and the vulnerability of faith as not being coercive are intrinsic to the gospel, and they are made more evident by the occasionalistic quality of the literature. When, for the sake of apologetic or missionary comprehensibility or for the sake of internal coherence, we step back from that concreteness and express ourselves in more general terms, it must not be with the thought that this will make the faith more credible. Apologetic rationalism, whether conservative like that of Clark or Van Til, moderate like Brunner, or liberal like Gordon Kaufman or David Tracy, is a rear guard exercise.

The real foundation, both formally and materially, for Christian witness is the historic objectivity of Jesus and the community he creates. Any other kind of "foundation" we can seek to make in a particular world is the footing for a bridge between that world and first-century Palestine.

By its nature, as a method seeking to reflect in its own structure the qualities of the text being read, "biblical realism" must be pluralistic with regard to styles and formulation. Therefore, it will, not by accident or misunderstanding but by virtue of its structural commitments, fall short of meshing satisfactorily with the methodological assumptions of scholastic orthodoxy which is committed to constructing a system which ideally would be rationalistic, stable, and closed. The reason for this flexibility of method is not a desire to be "liberal" either in the sense of an optimistic vision of human nature in general or in the more restrictive methodological sense of being optimistic about the power of one's critical tools. The reason is, rather, modesty about the power of our human instruments of interpretation, which leads appropriately, in the face of the choice which God obviously made to become manifest through a multiplicity of literary forms that are mostly narrative in framework and doxological in tone, to skepticism about the adequacy of any system-building of our own. Only in that way can the Bible be served and not become the servant in a communication event. Just as we are willing to receive our message from an authority we do not challenge, so we should properly subordinate our methods. Rational scholastic orthodoxy errs in filtering the given texts through the grid of its independent ordering operation.

This is not to say that the questions with which scholastic orthodoxy was concerned can be shrugged off as unreal or uninteresting. It must be doubted, however, that they must always come first or always be answered in the same way. The authentic prolegomenon is not the rational presupposition of another axiom which alone would permit us to say what we want to say. What needs to be said first is that we are already together in the believing community, praising God and supporting and admonishing one another.

Although some of its critics make that accusation for their own reasons, there is nothing about this "biblical realist" position that is primitivistic in the sense of promising that it would be possible to recreate a first-century world or a first-century world-view or a first-century church. No such naive vision is intended. In fact the biblical realist position is only possible as a post-critical phenomenon. It is scholastic orthodoxy which is naively pre-critical when it assumes that the scriptural text standing there alone can be interpreted faithfully and can be equated with our systematic restructuring of its contents. What is at stake is not whether the Bible can be interpreted at this great distance without linguistic and hermeneutic tools but whether, at those points where it is clear what it says, we are going to let that testimony count rather than subjecting it to the superior authority of our own contemporary hermeneutic framework.

It is also not accurate, although there are also some critics who for their own reasons make that claim, that this view includes any disrespect for human rationality, for the natural knowledge which we share with our unbelieving neighbors, or for the appropriateness of meaning systems not derived only from the gospel. This position is one which can only be exposited with the aid of rationality in all its identifiable forms. It involves as well more claims upon an esthetic sensitivity, also a form of natural culture, than do some earlier views. A commitment to biblical realism will heighten rather than weaken our ability to converse with our neighbors in their own language, if we become clear about the differences which distinguish one language game from another. I grant that some Barthian rhetoric, which I would reject if it be taken as systematic theology, although it may be quite appropriate as pastoral theology (e.g.,

Barmen), may have played into the hands of this misinterpretation. The point is not that all the truth is in Jesus or in the Bible. It is that the truth which is in Jesus is the truth that matters the most, which must therefore regulate our reception and recognition of other kinds and levels of truth rather than being set in parallel or subordinated thereto.

Perspicuity and Change

In describing the need for criteria within the corrective task, I noted that to know what "Jesus Christ" means requires acquaintance with a widening circle of "assumptions and prerequisites, cultural backgrounds, and definitions of concepts." No text has a clear meaning without a dictionary to define its terms. There is no infallible "dictionary," not even in the minimal literal sense of a collection of definitions for specific words and even less in the wider sense of what symbols, sentences, and social structures mean. Therefore, the choice made by God to use human events and human reporting of those events makes the task of faithful interpretation endless. On a given issue one can, by continuing dialogical disciplines, approximate more and more the confidence that one understands basically what the original testimony meant. But at the same time new issues arise and new challenges are addressed to old formulations in such a way that the task is never finished.

With regard to translation in the literal sense, Eugene Nida used to say regularly that no translation from one language to another can ever be perfectly accurate, but that in every specific interlinguistic interface it is possible to find a substantially adequate rendering of the central point of the original text. What is thus said about moving from Greek to Swahili or Chinese can also be said *mutatis mutandis* of restating in 1983 what was at stake when Jeremiah or John was writing. We can never know perfectly, but we can understand substantially. The disciplines of doing that may be exercised under the guidance of the Holy Spirit, but they are never infallible.

It is specifically with reference to future questions not yet

named that the Jesus of John 14—16 promised further leading
and "greater works." There is no reason to exclude the ministry
of theological articulation from the scope of this promise. It is
therefore inappropriate to accentuate, as has been done in some
past evangelical experience, the immutability of Christian truth
once formulated, as if that authority were enjoyed by our articulations rather than being reserved to the canonical texts themselves and the historical events behind them. Formulations can
and will keep changing and it is most fitting that we should
expect them to. The proper issue to be concerned about is the
ground rules and guidelines for articulating such changes, not
whether they should happen.

Having made use of the analogy to a linguistic model of
"translation," let me also suggest certain qualifications regarding
its adequacy. First we note those dimensions of the reading of
the canonical witness which are mentioned specifically in the
New Testament as distinct workings of the Holy Spirit. One of
these is the process of dialogue about moral matters for which
Jesus used the rabbinic expression "binding and loosing" and of
which he said that, when it is done in his name, it receives the
seal of his presence and stands in heaven. We may appropriately
read the narrative of Acts 15 as a specimen of God's keeping this
promise. An issue had been raised by the collision between the
missionary methods of Paul and his colleagues and the disciplin-
ary concerns of some people from Jerusalem. The matter was
given head-on attention rather than being dodged or papered
over. Arguments were brought to bear from experience and
from Scripture. Everyone who had anything to say was heard,
until the assembly fell silent. Then the concluding compromise,
proposed by the presiding elder of the host congregation, was
described as having "seemed right both to the assembly and to
the Holy Spirit." There is no tension or contradiction between
saying that this result was the work of the Holy Spirit and saying
that it was the result of proper procedures of conflict resolution
and decision making.

Secondly, we are explicitly urged to consider the variety of
gifts as one special sign of the guidance of the Spirit. The gifts

of prophet, teacher, moderator, etc., all contribute to the process of theological articulation. They contribute best if each has maximum liberty to contribute in its own way and if the exercise of those liberties is itself coordinated in the right way (which coordination is also one of the gifts). The one thing which the New Testament language on these matters gives us no ground for is the notion that the theological task could be exercised in isolation from the bearers of other gifts or from the surveillance of the total community.

In the spiral movement whereby the mind of the church constantly links the world's agenda and the canonical texts, one does find a degree of progress in any given context in becoming clearer both about what it is in the present challenge to which Scripture speaks and about what the answer is. This growing clarity cannot be imposed on other times and places, but we do learn about some of the priorities in our time and place if we keep the circuit open. That the God of the Bible cares about the future of this earth and the human race, rather than intending to leave it behind as a radioactive cinder in order for disembodied souls to enjoy themselves timelessly in a placeless heaven, is a truth which grows on anyone who reads the Scriptures with that question in mind, even though for centuries it was possible for readers not to notice that testimony, so thoroughly had they been taken in by neo-Platonism.

That the God of the Bible wants captives to be freed, the poor to be fed, and the exercise of authority to be accountable to those who are led is likewise becoming increasingly clear, though we knew something of it before theologians of the "Third World" made more of it. The agenda of oppression had been faced by Christian believers in other times—by the Lollards and Levellers, by Wesley and Finney. But in our age those themes have been given a much more acute vitality by spokespersons for the minorities and majorities whose human dignity has been denied by oppressive social structures. More than was the case for Wycliffe or Wesley (at least more in quantity if not in quality), this sensitizing impact of awareness has pushed readers of the canonical Scriptures to find new depth and breadth, new detail and sharpness, in the stories of Moses and Jesus and the apocalypse.

The biblical appeal of the contemporary theologies of liberation has once more given occasion to fulfill the promise of John Robinson that "the Lord has yet much more light and truth to break forth from his holy word." It is an affirmation and not, as many conservative evangelicals have reflexively assumed, a questioning of biblical authority when the language of liberation and empowerment prove fruitful in understanding further dimensions of what salvation always meant according to the scriptural witness, even though we had not previously been pushed to see it that clearly. It was the alliance of official Christianity with oppression which kept it from being seen for a millennium. One must assume as possible, and I would hope as likely, that there could be yet other such further clarifications ahead of us. Thus the function of the Bible is to continue correctively to stand in judgment on our past failures to get the whole point.

7   The Use of Scripture in the Wesleyan Tradition

DONALD W. DAYTON
Northern Baptist Theological Seminary
Lombard, Illinois

The more I have tried to comprehend the nature of
the Wesleyan tradition and to develop a theological method informed by its distinctive vision of Christianity, the more I have
had difficulty understanding my own tradition and myself
within the outlines of what most people seem to mean by evangelicalism. On one level this is very puzzling and perhaps ironic
because it would seem that the Wesleyan tradition ought to be
paradigmatic of what it would mean to be evangelical. After all,
John Wesley was perhaps the major figure in what came to be
known as the "Evangelical Revival," and the heyday of the evangelical experience in American life is often described by American church historians as the "Age of Methodism in America."

Because of this ambiguity we need to give some attention to
the question of in what sense the Wesleyan way of using Scripture in theology represents an "evangelical option." My own
efforts to probe the present and historical uses of the word
"evangelical" have caused me to wonder if it is possible to give
the word a common meaning applicable to all the contexts in
which it is used. I have come to agree with those who would
argue that evangelicalism is, to borrow a phrase from the British
analytical tradition of philosophy, an "essentially contested concept." This is to say that the core meaning of the word is necessarily under dispute—alternative visions of evangelicalism fill

the word with such different content that its use in other contexts is confusing without consideration of that transformation of meaning.

My own efforts to bring clarity to this discussion have centered on an analysis which suggests that the word evangelical is used in three primary ways. Each of the ways of using the word is derived from a historical paradigm and struggle in which there emerged an "evangelical" party. Because of the historical particularities involved in each period and the differing nature of the struggle in each case, these uses of the word evangelical convey a different vision of Christian faith. They arrange the elements of Christian faith differently and, as a result, use and understand the nature and purpose of the Scripture in significantly differing ways.

These three basic paradigms of evangelicalism derive then from the period of the Reformation centered in the sixteenth century, the "awakenings" of the eighteenth century, and the fundamentalist/modernist controversies of the last hundred years or so. Any effort to describe, and especially to contrast, these ways of being evangelical will necessarily be subject to the sorts of criticisms often leveled at efforts to think "typologically" or to describe "ideal types"; namely, (1) that the emphasis on defining major motifs may over-accentuate differences, (2) that the resulting analysis may be somewhat abstract, (3) that historical illustrations of the types will generally be mixed and intermingled, and so on. But I do believe that such a typology can bring clarity to many discussions, and I will attempt to describe my own emerging understanding of the use of Scripture in the Wesleyan tradition primarily through this sort of analysis.

The Reformation Paradigm

The Reformation defined itself basically over against Roman Catholicism. To be *evangelisch* was to be "protestant" and, more particularly, Lutheran. The core of this Protestant faith could be described in several ways, but perhaps the most useful is through the great Latin slogans of the Reformation: *sola scrip-*

tura; *sola Christe*; *sola gratia*; and *sola fide*. These expressions direct our attention to issues of authority and soteriology. On the level of authority, the Scripture is set over against reason and tradition (understood both ecclesiastically and as the cumulative and collected wisdom of personal experience). On the level of soteriology, the focus may be said to be on both the personal appropriation of grace understood christologically and the theme of "justification by faith alone." This has resulted in a way of understanding Christian faith that maximizes the "forensic" rather than the actual impact of grace and tends to contrast faith and reason, faith and works, and so on. In this way of conceiving evangelicalism the issues may be focused on questions of anthropology where the basic starting point is an Augustinian tradition of human inability (the "bondage of the will") leading as a necessary consequence to the classic Reformation articulations of election and predestination.

The "Awakening" or Wesleyan Paradigm

This paradigm was anticipated in the Puritan transformation of the Calvinist tradition and the Pietist reaction against the efforts of post-Reformation orthodoxy to articulate systematically the insights of the Reformation. A certain soteriological orientation was maintained, but there was a basic shift away from the organizing motif of justification—at least as understood forensically—toward themes of regeneration and sanctification. The result is basically a "convertive piety" with its call to self-conscious conversion, the experience of the "new birth," and a life of "holiness" that is demonstrably and empirically distinct from the rest of the world in its expression of "actual righteousness." The enemy in this paradigm is primarily a nominal Christianity that is not serious in its appropriation of the faith but is too often satisfied with orthodoxy that fails to make Christianity a genuine "disposition of the heart." This led to an activism that produced, at least within the Protestant experience, both the great missionary impulse and the massive efforts at social transformation not characteristic of Reformation Christianity.

And in the process there was an erosion of Augustinianism that emphasized the soteriological significance either of human will in a form of synergism or of human cooperation with the divine and a growing attack on such classic Protestant doctrines as limited atonement and predestination. This form of evangelicalism is so distinct from classical Protestantism that the Germans, for example, would not describe it as *evangelisch* but would speak of *Pietismus* or the Christianity of the *Erweckungsbewegung* (the "awakening movement").

The Fundamentalist Paradigm

Both of the above two paradigms of evangelicalism have faded into the background, especially in the American experience, because of another major controversy in the church—the fundamentalist/modernist controversy that may perhaps best be viewed as a fight over the extent to which the Enlightenment, the rise of the scientific world-view, and the emergence of a heightened historical consciousness require a theological reformulation of classical Protestantism. In the nineteenth century a growing secular rationalism, such new sciences as geology and Darwinism with their implications for traditional interpretations of the Scriptures with regard to human origins, the rise of biblical criticism, and so forth, all raised fundamental challenges to accustomed ways of conceiving of Christianity and especially biblical authority. The emerging struggles produced within American Protestantism two basic parties: the fundamentalists, who were committed to the defense of the shape of classic Protestantism and feared that any accommodation to these new currents of thought meant the demise of Christianity; and the modernists, who felt that intellectual integrity required some form of adaptation and rethinking of classical modes of articulating Christian faith. (Other issues were also at stake, especially a shift in eschatology in which premillennialism tended to erode the commitment to social reform and probably various sorts of social class sortings out, but the themes sketched above better represent the fundamentalist self-consciousness.)

Much intellectual confusion would have been spared if the label "fundamentalist" had been (properly I think) maintained. The problem, however, is that after World War II a party of fundamentalists again adopted the evangelical label to express a "neo-evangelical" agenda that included an intellectual apologetic for the theological articulation of classical Protestantism, a repudiation of fundamentalist separatism in favor of a more inclusive ecclesiology, and a renewed social agenda. Because many of the leaders of this movement had roots in the revivalist experience, as currently represented by the rise of Billy Graham, there were some points of continuity with classical evangelicalism, but the fundamentalist experience had shifted the orientation of this form of evangelicalism along a new axis. Now the fundamental issue had become the preservation of orthodoxy and the classical or pre-critical view of the Bible over against the liberal reformulators. The rallying cry became the "inerrancy of the Scriptures" (the doctrine that defined for its advocates the limits of the post-fundamentalist, "neo-evangelical" coalition which found expression in the National Association of Evangelicals, the Evangelical Theological Society, *Christianity Today*, and other institutions of the movement). Evangelicalism, in this paradigm, is now no longer a distinct theological tradition (i.e., "Reformation Christianity," though it tends to be dominated by a "Reformed" articulation of Christian faith) or a particular piety and ethos (as it tended to be in classical evangelicalism) but has become a theological position staked out between conservative neo-orthodoxy and fundamentalism on a spectrum from left to right that is defined essentially by degrees of accommodation to modernity. And, again, this form of evangelicalism so differs from the others that the Germans have had to invent a new word, *Evangelikal*, to describe the growing evangelical self-consciousness in Europe after the Lausanne Congress on Evangelization that represented the neo-evangelical coalition.

This is not the best place for detailed analysis of this typology and its strengths and weaknesses. The point here is basically that each way of conceiving of evangelicalism produces a different population when each net is used to pull out of both church history and contemporary experience a coherently related and defined subset. Thus consistent articulators of the Reformation paradigm tend to dismiss Roman Catholicism, liberalism, and Wesleyanism as equally unevangelical because they are predicated on a defective anthropology. Similarly, consistent advocates of the second paradigm find equally unevangelical all forms of nominal Christianity, whether Roman Catholic or Protestant, orthodox or liberal, and are likely to receive genuinely "born-again" Catholics, say from the charismatic renewal, as "evangelicals." And only when one begins to understand the neo-evangelical coalition in terms of its opposition to modernity can one comprehend recent convergences like the influx of neo-evangelicals like Carl F. H. Henry and faculty members of such colleges as Wheaton and Gordon into the orbit of the *New Oxford Review* with its roots in the reaction of the traditional (and high church) party within the Anglican tradition. Such illustrations could be extended indefinitely.

The Distinctive Shape of Wesleyan Theology

With this typology in the background we can better understand the shape of Wesleyan theology. Much of the distinctive way in which the Wesleyan tradition uses Scripture is wrapped up in theological context and method. Only as we grasp this more fully can we understand the significance of the Wesleyan mode of handling Scripture. Complete explication of the themes of Wesleyan theology would be beyond the limits of this essay. Here we will only hint at some of the basic differences that set the Wesleyan tradition off from the other two types.

Wesleyanism shares much with Reformation evangelicalism—so much so that many interpreters (William Cannon, Franz Hildebrandt, Philip Watson, George Croft Cell, and others) have emphasized the continuities and basically seen the movement as a recovery of the basic impulse of the Reformation. On some levels this is true. One may notice the personal soteriological orientation of both Wesley and Luther in the emphasis on the *pro me* significance of the work of Christ. One must also understand the Wesleyan movement as preaching a gospel of free grace that at times sounds very much like the Reformation theme of "justification by faith."

But there are other significant levels on which Wesleyanism must be understood as a corrective to the Reformation thought and even in many basic ways as a reversion to basically Roman Catholic patterns of thought. The "solas" of the Reformation are basically a disjunctive way of thinking while Wesleyanism is more conjunctive in its thought. While Luther was inclined to speak of faith *or* reason, gospel *or* law, faith *or* works, and so on, Wesley was much more inclined to speak of faith *and* reason, gospel *and* law, faith *and* works, and so on. It is true that Wesley had his Aldersgate experience under the influence of a public reading of Luther's preface to the commentary on the epistle to the Romans, but when he got around to reading the commentary he found Luther blasphemous in his treatment of law, works, and reason. Wesley was inclined to the text that the "law is established by faith" and was offended by the Lutheran denigration of the law and works. Several of Wesley's key texts were taken from the book of James which Luther so devalued. Indeed, it was characteristic of Wesley that he spoke easily the language of both the epistle to the Galatians and the book of James.

In most of these moves Wesley was more like the Roman Catholic tradition. Another way of saying a similar thing is to notice that, for the Reformation, faith tended to be the organizing virtue. But Wesley was quite clear that faith was instrumental to love. For Wesley love was the organizing motif of his thought. The image of God in Eden was the ability to love, and it was this ability to love that was lost in the fall. Justification brings forgiveness for Wesley, but the real point is the therapeutic work of grace in restoring the ability to love in regeneration and sanctification. The goal of the Christian life is to be found in the experience of "perfect love," and the eschatological hope is expressed in similar language. This is a significant shift of axis and a movement away from the "forensic" categories of the Reformation to the "organic" and "biological" categories of Pietism and some branches of the Reformed tradition. The emphasis is on regeneration more than justification, on the impartation of grace and virtue rather than its imputation. All of this may be viewed as corrective to the Reformation and something of a reversion to Catholic patterns of thought.

Such a shift has great implications for theological method in the Wesleyan tradition and for its view of biblical authority. It may be overstating a significant truth to notice that, in part because of the emphasis on faith, the generations after the Reformation were devoted to the clarification of the faith and they left us the legacy of great creeds and doctrinal symbols. The Wesleyan tradition, on the other hand, has left us a legacy of works of love—the crusade against slavery, concern for the poor, campaigns for the reform of society, and so on—in its effort to "spread scriptural holiness across the land and to reform the nation."

Unfortunately, historians of doctrine and theology have most often stood in the Reformation tradition and have concluded that Wesleyanism made no lasting theological contribution because its legacy was not one of speculative theology. Wesley did not play on their turf, and their usual response was either not to notice him at all or, if they did, to place him in the category of ecclesiastical leadership rather than theologian. But this is to miss much of the point. Wesley's mode of doing theology differed from theirs, but it was no less theological or rigorous. Wesley plumbed the whole of the Christian tradition and the Scriptures but bent this work to practical rather than speculative purposes—to issues of the shape of Christian life and existence. In all of this he was doing creative theological work and articulating a significant theological vision but not primarily in the mode of speculative theology.

Under the influence of the recent varieties of liberation theologies we are learning to appreciate this way of theologizing, and some of the more creative work in the interpretation of Wesley and the Wesleyan tradition has drawn on correlations of theological method with the liberation theologians. While there are of course many differences, there are also some significant convergences on the emphasis upon *praxis*, on the use of a different model than that of abstract truth being applied to a context, and so on. This work may be most easily seen in the report of the Sixth Oxford Institute of Methodist Theological Studies (1977), published as *Sanctification and Liberation* (Nashville: Abingdon, 1981) and edited by Theodore Runyon of Emory University. Again the common Catholic background of much, especially Latin American, liberation theology and the basically Catholic matrix of Wesley's thought—and these congruences—are not entirely accidental.

With regard to biblical authority the picture is similar. At many points Wesley sounds like a son of the Reformation in his emphasis on the finality of biblical authority and in his desire to be, in the much quoted phrase, a *homo unius libri* (a "man of one book"). But Wesley's conjunctive way of thinking puts Scripture in a larger context of authority quite different from that produced by the "solas" of the Reformation. Wesley was quick to castigate his ministers who read only the Bible. The Book could be understood only through the study of books. Wesley restored the Scriptures to a matrix of authority that gave a more positive value to reason, experience, and tradition. The Scriptures held pride of place in this matrix but in a conjunctive rather than disjunctive mode. This will be developed more fully momentarily in a fuller discussion of the Wesleyan Quadrilateral.

Similar contrasts may be drawn with the more modern fundamentalist paradigm of evangelicalism. Here the discussion is more complicated and perhaps more speculative. It is very difficult to try to understand how an eighteenth-century figure would have reacted to the later struggles of the nineteenth century and how the tradition should be interpreted with integrity in a new age. As a result the Wesleyan tradition, like most other classical traditions, has had both its fundamentalist and its more liberal wings of interpretation. But even the more conservative wings of the Wesleyan tradition (which because of their basically orthodox stance and their commitment to a "supernatural" articulation of Christian faith, have often felt some affinity with the fundamentalist wing of modern Protestantism) have not been able to find a home in the circles of either modern fundamentalism or more recently in neo-evangelicalism. This has been symbolized in recent years by the founding of the Wesleyan Theological Society. Some theologians in the Wesleyan tradition, especially those most under the influence of neo-evangelicalism, in the early years of the post-World War II Evangelical Theological Society attempted to work in the neo-evangelical coalition. But this was so dominated by modes of theology so foreign to the Wesleyan tradition that in little more than a decade the Wesleyan Theological Society was founded to begin to articulate its own style of theology.

There are still those, of course, who will argue that Wesley would find his place today among the fundamentalists. Wesley did make some comments that sound like the "slippery-slide" argument of Harold Lindsell: "If there be any mistakes in the Bible, there may as well be a thousand. If there be one falsehood in that book, it did not come from the God of truth" (citation from the standard edition of Wesley's journal, volume 6 [1915], p. 117, the entry having been dated Wednesday, July 24, 1776).

Wesley's comments on the Scripture often reflect the classical doctrines of the inspiration of the Scriptures and a view of them as the "oracles of God" directly. But, as with other classical figures like Luther and Calvin, Wesley reveals another side which is illustrated in his dealing with problems of chronology, his understanding of the biblical use of non-biblical sources, his judging of much of the Psalms as "unfit for Christian lips," and so on. These debates will no doubt continue as they do for other classical figures whom the fundamentalists wish to claim for their side of the argument. The growing consensus of the Wesleyan Theological Society is that the tradition is not well stated in the logic and ethos of the fundamentalist tradition. And the basic reasons for this are larger considerations about the shape of Wesleyan theology that set it apart from fundamentalism. Among these would be the following.

(1) The neo-evangelical tradition has its roots in the fundamentalist effort to preserve intact the structure of classical post-Reformation Protestant orthodoxy (indeed, it is here that the doctrine of inerrancy received its classical expression). This tra-

dition, however, produced the reaction of Pietism with its alternative strategy of how to "complete the Reformation." Wesleyanism stands in this latter tradition. It will be a while before the question is resolved about whether these traditions were significantly different in their approach to Scripture. Some would argue that Pietism merely assumed the orthodox doctrine of Scripture. I am more inclined to accentuate the differences. Orthodoxy tended to locate the doctrine of Scripture in theological prolegomena as the transcendent grounding of speculative reason; Pietism was more inclined to see in the Scriptures the charter of the church and consider it under a different theological locus. The traditions of exegesis of the key text of 2 Timothy 3:16 differ: orthodox exegesis (restated among the fundamentalists by old Princeton theologian B. B. Warfield) emphasized the once-for-all givenness and absoluteness of the process of biblical inspiration; Pietist exegesis (as illustrated by Bengel and adopted by Wesley and most of his followers) emphasized the ongoing process of inspiration in the church and the present work of the Holy Spirit in making the Scriptures alive and vital today. And perhaps most significantly we should notice that some would trace the emergence of early forms of biblical criticism to Pietism and its attack on the abstract doctrinal character of orthodoxy. There is a sense in which the intention of early biblical criticism was an effort to restore a "biblical theology" in which the Scriptures were freed from their dogmatic imprisonment. In all of this the Wesleyan tradition is more naturally seen in the Pietist rather than in the orthodox line.

(2) It is not often noticed that the Wesleyan tradition is the first major Christian tradition after the Enlightenment. In this it differs from classical Reformation theology, and we have already hinted that the difference may be seen in the different attitude that is taken in the Wesleyan tradition toward reason. The new social and intellectual context required a different articulation. And, again, the pietist and the enlightenment critiques of orthodoxy were often intermingled and mutually supporting. On the other hand, modern post-fundamentalist evangelicalism gener-

ally seems committed to the maintenance of the structures of classical Protestant theology in the face of enlightenment critique. These are quite different theological agendas and lead to different methods and concerns. The Wesleyan openness to reason and the fact that the Wesleyan tradition was more easily adapted (contextualized?) to the new intellectual environment, combined with the fact that Wesley did seem easily to appropriate the emerging biblical scholarship of his day, are grounds for suggesting that the Wesleyan tradition is more appropriately viewed as non-fundamentalist, even among those who wish to live in more direct continuity with the spiritual dynamic of the founder.

(3) Related to this enlightenment location of Wesleyanism is the fact that Wesleyanism differs from fundamentalism in its analysis of the human problem. Modern neo-evangelicalism focuses on the problem of belief and the maintenance of orthodoxy and makes the modern crisis of unbelief the key issue. While orthodox in a broader sense, Wesley did not locate the basic problem here. He was fond of quoting the suggestion of the book of James that the devils are orthodox but obviously not examples of true or scriptural Christianity. For Wesley, true Christian religion was not a matter of opinion or even of mere orthodoxy but more a matter of the will and a "disposition of the heart." This orientation and the fact that Wesley was working along a different axis of thought have meant that the Wesleyan tradition has not been so traumatized by the Enlightenment. The problem of Christian faith may be complicated by the rise of secular rationalism, and Wesley was quick to repudiate its manifestations in his own time, but the basic problem of Christian faith, at least as perceived by the Wesleyan tradition, remains the same both before and after the Enlightenment. And, on the other hand, since the Wesleyan tradition is working on a fundamentally different axis, it is more easily able to adapt to a new intellectual context.

(4) One may make the same point in a slightly different manner. Perhaps more significant even than the rise of the rationalism of the early era of the Enlightenment is the rise of the

"historical consciousness" of the late Enlightenment and the nineteenth century. Modern forms of biblical criticism, for example, are probably more clearly rooted in this development. Also a part of this was the emergence of the social sciences which, in the application of the psychology of knowledge and the sociology of knowledge to classical modes of thought, had a significant relativizing impact. One may view the fundamentalist wing of modern Protestantism as that branch which was unable to assimilate these modern forms of thought because of its roots in more rationally articulated forms of theology and its ahistorical and biblicist patterns of thinking. Certainly the recent neo-evangelical polemics against any forms of relativism or situationalism would seem to confirm this tendency. It could be argued that Wesleyanism is more capable of assimilating these modern modes of thought. One reason for this would be that, in the shift to regeneration, the category of change is imported into the center of Wesleyan thinking. This would be true both with regard to the individual, where the Christian life is developmentally described as a series of stages, and more broadly in society. Thus the Wesleyan tradition has an inherent affinity to historical process and movement, which puts it at odds with the more absolutistic traditions that try to deny relativity and the historical conditionedness of Christian life and thought. This may perhaps best be seen in the Wesleyan attitude toward the ministry of women. While the fundamentalist experience on this question has been quite slow in allowing the ministry of women, lagging far behind the churches of the mainstream, the Wesleyan churches have often been the pioneers of this practice, especially in the nineteenth century when the conservative Wesleyan churches were far in advance of the more established denominations. The Wesleyans did not see the biblical injunctions against the ministry of women as providing a norm and pattern for all time. Instead they saw the Bible as the medium of a new source of life and power which changed persons and the world so that application of the spirit of the Scripture could not be achieved by a mechanical application of the letter of the Scripture.

(5) All of this is to argue that the very logic of the Wesleyan tradition is basically at odds with the fundamentalist experience and that this extends to the understanding of the nature and function of Scripture. A final illustration will have to suffice. The fundamental contrast between Wesleyanism and fundamentalism (including neo-evangelicalism) became clear to me when I happened on two late nineteenth-century charts. The first derived from the dispensational pre-millennial tradition and was a classic dispensational chart of the outline of history and eschatology. (Ernest Sandeen has argued in his *Roots of Fundamentalism* that dispensationalism is in many ways the defining characteristic of the modern fundamentalist experience which lies behind neo-evangelicalism.) The second was a chart in the front of the classic statement of the Salvation Army by its founder William Booth, *In Darkest England and the Way Out*. It is hard to describe how violently different these are. The Wesleyan chart, as represented by the Salvation Army, pictured sin in historically concrete terms: infidelity; drunkenness; greed; oppression; racism; etc. The "salvation" pictured was also historically concrete and actual, involving a range of dimensions from personal salvation and transformation through all kinds of social agencies and reform from credit unions for the poor to day care centers for working mothers. By contrast with this vision, embedded as it was in history and actual transformation, the dispensational chart appeared contrived, ahistorical, and almost gnostic in character. The function of Scripture—its role, its product, its use—is fundamentally shaped by these differing contexts.

The Wesleyan Quadrilateral

In summary, then, of what has been hinted at above we should note that, as much as theological method has been formulated in the Wesleyan tradition, it has often been described in terms of the Wesleyan Quadrilateral of Scripture, reason, tradition, and experience. Wesley does not use this formulation in his own writings, but it does echo patterns of thinking that are demonstrably characteristic of Wesley. One of his major treatises, for example, was entitled *The Doctrine of Original Sin, According to Scripture, Reason and Experience.* This title does not fully reproduce the quadrilateral, but the terms change in various of Wesley's statements and usages so that the quadrilateral may be said to systematize Wesley's thought and to describe the method of theological reflection within the Wesleyan tradition. Only very recently, with the formation of the merged United Methodist Church in 1968, has this really been formalized in a statement of "Our Theological Task" which appears regularly in *The Book of Discipline,* though similar analyses have been developed elsewhere, for example, in Colin W. Williams, *John Wesley's Theology Today.*

This articulation speaks quite self-consciously of four norms or sources of theology. Within these it is generally understood that Scripture is the "norming norm" or the fundamental authority in theological reflection. But the Wesleyan vision includes a high respect for the tradition of the church as a source for theological formulation and a willingness to be judged by it, though flexibly, with Scripture as the final judge of the value of tradition. We have already indicated Wesley's more positive appreciation of reason, especially as a tool of reflection and analysis; one of his most characteristic types of writing was various "appeals" to "men of reason and religion." And, finally, Wesley not only wished to find true religion expressed experientially, but he also had a more positive role for experience in judging and correcting his theological formulations.

We have already provided several brief illustrations of how these norms have influenced theological reflection within the Wesleyan tradition. A final illustration will have to suffice. One place to see easily the variety of theological norms coming into play is in Wesley's *Plain Account of Christian Perfection,* perhaps both the key text for those who wished to sustain continuity with the spiritual experience of classical Wesleyanism and a source of much controversy with outsiders who found the key doctrine of the Wesleyan tradition offensive. In this tract Wesley seems to come to his high ideal of "perfect love" in his reading of Scripture informed by a variety of the great spiritual teachers of the church who emphasized similar themes. His understanding of the possibility of the achievement of this ideal and the fact that it often was achieved in a "crisis experience" seems to be elaborated out of an analysis based on the collected experiences of a number of his followers—a sort of "phenomenology of Christian experience." And in the process he appeals regularly to what is required by logic and reason, as well as to themes of a sort of natural theology in which he makes analogies to the experiences of birth and death. The result is a very subtle interplay of theological norms and sources that Wesley understood to be guided and directed by the Scriptures.

Much of the debate about the Wesleyan Quadrilateral has centered on the theological pluralism that it necessarily leads to. The interplay of the various sources is subtle and the judgments are often "aesthetic" and dependent upon a variety of factors that include the personal history and psychology of the theologian as well as the extent to which the sources have been grasped and understood. This is certainly an issue, but it is both a strength and a weakness at the same time. From one angle the use of the quadrilateral merely brings to self-consciousness factors that seem to be present in all theological reflection, even among those who deny that they are operating with multiple norms. And it is precisely because of these dimensions that Wesleyan theology can assimilate modern patterns of thinking and can find contextualization in a variety of situations. It is for such reasons that I have found within the Wesleyan tradition a useful pattern of theological reflection and the resources for trying to think theologically in the modern world.

8 An Evangelical and Catholic Methodology

ROBERT E. WEBBER

Wheaton College
Wheaton, Illinois

I approach the question of the authority of the Bible in the dual role of one who is a committed evangelical Christian and one who does historical theology. As an evangelical, I regard the Scriptures to have the place of supreme authority in the life and practice of the church. I believe the church as well as the individual Christian owes no ultimate obedience to any earthly authority, whether government, reason, conscience, or custom.

As one who does historical theology, I believe evangelicals who commit themselves to Scripture as the ultimate authority in faith and practice cannot afford to separate Scripture from the whole circle of theological concerns and the history of the church of which it is a part. The Bible does not stand alone. It is not a book of rational propositions which can be scientifically analyzed and systematized into a universally accepted textbook of theology. It is a dynamic book related to specific historic events, characterized by a central religious message, and, although divine in nature, the product of circumstances with a human side. Further, it belongs to the church as its unique possession and ought not to be interpreted today apart from the experience given to it in the history of the church's liturgy, creeds, confessions, interpretation, and the common faith of two thousand years of believers.

Thus the Scripture belongs to a community—a community

of theological ideas such as the church's thinking about God, Christ, the Spirit, salvation, the sacraments, the last days, and tradition. It also belongs to a community of people—saints, Fathers, martyrs, Popes, reformers, theologians, the common folk. Consequently the issue of its authority is bound together with more than that which can be seen by the eye, heard by the ear, or understood with the mind. Any attempt to reduce the issue of authority to a single issue or a manageable dogma is an insult to its complexity and a human impertinence. Yet, to do theology is to run such a risk.

My historical understanding is that the church has always struggled with the problem of authority and solved it in different ways. Thus in the history of the church different views about the Bible exist among equally committed Christians. Nevertheless, in order to avoid a relativistic approach which says "any approach is as good as the other," I have made the choice to plant my feet in the ground cultivated by the early church. While I do not wish to absolutize their conclusions, I do regard the consensus of the Fathers as an important element in the interpretation of scriptural themes and in the current debate about authority in the life of the church.

My method of doing theology is one that recognizes the value of tradition. In order to explicate this view, I will first give an example of my theological method as evidenced in a paper originally published in the *TSF Bulletin* (volume 7 [September-October 1983] pp. 8–10) entitled "Worship: A Methodology for Evangelical Renewal." The essay appears here, in a slightly different form, with the permission of the Theological Students Fellowship. Second, I will reflect on my approach to worship and, in that way, clarify my view of the relationship between Scripture and tradition in doing theology.

Worship: A Methodology for Evangelical Renewal

Trend watchers are telling us that the next important issue in evangelical churches is worship. Rumblings of discontent are already being heard in the church. Some are talking about boredom with sameness, others are concerned over the lack of relevance, and many feel the need to become worshipers but can't find the words or concepts to articulate their need or signposts to direct this search. Unfortunately our evangelical seminaries are not prepared to offer our churches adequate leadership in worship.

I speak from experience. I graduated from three theological seminaries without taking a course in worship. Even though I was planning to become a minister, no one ever sat me down and said, "Look, worship is one of the most central aspects of your future ministry. Now is the time not only to learn all you can about the subject but also to become a worshiping person so you can offer mature leadership to your congregation." The simple fact is that my seminary professors themselves knew little about the subject. Unfortunately my seminary education left me with the impression that the only important matter in morning worship was the sermon. All else was preliminary. Pick out a couple of hymns. Say a few prayers. Get through the announcements. Let the choir sing. And now, here comes what we all came for—the sermon! I say heresy, bunk, shame!

In this article it is my intention to speak to evangelical seminaries and seminarians in particular because they more than any other grouping of seminaries have neglected the subject of worship. They have relegated it to the corner of the curriculum, treating it with indifference and a degree of relative unimportance.

Therefore it is my purpose to argue for something more than the mere inclusion of worship courses in the curriculum. What is needed within seminary education is a recognition of worship as a legitimate discipline among other disciplines. Because worship has been, as one student remarked, "neglected by evangelicals for centuries," we need to find a methodology for the study of worship before we begin to tackle the subject.

Unfortunately, in the curriculum of most evangelical seminaries worship is relegated to the practical department and treated as a matter of technique and style. This approach must be challenged by the students who are being shortchanged in their education and preparation for ministry because worship is a field of study in its own right. Indeed it is an interdisciplinary study demanding expertise in biblical, historical, and systematic theology as well as the arts, practical expertise, and personal spiritual formation. Thus worship, or more properly *liturgics*, must be regarded as one of the most vigorous and demanding of the seminary disciplines. It must be taken off the back burner and given its rightful place in the seminary curriculum.

But what is the methodology by which this renewal in worship can be accomplished? It is, I believe, threefold: we must simultaneously strip away our false conceptions, re-learn the meaning of worship, and apply the newly acquired principles of worship to our contemporary evangelical communities. In this paper, I intend to sketch out the context of this threefold method in a preliminary way.

Stripping Away False Conceptions of Worship

The method by which I propose stripping away false conceptions of worship in the evangelical community is through a historical examination of Protestant-evangelical worship from the Reformation to the present. My own study in this area yields two general theses. The first is that there is a radical difference between the worship of our sixteenth-century evangelical forefathers and contemporary evangelical practice. The second is that Protestant-evangelical worship has followed the curvature of culture rather than being faithful to the biblical, historical tradition of the church. A brief examination of these two theses is in order.

First, the gap between present evangelical worship and the practice of the Reformers can easily be seen through an examination of the Reformation liturgies. Pick up any of the liturgies such as Martin Luther's *Formula Missae* of 1523, Martin Bucer's *Strasbourg Rite* of 1539, John Calvin's *Form of Church Prayers* of 1542, or something as late as Richard Baxter's *The Reformation of the Liturgy* of 1661, and the difference can readily be seen. I find, for example, the five following characteristics in these liturgies: (1) an affinity with the liturgies of the ancient church;

(2) an order that follows the pattern of revelation and Christian experience; (3) a significant emphasis on reading and hearing the Word of God; (4) a high degree of congregational involvement; and (5) a view of the Lord's Supper which affirms its mystery and value for spiritual formation.

By contrast my experience in many evangelical churches is as follows: (1) a radical departure not only from the liturgies of the ancient church but from those of the Reformation as well; (2) confusion about order; (3) minimal use of the Bible; (4) passive congregations; and (5) a low view of the Lord's Supper.

Historical research must ask: How did this change occur? What are the cultural, social, religious, and theological factors which contributed to these changes? How has the actual character of worship changed over the last several centuries? What do these changes mean for the corporate life of the church today?

It is not my intention to answer all these questions. Indeed, considerable historical work must be done in the evaluation of Protestant worship during 1600–1900 before a full and adequate answer is available. However, my preliminary work in this area leads me to assert the second thesis, namely, that evangelicals have followed the curvature of culture. A few illustrations will illuminate this point.

As the meaning of worship became lost among various groups of Protestant Christians, the shape of worship was accommodated to the overriding emphasis within culture. For example, the first significant shift occurred with the introduction of the print media through the Gutenberg press. Protestantism, which can be characterized as a movement of the word, led the way in the shift from symbolic communication of the medieval era to the verbal communication of the modern era. Because words were regarded as higher and more significant vehicles of truth than symbols, images, poetry, gesture, and the like, all forms of communication other than the verbal became suspect. Consequently, Protestant liturgies were not only word centered but attached great religious importance to the verbal content of worship.

A second shift occurred as the result of the Enlightenment. The concern for rational, observable, and consistent truth, which grew out of the empirical method, gradually influenced worship. The essential feature of worship was the sermon. All else sank into relative unimportance. In Puritan circles sermons were sometimes three hours in length with a break in the middle. They were often exegetical and theological dissertations that would be considered beyond the grasp or care of the average lay person today.

Another shift in worship can be observed as a result of the rise of Revivalism. The field preaching of the evangelists gradually replaced the morning service, making Sunday morning a time for evangelism. Although preaching still played a central part, one focus shifted from information directed toward the intellect to an emotional appeal aimed at the will. The climactic point became the altar call to conversion, rededication, consecration to ministry, or work on the mission field.

Today another shift is taking place resulting from the current revolution in communications. The entertainment mentality which thinks in terms of performance, stages, and audiences has been making its appearance in local churches. Consequently, evangelical Christianity has produced its Christian media stars. Unfortunately many churches are following the trend by "juicing" the service with a lot of hype, skits, musical performances, and the like, which will attract the "big audience."

My concern is that this kind of evangelical worship represents not only a radical departure from historic Protestant worship but also an accommodation to the trends of secularization. Thus, worship, which stands at the very center of our Christian experience, having been secularized, is unable to feed, nourish, enhance, challenge, inspire, and shape the collective and individual life of our congregations in the way in which it should. Consequently the whole evangelical movement suffers.

How will change be brought about? While that is not an easy question to answer, it does seem that the second step toward worship renewal ought to be a concerted effort within our seminaries to recover the biblical-theological meaning of worship and to trace its historical development from Pentecost to the Reformation.

Restoring a Biblical-Theological and Historical Perspective of Worship

As evangelicals we must acknowledge that the true character of worship is not determined by people but by God. Much of contemporary evangelical worship is anthropocentric. The biblical-theological view of worship, however, is that worship is not primarily for people but for God. God created all things, and particularly the human person, for his glory. Thus, to worship God is a primary function of the church, the people who have been redeemed by God.

The meaning of the Greek word *leiturgia* is work or service. Worship is the work or service of the people directed toward God. That is, we do something for God in our worship of him. We bless God, hymn him, and offer him our praise and adoration. But worship is not without reason. We do this because God has done something for us. He has redeemed us, made us his people, and entered into a relationship with us.

Consequently the biblical rhythm of worship is on doing and responding. God does. We respond. What God does and is doing happened in history and is now told and acted out as though it were being done again. The unrepeatable event is being repeated, as it were. And we are present responding in faith through words, actions, and symbols of faith.

There are two parts to this biblical-theological view of worship that need to be examined. First, worship is grounded in God's action in Jesus Christ which, although it occurred in the distant past, is now recurring through the Holy Spirit in the present. The point is that worship is rooted in an event. The event character of worship is true in both the Old and the New Testament. In the Old Testament the event which gives shape and meaning to the people of God is the exodus event. It was in this historical moment that God chose to reveal himself as the redeemer, the one who brought the people of Abraham, Isaac, and Jacob up out of their bondage to Pharaoh with a strong arm. They then became his people, the *qāhāl*, the community of people who worship him as Yahweh. Thus the Tabernacle and, later, the Temple, the feasts and festivals, the sacred year, the hymnic literature and psalms of thanksgiving revolve around the God who brought them up out of Egypt and made them his people.

The same is true in the New Testament. In the Christ event God is shown to be the loving and compassionate one who came to free humankind from the kingdom of evil. In the birth, life, death, and rising again of Christ Satan was vanquished. Christ was demonstrated as the Victor over sin, death, and the domain of hell. Consequently the worship of the primitive Christian community was a response to this event. Hymns, doxologies, benedictions, sermons, and symbols of bread and wine all flow from this event and return to it in the form of proclamation, re-enactment, remembrance, thanksgiving, and prayer.

The second biblical-theological part to Christian worship is the understanding that the church as the corporate body of Christ is the response to the Christ event, and thus the context in which the Christ event is continuously acted out. Thus the phenomenon of the Christ event does not stand alone. There is another event which happened simultaneously with it, an event which is intricately connected and inextricably interwoven with the Christ event. It is the church, the new people of God, that people through whom the Christ event continues to be present in and to the world. The church is the response to the Christ event. It is that people whose very essence cannot be described or apprehended apart from the Christ event. These are the people in whom Christ is being formed and without whom the fullness of Christ cannot be made complete. It is the *ekklesia*, the worshiping community.

Therefore, the two fundamental biblical-theological axioms of worship which are basic to worship renewal are rooted in the Christ event which the church, as the unique people of this event, is called to celebrate. These axioms are radically evangelical, yet I dare say they have been lost to our churches that have turned worship into a time for teaching, evangelizing, entertaining, or therapy. Methodologically worship renewal must begin with a fresh rediscovery of *Christus Victor* and of the church as the community in whom the Christ event is celebrated to the glory of God.

The second methodological concern has to do with the recovery of that rich treasury of resources handed down to us by the experience of the church. I find American evangelicalism to be secularized in its attitude toward history. There is a disdain for the past, a sense that anything from the past is worn-out, meaningless, and irrelevant. There seems to be little value ascribed to what the Holy Spirit has given the church in the past. It is all relegated to tradition and dismissed as form. At the same time, no critical examination is directed toward present distortions which have been elevated without thought to a sacred position. Evangelicals who want to restore true worship must therefore abandon their disdain of the historical and return to a critical examination of the worship of the church in every period of history.

It must be recognized that there is a normative content to worship that is found in the worship experience of the church everywhere, always, and by all. This is the content of word, table, prayer, and fellowship (see Acts 2:42). The public worship of the church cannot happen without these elements, and it is preferable that they all be present in public worship. Further, in the same way that the church has wrestled with its understanding of Christ and the Scripture through creeds, commentaries, systematic theologies, and the like, so also the church has developed ways to do its worship. These include structural forms, written prayers, hymns, rules for preaching, the church year, the lectionary, and numerous symbolic ceremonies. Interestingly, in the early church these resources were being developed at the same time that creedal statements were coming into being. Yet, we evangelicals who affirm the Nicene and Chalcedon creeds and boast that we remain faithful to their intent are proudfully neglectful of the liturgical forms and theological perception of worship shaped by some of the same Church Fathers.

Specifically we need to recognize that those who have gone before us, those who have wrestled with the meaning and interpretation of the faith in creeds and liturgy, were women and men of faith. To accept the creeds, on the one hand, and reject the liturgies by inattention that often expresses itself in disdain, on the other, is contradictory and unwise. For orthodoxy was primarily given shape in the liturgy, and the creeds were originally part of the larger liturgical witness. We recognize that the early church was unusually gifted with the spiritual leadership of Justin, Irenaeus, Tertullian, Athanasius, John Chrysostom, and Augustine. Yet we neglect to study the worship of the church which reflects their faithfulness to Christ and the orthodox tradition.

Nevertheless the Scripture is still the judge of all liturgies. To be sure, there are liturgies which fail to hand down the orthodox tradition. For example, liturgies which reflect an Arian Christology or those medieval liturgies which clearly reflect a sacrificial notion of the Eucharist must be judged by the orthodox tradition. But the task of critical evaluation of the older liturgies sharpens our ability to offer constructive and critical evaluation of contemporary worship. For, without a knowledge of the worship experience of the church throughout history, we are left without adequate tools for either critiquing contemporary worship or reconstructing a worship that is faithful to the Christian tradition.

In terms of tradition we must be able to distinguish different levels and, thus, to attach a corresponding scale of values to them. If we think in terms of a series of concentric circles, the apostolic traditions must be central. The apostolic tradition includes the word, table, prayers, hymns, benedictions, doxologies, and the like, as that content which proclaims both the Christ event and the relationship which the church sustains to God. A second concentric circle includes those traditions which are universally accepted and practiced by Christians. Such things as creeds, confession, the kiss of peace, the Lord's prayer, the *gloria in excelsis Deo*, and the church year belong here. In a third concentric circle we may place those traditions which are peculiar to a particular grouping of people such as the Orthodox Church in the East, the Catholic Church in the West, or one of the many Protestant denominations. Matters such as vestments (or no vestments), bells, architectural style, inclusion of the little entrance or the great entrance, musical tones, and issues regarding kneeling, standing, or raising hands during prayer are all matters of cultural and stylistic preferences. And, finally, in a fourth circle one may place those specific customs that are peculiar to a local congregation. Certainly, when we recognize the original impulses from which these ceremonies derive, we may see them for the most part as expressions of faith, witnesses to the importance attached to Christ and his redeeming work. Our task is not to be judgmental in a manner of spiritual superiority but to dig beneath the traditions to recover the spirit that originally animated them, so that we too may share in the original dynamic that enlivened the telling and acting out of the Christ event in another time and another place or among other Christians who expressed their response to the Christ event in a way foreign to our experience.

In sum, the methodological approach to worship renewal needs to be rooted in a thoroughgoing biblical-theological and historical understanding of Christ and the church. Now the question is: What kinds of changes may occur in evangelical worship as a result of this methodological approach?

Applying the Biblical-Theological and Historical Methodology

Changes do not come easily in any aspect of the church. Worship is no exception. Nevertheless I foresee the methodology which I have proposed challenging evangelical worship in at least six areas.

First, it will challenge the understanding of worship. I find that evangelicals frequently exchange true worship for the substitutes mentioned in the first section. Those evangelicals who are thinking about worship tend to think almost exclusively in terms of worship as expressing God's worth. While it is essential to recover worship as directed toward God, it is equally important to rediscover the content of that worship. That content may be summarized this way: In worship we tell and act out the Christ event. In this action God is doing the speaking and acting. Consequently we respond to God and to each other together with the whole creation to offer praise and glory to him. (This is a basic definition of worship which needs to be unpacked for a full appreciation of its content.)

Second, evangelicals will be challenged in the area of structure. Evangelical services lack a coherent movement. There seems to be little, if any, interior rhythm. Historical worship, on the other hand, is characterized by a theological and psychological integrity. Theologically, worship is structured around God's revelation in word and incarnation. This accounts for the basic structure of word and table. Psychologically, the structure of worship brings the worshiper through the experience of his or her relationship with God. It follows the pattern of coming before God in awe and reverence, confessing our sins, hearing and responding to the Word, receiving Christ in bread and wine, and being sent forth into the world.

Third, evangelicals will be challenged in the matter of participation. I find evangelical worship to be passive and uninvolving. The worshiper sits, listens, and absorbs. But seldom does the worshiper respond. As in the medieval period, worship has been taken away from the people. It must be returned. Participation will be recovered as the dramatic sense of worship is restored. Further, the participation of the people can be enhanced through the use of lay readers and preachers, congregational prayer responses, Scripture responses, antiphonal readings, affirmations of faith, acclamations, the kiss of peace, and increased sensitivity to gestures and movement.

Fourth, a study of the past will sensitize evangelicals to the need to restore the arts. One of the great problems within the evangelical culture is a repudiation of the arts in general—more specifically, the failure to employ the arts in worship. This disdain toward the arts is deeply rooted in a view that consigns material things to the devil. The pietistic and fundamentalistic backgrounds to modern evangelicalism are addicted to the erroneous view—dualism—that sets the material against the spiritual. Consequently, art, literature, music, and the like, are frequently seen as the vehicles of evil, as means through which people are lured away from spiritual realities to mundane physical attachments.

The repudiation of the material is in direct contradiction to the incarnation and to the stand taken by the church against Gnosticism. Consequently, the visible arts as well as theatre, the dance, color, and tangible symbols have historically had a functional role in worship. Space, as in church architecture, is the servant of the message. The design and placement of the furniture of worship, such as the pulpit, table, and font, bespeak redemptive mystery. The use of color, stained-glass windows, icons, frescos, carvings, and the like, is a means by which the truths we gather around in worship are symbolically communicated. Worship not only contains elements of drama but also is a drama in its own right. It has a script, lead players, and secondary roles played by the congregation. (Neglect of these matters within our evangelical seminaries and churches have weakened worship and the message it conveys. Consequently a program of liturgics must take these matters into consideration.)

Fifth, evangelicals will be challenged to reconsider their view of time. We practice a secular rather than a sacred view of time. The restoration of the church year and preaching from the lectionary are vital to worship renewal. The church year provides an opportunity for the whole congregation to make the life of Christ a lived experience. It is not merely an external covering of time, but the very meaning of time itself. During the church year we enter fully into the anticipation of Advent, the joy of Christmas, the witnessing motif of Epiphany, preparation for death in Lent, participation in both the resurrection joy of Easter and the reception of Pentecost power. Surely it is an evangelical principle to live out the life of Christ. Practicing the church year takes it out of the abstract and puts it into our day-to-day life in the world.

Sixth, a recovery of true worship will restore the relationship between worship and justice. Worship affects our lives in the world. It is not something divorced from the concerns of the world. Because Christ's work has to do with the whole of life, so also worship which celebrates that life, death, and resurrection relates directly to hunger, poverty, discrimination, human suffering, and the like.

Conclusion

In this paper I have attempted to outline a methodology for worship renewal. My concern is that evangelicals who are now beginning to rediscover the theme of worship will offer a superficial approach to worship renewal. This fear arises from my understanding of the ahistorical nature of evangelicalism. Our disdain for the past will prevent us from being open to the rich treasury of the historical understanding and practice of the church. This we must change.

Methodological Reflections

Since my approach to worship betrays a dependence on early church tradition, it is incumbent upon me to defend my use of tradition in relationship to the Scripture. Do I set tradition above Scripture or even alongside of Scripture? Can I use tradition and still claim to be evangelical? Why is the tradition of the early church any better than any other tradition? In order to answer these questions I will formulate and answer three questions in particular: (1) How can I call myself an evangelical when tradition plays an important part in my theological method? (2) Does my method elevate tradition over Scripture? (3) Why choose the tradition of the early church over that of another era?

How Can I Call Myself Evangelical When Tradition Plays an Important Part in My Theological Method?

In the first place, it is necessary to define the word "evangelical." The word is used in four ways: (1) linguistic; (2) historical; (3) theological; and (4) sociological. Linguistically the word evangelical is rooted in the Greek word *evangelion* and refers to those who preach and practice the good news; historically the word refers to those renewing groups in the church which from time to time have called the church back to the *evangel*; theologically it refers to a commitment to classical theology as expressed in the Apostles' Creed; and sociologically the word is used of various contemporary groupings of culturally conditioned evangelicals (i.e., fundamentalist evangelicals, Reformed evangelicals, Anabaptist evangelicals, conservative evangelicals). Each group has its own ethos, its own "popes" and authoritative methods of interpretations. The question really is: how can I as a member of the Wheaton community and conservative evangelicalism make a break with the fathers of neo-evangelicalism (i.e., Carl F. H. Henry) and advocate a method contrary to the authority they exercise over the evangelical subculture of which I am a part?

My answer to this question is somewhat complicated. Let me attempt to make it clear. It arises out of my method of doing theology, which consists of the following fourfold criterion of judgment:

1. Is it rooted in the Scripture?
2. Does it enjoy historical verification?
3. Is it theologically consistent with orthodoxy?
4. Does it have contemporary relevance?

In my opinion the conscious or, in some cases, the unconscious method of most evangelicals follows the same fourfold criterion as I have set forth above. The difference between us is located particularly in questions two and three. While my point of reference historically and theologically is the early church, most evangelicals make their historical and theological criterion in a much later time, say with the Reformation, with seventeenth-century orthodoxy, with Wesley, or with nineteenth-century Princetonian theology.

My contention is that theological thinking about apostolic uninterpreted truth is filtered through a system of thought (Plato, Aristotle, Descartes, Kant, Scottish Realism, existentialism, Whiteheadian physics, etc.) and that the system of thought itself is gradually treated as authoritative. Thus, the difference between theologians is not always over truth but is often over the system that delivers the truth.

I do not believe theology is an exact science. It is neither an inductive nor a deductive science, as some may argue. Rather, theological thinking is a discipline which involves concept formation and the development of a conceptual scheme. Theology makes use of conceptual models which may be drawn from extra-biblical sources.

Theology may therefore be defined as human thinking about truth. Truth is Jesus Christ specifically and the Bible more generally. People, synods, councils, and the like, who reflect on Christ and the truth, give us theology. Consequently theologians such as Aquinas, Calvin, Luther, and Barth give us systematic thinking about truth which we call theology.

If this is true, it follows that the most conservative method of doing theology is to go back into history to a time when the tradition of faith carries the least amount of cultural baggage. Further, it means that all systems and persons who seek to be faithful to the original deposit are evangelical in the linguistic and theological sense. Consequently, I can affirm the evangelical nature of any one of the many different sociological groupings of twentieth-century evangelicals, the evangelical nature of the Reformers, and the evangelical basis of Catholic or Orthodox theology. The only groups within Christian history that are not evangelical at bottom are those who deny apostolic Christianity or those who so thoroughly reinterpret it through their conceptual grid (i.e., Gnostics, anti-supernatural liberals) that it ceases to retain integrity with apostolic intent.

In worship this means that any Christian group that uses the Word, prayer and the table at least has the basic elements of worship. However, when these elements of worship are filtered through contemporary cultural grids, such as educational, evangelistic, entertainment, or psychological purposes, the apostolic intent of worship may become lost. Consequently, the historical point of return to uncover apostolic intent is most likely not Wesley, Calvin, or Aquinas. Rather, it is best to get as close to the original source and intent as possible, namely, the Church

Fathers who sought faithfully to deliver the apostolic order, intent, and meaning of worship. Thus a return to the tradition of the early church cuts through later accretions and developments, exposing the ways in which they have departed from apostolic intent while at the same time reviving the current practice of worship through the rediscovery of the apostolic intent preserved by the Fathers. I believe this method is truly evangelical, in the best sense of the word. I advocate this method, not over minute issues of interpretation, but with regard to the big questions—theological matters such as the canon, major doctrinal issues, ethics, and liturgy.

Does My Method Elevate Tradition over Scripture?

The original meaning of the word tradition is a key to understanding the relationship between Scripture and tradition. The Greek word *paradosis* is used throughout the New Testament to mean "hand over" (see for example Mark 1:14; Eph. 4:19; 5:2; Acts 15:26, 40; 16:4; Matt. 25:14; Luke 4:6; 1 Cor. 15:24). In terms of Christian belief it is used by Paul when he directed the Thessalonians to retain hold of the "traditions" which he had taught them by word or pen (2 Thess. 2:15); it refers to the faith content of his preaching in Corinth as evidenced in his comments in 1 Cor. 11:2, 23; 15:3. He had "handed over" to the Corinthians various "traditions" which had been entrusted to him by others. Further, according to Luke original eyewitnesses had "handed over" information to him (Luke 1:2), and according to Jude the faith could be described as that which had been "handed over" to the saints. Finally, the notion of "handing over" the faith through the centuries was expressed by Paul when he admonished Timothy to "hand over" the tradition of faith which he had received from Paul's teaching (1 Tim. 2:2). This sense of "handing over" the truth which had been passed down from the Apostles became prominent in the second-century battle with the Gnostics. It accounts for the development of the earliest form of apostolic traditions and apostolic succession among the early Church Fathers, particularly in Irenaeus' *Against Heresies*.

In doing theology, it is important to develop a phenomenological description of the way in which a Christian truth or practice may have developed in the primitive Christian community and on into the second century and beyond. Part of the theological task is to reconstruct this development in search of the apostolic faith and practice which was "handed over" to the next generation. In broad strokes the unfolding of the tradition may be outlined as follows:

1. The tradition of the Christian faith is Jesus Christ who was born, lived, died, and was resurrected.
2. Oral and written accounts about Jesus Christ began to appear immediately. Some were true; others were false.
3. The church, which is Christ's body, was given the responsibility of handing Jesus Christ over from generation to generation.
4. The Apostles, as authoritative leaders in the church, were faced with the immediate responsibility of interpreting Christ and handing him down accurately.
5. The context in which this interpretation was initially forged out was mainly in the worship of the church. The primitive Christian hymns, creeds, doxologies, benedictions, catechetical literature, and apostolic interpretations belonged to the liturgy of the church. Thus, worship was the context in which Christ became a lived experience and a confessional reality.
6. The Scriptures, which came later, were the written product of this process. They contain the authoritative accounts of Christ together with the apostolic interpretation of Christ. Thus, Scripture is tradition; that is, it hands over Jesus Christ.
7. The development of theology in the early church is intricately related to the development of Scripture as the church's authority. For, fundamental Christian thought (as articulated in the ecumenical creeds) and foundational Christian practice (such as worship and ethics) are more detailed reflections of apostolic teaching and practice. Early Church Fathers were not creating something new. Rather, they were extracting and

expanding apostolic teaching. In the fourth century Athanasius sums up this process in these words: "The actual original tradition, teaching, and faith of the Catholic church, which the Lord conferred, the apostles proclaimed, and the Fathers guarded" (*Ad Seraph.* 1.28).

In brief, the process above applies to worship in the following manner. The Holy Spirit gifted the Apostles with an understanding of Christ. This understanding was proclaimed and acted out in worship. The material of worship, such as hymns, creeds, benedictions, baptism, Lord's Supper, and catechetical material, became part of the Scripture. The order and practices of worship, which are somewhat hidden within the Scripture, are more clearly elucidated in the writings of the Fathers. Thus, insights into worship provided by the Didache, Justin, Tertullian, Hippolytus, and others are rooted in apostolic authority. Consequently the major outline and understanding of worship developed by the Fathers constitute an authoritative guide for worship renewal today.

What may be observed here is a process of authority related to tradition. It is the apostolic witness that is authoritative. The Bible is authoritative because it preserves and hands down this witness. The description of worship by the early Church Fathers is authoritative insofar as it remains faithful to the apostolic authority preserved in the Scripture. Thus, the Scripture is the judge of early Christian thought and practice as well. The task of the liturgist who must be conversant with both biblical and patristic sources is to discern where, when, and how early Christian worship expands scriptural teaching and thus becomes normative. The liturgist must also be able to discern where, when, and how worship practices become extra-biblical and, thus, relegated either to the realm of *adiophora* or erroneous practice.

In conclusion, the importance of early Christian worship for worship renewal today is in direct relationship to the degree in which the early church remained faithful to the apostolic tradition preserved in Scripture. If we assume that critical reconstruction of ancient worship demonstrates its form and content to be faithful to the apostolic practice in the main, ancient worship becomes an authoritative guide for worship renewal today. In this way the New Testament concept of tradition as that which is "handed over" is maintained and preserved.

Why the Early Church over That of Another Era?

It must be stated that the Fathers of the early church era were just as subject to its cultural milieu and conceptual systems as we today are subject to ours. The theology of the early church was forged out in the context of the mystery religions, polytheism, Gnosticism, cults such as Manichaeism, and the philosophy of Plato, Aristotle, Stoicism and neo-Platonism. To assume that the early Fathers were immune from these influences or that traces of this cultural milieu are not to be found in the writings of the Church Fathers would be naive indeed.

However, I would join those who argue that the ancient church, being in such close historical, geographical, linguistic, and conceptual proximity to the New Testament era and to its parent religion, Judaism, is characterized by a sustained attempt to remain faithful to the apostolic tradition. Consider, for example, the following six ways in which this may be demonstrated.

First, the early church was responsible for summarizing the general doctrines of the faith in creedal form such as the rule of faith, the later Old Roman Symbol, and finally the Apostles' Creed. To this day the whole church frequently confesses its faith in God within the liturgy by reciting the Apostles' Creed.

Second, we recognize the early church's part in the development of a canon. This was a process occurring after the apostolic age and one which took several centuries. Yet, in more than fifteen hundred years since the affirmation of this canon it has not been repudiated even though it has been the subject of controversy and continual scrutiny.

Third, the early church's ecumenical creeds have given definition to a trinitarian concept of God (Nicene Creed) and to an affirmation of the human and divine natures in the person of

Christ (Chalcedon Creed). While these creeds are written in the Greek language and use Hellenistic concepts, they preserve and even expound on the biblical kernel of truth they seek to explain. In spite of our contemporary questions they remain models of theological thought and methodological inquiry.

Fourth, the ancient church has provided foundational thought on ecclesiology, ministry, and sacraments. While less binding on the thinking of all Christians than are the Nicene and Chalcedon creeds, this thought has nevertheless become foundational for all future thinking on these subjects.

Fifth, the ethical approach of the first three centuries to war, abortion, infanticide, marriage, and numerous other subjects and its thinking about the church's relationship to society in general and to the state in particular have shown how penetrating early Christian thought is in the social, political, economic, and psychological areas of human existence.

Finally, during the same era, the church was wrestling with its worship. The form of worship, together with the approach to baptism, eucharistic prayers, sacred year, architecture, the lectionary, and ceremony, was being developed at the same time as were the creeds, canon, and ethics.

My argument is that the early church has defined the theological issues and set out the limits of orthodoxy. Anyone who defends the canon, subscribes to the Apostles' Creed, advocates the Trinity, or adheres to the full humanity and divinity of Jesus is already more than a New Testament Christian by virtue of having passed over into the fuller definition given to orthodoxy by the ancient church. Orthodoxy is a tradition developed by the early church that stands in apostolic continuity. Nevertheless, as an extension of the biblical principles, these areas of theological thought as defined and expanded by the early Church Fathers represent a movement beyond that conceived by the New Testament church. Further, the work of the Fathers represents foundational Christian thought which has been the subject of interpretation, reinterpretation, and debate throughout the history of the Christian church. Thus the importance of the Fathers and ancient Christian thought is difficult to question.

I agree with Paul Tillich who once said that no one should dare to wrestle with modern Christian thought until after having mastered classical Christian thought.

Finally, let it be stated that the value of early Christian thought finds expression in contemporary renewal, especially in the areas of liturgy and the rites of initiation (baptism, confirmation, Eucharist). The cutting edge of contemporary thought in these areas is historical thinking. The architects of Vatican II went back to the early church to discover its heart. We would do well today to do the same. This period represents the common roots of all Christians. Thus, to give more weight to this period of theological thought is to be orthodox, evangelical, and ecumenical.

Conclusion

I have attempted to illustrate and defend an evangelical and catholic method of doing theology. My argument is that the evangelical content of Christianity is rooted in the apostolic interpretation of the Christ event which, in the developing sources of the church, is contained in Scripture. The theological themes of Christianity have been further defined and elucidated in the creeds and practices of the ecumenical church of the first six centuries. This catholic interpretation which, as Vincent of Lérins stated, is believed "everywhere, always and by all" constitutes orthodox thought and practice. It is the tradition (that which has been handed over) of the church which has been transmitted through the centuries in a variety of conceptual models and in just as many social, cultural, and political milieus. Our theological task today is not to invent new theologies and practices but to remain faithful to that which has been handed over as we seek to hand it over today through the grids of our time and place.

9 How Does the Bible Function in the Christian Life?

WILLIAM A. DYRNESS
New College Berkeley
Berkeley, California

> The Lord has more light and truth yet to break forth out of his holy Word.
>
> John Robinson

To begin our discussion of Scripture with the question of how we use the Bible in theology may in itself be misleading. It might imply that Scripture is something I control and which I can manipulate according to my needs. But if the Bible is God's word and therefore a powerful presence in my life, the proper question may be: how does God's word use me? In any case a study of the function of the Bible must begin with the recognition that the Bible cannot be considered in isolation from my life and faith and that of the community of which I am a part. It will be my purpose to argue in this chapter that the Bible does not function in a vacuum and that statements about its power and authority must reflect on its context as well as its nature.

The model I would propose in the use of Scripture might be called the interactionist model.[1] This way of thinking suggests that Scripture actually functions in an interaction between my own experience, the encounter with the text, and the reality of God through this. I will argue that my experience with Scripture will certainly come to include theoretical knowledge about Scripture but that this only becomes relevant in the light of my concrete experience with the truth of Scripture, much of which can never be fully articulated. Indeed, as the reader becomes mature in Christ, it is the actual experience of scriptural truth that is more important. For it is this that enables the reader to judge more clearly the organic meaning of Scripture. Contrariwise, when theoretical constructs about Scripture continue to dominate we run the risk of limiting the Holy Spirit's use of the Bible to particular modes of working, and thereby we fail to allow new light and insight to break upon us. We will seek to present this model in three parts—telling our story, hearing God's story, and allowing these stories to merge.

We Begin by Telling Our Story

To understand Scripture properly we must begin not with a doctrine of Scripture but with our life in the world. This follows not only from the importance of our particular starting point but also from the way we come to know anything at all. A recognition of this fact has been reflected in recent studies in theological method. For example, Bernard Lonergan points out, "A theology mediates between a cultural matrix and the significance and role of a religion in that matrix."[2] Previously, he notes that culture was understood in a classical sense: classical values were viewed as static and unchanging. Now we have come to see culture more empirically as the changing values and meanings that inform a way of life. Our faith therefore is necessarily expressed and understood in terms of our particular setting. This need not be seen as a handicap; it is rather a recognition of our existence in society and history. This means moreover that our reflection on and use of Scripture must also take their impetus and starting point from the forces that shape our consciousness. In our day particularly momentous and complex issues face us—diminishing resources, economic affluence and poverty, and arms escalation, to name only a few. On a personal level many people carry heavy burdens of suffering or discouragement. These factors are surely relevant to the way we use Scripture.

This particularity of our starting point has been highlighted by the social and historical sciences. These show us the ways we are products of our environment and the history and traditions lying behind it. We must begin here because we simply cannot begin anywhere else. We cannot jump to some privileged place of neutrality or complete objectivity. We can neither close out all sense data (as Descartes wanted to do) nor bracket all ultimate questions (as Husserl sought to do). Nor do we perceive our life in discrete impressions (as Hume claimed) or in individually verifiable facts (as the logical positivists insist). Rather we are aware of a totality of experience making a dynamic whole. And it is within this context that we must live as responsible persons.

Rudolf Bultmann has been one theologian anxious to recognize the role that our modern pre-understanding plays in the interpretation of Scripture. He insists that it is impossible for a modern person who uses electricity and jet planes to understand the New Testament as it is written. In contrast to people in biblical times "modern man acknowledges as reality only such phenomena or events as are comprehensible within the framework of the rational order of the universe . . . the thinking of modern men is really shaped by the scientific world-view, and . . . modern men need it for their daily lives."[3]

Now it can hardly be doubted that whatever modern people comprehend must be put in terms that are congruent with other things they know to be true. Just as Scripture must be put into a language we can understand, so it must be translated into a cultural framework we can relate to. But it does not follow that our framework of understanding, any more than our language, is fixed and unchanging. Bultmann has followed Kant here in making our point of view into a normative and critical principle.[4] We must allow that the framework in which we see things needs correction or indeed transformation. As Peter Berger comments, "We must begin in the situation in which we find ourselves, but we must not submit to it as to an irresistible tyranny."[5]

In another place Berger elaborates this caution. He notes that modern (Western) consciousness may find traditional conceptions of God and the supernatural highly improbable. Long held and highly dispersed habits of thought may incline the average person toward secularism and naturalism. But this interesting and helpful sociological analysis is purely descriptive. These methods uncover the habits of thought with which the average person approaches Scripture. These mind-sets may well be hostile to the truth of the Bible; indeed, its messages may often be dismissed out of hand. But this does not mean that Scripture must be ignored or transformed to suit our way of thinking. It is possible of course always to assume in principle that one's modern ideas are right, but this does not put one in a position to learn much of anything new. The defect, after all, Berger points out, may lie in the modern consciousness and not with the truth of Christianity.[6] Though we must recognize where we are in our thinking, we must always be open to change or to altering our point of view if growth and maturation are to take place.

But it is clear that we ignore our presuppositions to our peril. As we noted, looking at Scripture in isolation from its context may tempt us to overlook the mind-sets and cultural predispositions with which we come to Scripture. We may then be blind to our tendency to focus on particular themes in the Bible while overlooking others. While teaching in Asia I became aware how often Western readers tended to see the truth of Scripture in abstract terms, while Asian readers tended to focus on narrative and concrete images. They did not find it necessary, as we do, to isolate single meanings and eliminate nuances and allusions. I have even heard of a situation in Africa where believers are particularly attracted to the genealogies in the Old Testament. Surely, they insist, here is a sign of authenticity.

The other side of this same point is that by ignoring the particular settings in which Scripture is read we risk losing the richness that varying perspectives may bring to our understanding of the truth of Scripture. Although we are sinners and we live in a fallen world, because of God's sovereignty and providential presence, there is always positive value in what we bring to Scripture.[7] And we must not be ungrateful for these preliminary signs of God's grace.

On a more personal level individuals may be more conscious of some immediate need or crisis which motivates them to turn to Scripture in the first place. As God heard the cries of the Hebrew people suffering under oppression in Egypt, so also God hears the cries of people today and sees their tears. It would be both inhuman and theologically deficient to fail to take such predispositions into account, for these are the particular openings which give opportunity for Scripture to speak with special power.

In summary we may say that, since we are products of our setting and the particular values of our community, it is this concrete experience which we must bring to Scripture and in terms of which we must understand its message. The principle at stake here is what the Reformers called the perspicuity of Scripture. The truth of Scripture is accessible and clear to all who can read it for themselves. When we by contrast present Scripture in the first instance in terms of some particular theological framework or in the light of specialized or critical issues, we not only fail to address the questions that trouble us, but we may also place a barrier between the reader and the text of Scripture. It might even be argued that much that passes for biblical study in our seminaries and graduate schools has in fact the effect of creating barriers between the lay reader and the Bible.

The use of Scripture, however, is not a special property of professional interpreters; it is a function of the whole body of Christ. Professional exegetes have the important role of helping Christians to learn to read Scripture for themselves. They provide historical and corporate perspectives which protect from individual excesses. This extremely important process is described in Ephesians 4:11–16. There it is clear that the goal of ministry is the maturity of the whole body. The gifts poured out on the church by the ascended Christ have as their final goal that "we all reach unity in the faith and in the knowledge of the Son of God and become mature, attaining to the whole measure of the fullness of Christ" (vs. 13, NIV). Those whom we call professional exegetes are then servants of the church who are to help people read Scripture in the light of their own questions—

not in the light of problems scholars (or their German teachers!) say are important. It does not take much interaction with lay readers to see how enormously different are the problems they see in Scripture from those theologians are taught to see. One often hears the lament that theology has not penetrated into our churches. The reason for this may in part lie here: individual Christians must be challenged to reflect on their commitment and to work from a biblical point of view.[8] For authentic commitment will always be relative to times and places. Indeed the biblical picture portrays a God who wishes to enter fully into the fabric of human life—one who leaves the ninety-nine in the fold and goes out and seeks the one sheep that is lost. So today we must believe that God is seeking us out, coming to us where we are and seeking to bring redemption into our lives, our homes, and our communities. But how does Scripture mediate this coming?

Scripture Functions in Allowing Us to Hear God's Story

In various ways the Word of God comes into our situation. But as we are exposed to it we soon learn that it does not come simply as another source of knowledge about ourselves or the world, but as a dynamic call which demands a response. This awareness comes from the interaction of two factors in the text. First, we see in Scripture particular people and communities that represent times and places very different from our own. Yet they are seen to be real people who cry and laugh just as we do. Second, we find God coming to them, speaking to them, and interacting with them in pursuit of his good purposes. These purposes are realized in a series of events that Gabriel Fackre calls the red thread through Scripture—the central and defining narrative of Scripture, what we might call God's story of redemption or renewal.

We find in Scripture a God who is actively present not only as the creator but also the sustainer of this order of things. We see God enter history, meet people where they are, but actively transform situations in which he is present. Both elements of the record are indispensable. It is a real human world we meet with. The authors of Scripture give an authentic witness to the crucial events of God's redemptive program climaxing in the life, death, and resurrection of Christ. As Conrad Boerma puts it, "From within their own social situations its authors described how God changed their world. . . ."[9]

This human point of view calls for further elaboration, for one often sees reference to the cultural and historical conditionedness of Scripture as though it were a cause for concern. The particularity, it is held, is a source of problems for the interpreter. Indeed, one is led to believe that the ideal form of revelation would have been a set of abstract propositions. I believe it is time that we saw the mistake in this line of thinking. Because of the particular intellectual heritage that we enjoy in the West, we have come to believe that propositional statements are the purest form of truth. In fact, however, the proposition most often reflects the abstraction of truth from its circumstantial expression. Now one ought not belittle the factual or cognitive dimension of Scripture. There are statements of fact which reflect the transcendent purposes of God, but these are often given figurative, poetic, or ironical expression. And they always have a historical and cultural context. As Bernard Ramm put it a generation ago, "propositional revelation" is an unhappy expression because "it fails to do justice to the literary, historical and poetic elements of special revelation."[10]

In fact the conditionedness of Scripture is an asset to interpretation rather than a liability. The particular and circumstantial expression of revelation underlines the truth that God has entered into actual history and has made himself known to particular people at special times and places. All of this is a great advantage. For we too are subject to historical exigencies and cultural patterns. And, if it can be shown that God spoke to such a people in the past, we can more readily believe that the living Lord of history can come into my life today and transform it by his presence. Indeed we may well discover in those biblical figures our own historical "roots." It is precisely the struggle of real people with God's word and, in turn, God's patience and mercy toward them that can, as Hebrews 11 shows, stand as an example for us.

But we must go beyond this. For the important thing is not merely that God spoke to actual people and entered real events. Rather, it is what God has said and done in those events. For in creation, in the call of Israel, in the life and work of Christ, and in the pouring out of the Holy Spirit on the church we find the great defining events of all histories and the story around which we must in our turn orient our lives. Initially, however, in these events and their interpretation we discover an alien voice. We encounter something completely outside our experience that forces us to say with Nicodemus, "How can these things be?" Moreover in this strange order of things I am confronted with a personal God who not only called Abram out of Ur, but is clearly seeking me in the ministry of Jesus Christ. By reflection on this God and his interaction with his people, I am led to see myself not only as misinformed about this or that fact about the past but also as a sinner, someone standing guilty before a holy God. I come to see that my need is not more information, as I might have thought, but conversion, which I could never have guessed. Scripture's own witness is very clear about the purpose of the written word—"these [signs] are written that you may believe that Jesus is the Christ, the Son of God, and that believing you may have life in his name" (John 20:31). This experience with Christ is ultimately the source of power that is often associated with Scripture (Rom. 1:16; 2 Tim. 3:15–17; Heb. 4:12). This too was a common emphasis in the faith of Reformation churches as M. E. Osterhaven explains: "Scripture presents a unified message concerning God's grace made manifest in Jesus Christ and the Christian's call to live unto him. That is the Bible's single theme, and everything drawn from Scripture must be related to that theme."[11] It is this message of the finished redemptive work of Christ which we call God's story and which is the absolute unchanging element in Scripture.

So in the encounter with the Bible I come to see that the dependence on its truth must be of a wholly different kind than my relation to other sources of truth. Here is a claim before which I cannot remain indifferent, here is a call which I cannot ignore. Moreover, in responding to this truth in faith we find that it snatches us from ourselves, as Luther put it, "and places us outside ourselves, so that we do not depend on our own strength, conscience, experience, person, or works. . . ."[12]

Now we are in a position to understand the Reformation slogan, *sola scriptura*. While we began in a situation in which both our experience and Scripture play a role, we are driven to the place where Scripture is seen to possess a unique authority and where my experience is subject to transformation. Only Scripture possesses this power to renew us by virtue of its message of the gospel. However, the truth of the gospel cannot have its full impact on my life apart from a real interaction with my experience. Notice that we are not saying that revelation occurs in this interaction, but that the meaning of revealed truth is only appropriated in this process (what we traditionally call illumination). Moreover, we are affirming that only through this process does God confront people during these last days while we await the return of Christ. This differs in no substantial way from the Reformers' teaching on Scripture. For Calvin, though the word of God is the only reliable source of knowledge of God, its authority is realized in the reciprocal relation between the word and the spirit as these are active in the life of the church.[13]

Another way of putting this is to emphasize that the authority of Scripture is self-authenticating. This is not to say we are made to have some mystical experience of certainty, but that through the ministry of the Holy Spirit we are made to taste the reality— in our own life and times—of God's goodness and love manifest in Jesus Christ. It is primarily through the experience of God's power, whereby our lives are affected in a concrete way by God's presence, that we come to understand its authority. John Calvin put this well when he reminded us that "the word of God is not intended to teach us how to chatter, or to make us eloquent or subtle, but to reform our lives."[14] And, we might add, to reform the lives of our families and communities.

I believe it is important to recognize that our view of the authority of Scripture results not only from what the Bible teaches about itself but also from the way the Bible has functioned in the experience of the church. The reflection on this scriptural self-witness and our continuing experience with the text lead to our confession of the nature of Scripture. Of course our doctrine of inspiration does not grow out of our experience with the Bible, but from the teaching of Scripture itself. But that truth does not become actual apart from a real interaction between the text and my experience. The authority of Scripture may certainly be understood theoretically. But this expression of things is a second-order reflection upon the actual course Scripture takes in the life of the believing community. The authority of the text is a comprehensive one involving theoretical and experiential factors by which God moves us through the Holy Spirit to transform our lives, initially by conversion, then through the discipleship that necessarily follows this. Our reflection upon this is meant to illumine our experience and not to replace it.[15]

Let us summarize where we have come. Our understanding of the function of Scripture must be carried out in the light of the particular situation in which we find ourselves. The word of God enters this situation through preaching or private reading. There we meet a God who has entered into a unique relationship with a particular people at a special time, a people who are in many ways like those I know. In these events God shows himself Lord and, in his Son, a Savior who seeks me and calls me to follow him in the particular place I find myself. The authority of Scripture is mediated to me by my actual experience of power whereby the Holy Spirit renews my heart (the process the Reformers called the internal witness of the Holy Spirit). In this experience I find my habits of thought and even my personal crises challenged and confronted by a whole new order which we have called God's redemptive story. The challenge now becomes to see my own story, with which I began, in terms of God's story which has now grasped me and taken me out of myself.

Scripture Functions as God's Story and Mine Merge

The final stage in the interaction between Scripture and the believer occurs when I see my story and the story of God in the Bible as a part of a single story. The goal is not only a deeper understanding of the truth of Scripture but also a more comprehensive experience of the grace of God which is revealed therein. Few would care to argue that the goal of Scripture is a deeper embodiment of God's grace, what Scripture calls Christian maturity, becoming like Christ (Eph. 4:15). But we have not done enough to draw out the implications of this for the use and interpretation of Scripture. For, as we are drawn into the full meaning of the central events of Scripture, we see that a continuing response is called for and therefore an ongoing experience (interaction) with the text. This truth enters our experience with cognitive weight but also with symbolic richness and spiritual power.

In this process of interaction with Scripture we must guard against two dangers both of which have been prominent in our Christian communities. On the one hand, since we wish to continue to learn and grow, we ought never to fix our experience with Scripture in such a way that a given Christian practice becomes normative. I am not speaking here of the norms of Scripture which do not change. But I am referring to our practice of understanding and applying these norms to a particular time and place. The methods of study and interpretation, just as much as the cultural expression of Christian truth, must be seen as relative to times and places. For, just as at the beginning our modern secular world-view must not be allowed to determine what Scripture will say, so also no stage of Christian growth can be allowed to impede further growth. For, as Paul reminds us, we all see through a glass darkly and we must always be open to further clarity.

On the other hand, in our questioning of Scripture we must never fix in advance what Scripture will say. We will surely have our confessions and our convictions that God's word is dependable and sure. Scriptural truth does not fundamentally change at the whim of the interpreter. But when we have reached that point where we believe that Scripture has said its last word to us and we are always sure what its message will be, when all around us major events are causing great changes in our understanding of ourselves and our world, then we may be limiting the actual authority of Scripture in our lives. For a progressive understanding of Scripture issues in an ever deeper reflection on our daily lives. Our goal is progressively to interpret our vocations, our personal and family lives, in the light of God's program. We come to see our unfolding story as a part of God's story. For Scripture is given not primarily to inform me but to interpret me and my world. As far as I am personally concerned, Scripture has been given for the sake of *this world in which I live*, for it is this world which Christ came to redeem and where we pray to see God's kingdom come.

Just as the Beroeans of Acts responded to the events around them by searching the Scriptures daily to see if what Paul said was true (Acts 17:11), so we must interpret our experience afresh in the light of God's word. It would be foolish indeed to ignore the experience of past Christians and their confessions of faith, for this is all relevant to our own confession. We are products of one or another tradition of Christian experience and we surely find there rich resources for our present understanding. But we best honor these examples by bringing even these creeds and confessions to Scripture to see if there is genuine congruence. For only here, we believe, God speaks with the authority that has transforming power.

Paul reminds us in 1 Corinthians 1:28 that the lowly things of this world which God chose are to "break up the existing state of things" (author's translation). This lowly gospel message continues to break up existing states of affairs. As the Reformers put it, the church therefore is "always being reformed" by the word of God. "Scripture is in the hands but not in the power of the Church,"[16] notes Karl Barth. The reason for this is that the great purpose of God outlined in Scripture is not limited to Bible study or even missionary work. These vital activities are signs of the final goal—a kingdom of righteousness in which all things are brought under the rule of Christ (Eph. 1:10). This will not be realized completely until Christ comes again but we must be seeking to bring about intimations of that kingdom by the power of the first fruits of Christ's reign already present in the Holy Spirit.[17] What is relevant for the function of Scripture is that the great culmination which God holds out for us involves both his story and ours in glorious interrelationship. If this is so, we cannot fully appropriate the truth of Scripture unless this relationship is already experienced—unless, that is, God's story has in fact become our own story.

This means that Scripture will function much more like a musical score than a blueprint for our lives. A score gives guidance but it must always be played afresh. Seeing Scripture as a blueprint not only overlooks the reality of historical change and the changes in consciousness that result from this but also misunderstands the way God works. It implies a static understanding of culture in which God cannot do something new which is consistent with Scripture and thereby provide a fresh musical interpretation which reflects modern sensitivities. Paul implies that it is just such experiences which have been made possible by the cataclysmic death and resurrection of Christ and which will be climaxed by that final renewal, the second coming.

The goal of the interaction between Scripture and the Christian community then is that the power of the gospel become operative in the life of that community. In one sense we can say that the authority of Scripture is actual not only where Scripture is acknowledged and read but also where its power is seen. This is to say also that God's redemptive program and story is continuing exactly where this power is manifest. This process of understanding can be seen to involve several levels. First, there is the careful exegesis of Scripture and the historical and cultural study necessary to this. But this process must continue through the actual "hearing," in the biblical sense, of God's word. The words we read must be seen as a summons to discipleship. Nor is this merely an application of the truth of the text. For much in Scripture cannot be understood apart from the active obedience to the voice that speaks there. This experience will then, in turn, provide a further context in which Scripture is read anew. The goal is that envisioned by the prophet Jeremiah (31:33–34): God's law is to be written on our hearts, so that it not only permeates our thinking but also becomes our very life and breath.

This process from start to finish is carried on in the fellowship of believers, so that the interaction and the growth that results has a horizontal and a vertical dimension. This point is so important that it bears emphasis. While we are sometimes under the impression that our problems and our faith are a private affair, this is an illusion. We are always dependent on our culture and support communities. To one who believes in Christ, the corporate dimension becomes even more important. For it is the wisdom and maturity of the body of Christ as a whole that the Holy Spirit is working toward. And for this project all the varied gifts are pressed into service. This not only protects us from individual aberrations but also ensures that every member is fully involved in the process of growth toward maturity in Christ. The use of Scripture must be understood as a controlling norm in this process.

This brings us back to our opening statement—Scripture is given because God wants people who are growing up into maturity in Christ. In the nature of the case this cannot be a matter of rules or of a specified understanding of Scripture. To the mature person, analytic skills are important and understanding is essential, but these are only part of a holistic understanding of life that is generated from actual experience with God and the Word. The process of maturing involves a movement from viewing situations as a collection of equally relevant facts to seeing the world as an organic whole in which only certain parts are relevant at a given moment.[18] This includes a developing sense of which aspects of biblical truth relate to a particular circumstance.

This is not the place to draw out the implications this view has for our practice of hermeneutics and biblical interpretation. But we can at least predict with confidence that our life of obedience will surely have its impact on our methods of interpretation just as our earlier reading of Scripture had its impact on our lives. This may suggest a preference for inductive types of study which approach texts with openness. It will underline the historical dimension of theology that looks to previous stages in the interaction with Scripture, both as part of our story and a commentary on God's story. All our study will be seen as a goal to our mission and our growth. Our Christian lives will involve a continuing dialogue with Scripture. With growing maturity will come an increased power of judgment (1 Cor. 2:15–16). This is why Donald Bloesch can say "only reflection [on Scripture] done in faith can grasp what is of abiding significance and what is marginal and peripheral."[19]

In our interpretation of Scripture, understanding will result from and not just precede our actual obedience. The light will grow; understanding will deepen within the community as we seek to engage ourselves in God's program. This implies that we may at times take risks and follow out our commitment beyond what is immediately clear. After all, our world makes unique demands, and it challenges us in subtle and unpredictable ways. Our reading of Scripture must give God room for the unique and exciting. It must reflect that of the early Christians of whom it is said, "They turned the world upside down."

The reading of Scripture in this way will require a response of the whole person as well as of the whole community. The Holy Spirit does use rational factors to speak to us through the Word. Commitment is a rational event, but it is something more as well. As Pascal says, "Faith indeed tells what senses do not tell, but not the contrary of what they see. It is above them and not contrary to them" (Pensées, 265). We will want to reflect on Scripture in a systematic way, but this will not be done in isolation from personal and social factors. Equipping the saints is a matter of training not only minds but also hands, eyes, and even reflexes. This is a process that is always begun afresh with each generation, and it results from an interaction between Scripture and the believing community that is never finished. For, as Karl Barth argues, only in this way are we true not only to the nature of Scripture itself but also to our link with the Church in every age:

> The Church is most faithful to its tradition, and realises its unity with the Church of every age, when, linked but not tied by its past, it to-day searches the Scriptures and orientates its life by them as though this had to happen to-day for the first time. And, on the other hand, it sickens and dies when it is enslaved by its past instead of being disciplined by the new beginning which it must always make in the Scriptures. . . . The principle of necessary repetition and renewal, and not a law of stability, is the law of the spiritual growth and continuity of our life.[20]

10 The Nature and Function of Theology

DAVID F. WELLS

Gordon-Conwell Theological Seminary
South Hamilton, Massachusetts

> Two preachers articulate contrasting views of authority in a
> well-known woodcut from the sixteenth century. The Ro-
> man Catholic is arrogantly wagging his finger at the congre-
> gation and saying, "*Sic dicit Papa.*" The Protestant, his finger
> humbly pointed at the page of Scripture, declares, "*Haec dicit
> dominus de.*" The artist, needless to say, was Protestant!

Like so many other slogans, however, the Protestant Reformers'
sola scriptura both revealed and concealed important issues. What
it revealed was their conviction that Christian theology in its
form and substance as well as its function in the church must be
determined by God's authoritative Word, the written Scriptures.
Given the sufficiency of Scripture, "whatsoever is not read
therein," declares Article VI of the Thirty-nine Articles, "nor
may be proved thereby, is not to be required of any man, that it
should be believed as an article of faith, or be thought requisite
or necessary to salvation."[1] What the slogan concealed was the
complexity of the process involved in understanding God's
Word in the context of cultures far removed in time and psychological texture from those in which the revelation was originally
given. It is this complexity which I wish to analyze in order that
I may say how it is that evangelical theologians today ought to
construe the significance of the *sola scriptura* principle for their
work.

The Nature of Evangelical Theology

The nature of evangelical theology is determined for it by the nature of that Word of which it is the exposition and application. The Word of God is the unique, written disclosure of God's character, will, acts, and plans. It is given so that men and women who have come to faith through its teaching might learn to live in God's world on his terms, loving and honoring him in all that they do and seeking to make known to the world his law and gospel. That is the purpose of God's revelation and the task of theology is to facilitate this.

This facilitation begins with the recognition of the bipolar nature of biblical revelation. Biblical revelation was given in a particular cultural context but it is also intended to be heard in our own context. This revelatory trajectory, then, has a point of origination and a point of arrival. It is the fact of inspiration and the contemporary work of the Spirit which secure a consistency between its *terminus a quo* and its *terminus a quem*. The work of the Holy Spirit was such that the responsible human agents who were used in the writing of Scripture were able to employ cultural materials and, indeed, to shape the revelation in terms of their own understanding, but what God the Spirit willed should be revealed was exactly what was written, and the content and intent of this revelation were alike transcultural. The biblical revelation, because of its inspired nature, can therefore be captive neither to the culture in which it arose nor to the culture in which it arrives. It was not distorted as it was given, nor need it be distorted as we seek to understand it many centuries later in contexts far removed from those in which it was originally given.

The bipolar character of revelation is what Krister Stendahl appears to have had in mind in the distinction he has drawn between what Scripture "means" and what it "meant."[2] Unfortunately, however, this is a distinction which can be misunderstood. Much modern theology is of the opinion that contemporary meaning is largely uncontrolled by and different from biblical meaning. What Scripture says, it is argued, is to be determined by the cultures in which it was given and what it means is to be determined by, and not merely related to, our own modern culture. This approach destroys any meaningful understanding of the Spirit's work in inspiration and illumination.

It is the task of theology, then, to discover what God has said in and through Scripture and to clothe that in a conceptuality which is native to our own age. Scripture, at its *terminus a quo*, needs to be de-contextualized in order to grasp its transcultural content, and it needs to be re-contextualized in order that its content may be meshed with the cognitive assumptions and social patterns of our own time. This process, I suggest, is helpfully illustrated by the way in which our electronic media work. Prior to the electronic age there were only three factors involved in communication: the orator; the speech; and the audience. With the new media the orator has become the sending source and the audience is the receptor. The speech has become a message which now also has to be encoded by the sending source and decoded by the receptor. In all, then, there are now five components in the process. With a little adaptation this model might graphically represent the theological task[3] in this way:

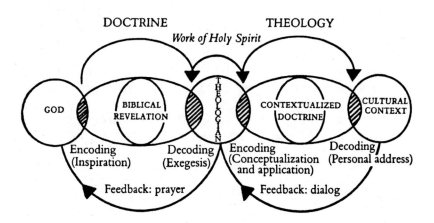

It is now my purpose to examine this process, focusing principally on the two poles or foci in the theological task. This I wish to do by redefining, for the purposes of this essay, my use of two words: doctrine and theology.[4]

Doctrine and the Pole of Revelation

Doctrine is what the Bible says on any subject. We speak of "the doctrine of the atonement," "the doctrine of Christ," or "the doctrine of God," and what we have in mind is the collective testimony from the various biblical authors as to what should be believed about the atonement, about Christ, and about God. The word *doctrine* is therefore being used in a way that is flexible enough to accommodate the variety of biblical teaching on these and other subjects as well as the factor of development in some themes as we move from the Old Testament into the New Testament. Our doctrinal categories can be neither artificial, so as to impose an order on the biblical revelation which is not itself a part of the revelation, nor wooden, so as to exclude testimony which does not fall within the prescribed pattern. The doctrinal form must arise from and faithfully represent the revelatory content which the doctrine is seeking to present. This question, of how doctrine should be derived, now needs to be addressed more specifically, first positively and then negatively.

Principles of Construction

The process of deriving doctrine has three facets to it. These facets are not so much stages, distinguished from one another in a chronological sequence, as they are characteristics of a single process and as such always function together with each other in any healthy formulation. These facets or characteristics may be designated as the scientific, artistic, and sacral.[5]

The use of the word *scientific* in this context is undoubtedly provocative. It may conjure up memories of an earlier phase in American evangelical theology in which theology was customarily spoken of as being a science[6] or a still earlier phase in which theology used to be described as the "queen of the sciences." Nothing so triumphalistic is in mind here! There is, however, an analogy between the two activities which is helpful to observe.

In both cases there is objective data which needs to be understood, organized, and explained. The explanation with the greatest plausibility is the one which best explains the most data. Whether one is dealing with scientific hypotheses and theories in the one case or doctrines in the other, the explanation must always remain subservient to and open to correction by the data being explained. Scientific theories cannot be sustained in cavalier disregard for the facts and neither can doctrines. Both the foundation and the parameters of any doctrinal formulation must be provided by careful, honest, skillful exegesis. Doctrine which is not at its heart exegetical is not at its heart evangelical; doctrine which develops a life of its own and blithely disregards what Scripture says is also blithely disregarding what God says. That is what it means to have an inspired Scripture and this is the import of the *sola scriptura* principle for doctrine.

It is a myth, however, to suppose that this process, either in science or in biblical study, proceeds merely according to external laws without reference to the inner life of the interpreter! It is for this reason that, in addition to the scientific dimension, mention is here made of the artistic and sacral.

By the word *artistic*, what is in mind is the place of understanding and even of self-understanding in the construction of doctrine. For, in the nature of the case, the fruit of exegesis has to be constructed into a synthetic whole and that construction is significantly affected by the pre-understanding, the presuppositions, the experience, and the psychology of the interpreter. The ideal we need to hold out to ourselves, then, is that of faithful resonance between the realities being spoken of in Scripture and our own understanding of those realities. An interpreter whose grasp of the life and meaning of sin is shallow will, for example, almost inevitably understand the teaching of Scripture on sin in a shallow manner and the doctrinal structure which results will be correspondingly deformed. The interpreter's cognitive presuppositions and his or her spiritual capacity for understanding the truth of God are fundamental in the formation of doctrine.

This, however, leads naturally into the third factor, the sacral. Martin Luther declared that he had learned from Psalm 119 that the three factors indispensable to the construction of "right theology" are *oratio*, *meditatio*, and *tentatio*. What he meant was that our entire doctrinal endeavor must be understood in the context of knowing God, as an exercise in spirituality, as an expression of our love and worship of God. This is an aspect of the theological task, I dare say, which has largely vanished from most learned discussions.

Meditatio,[7] if I may begin here, is the reading, studying, contemplation, and inner digestion of Holy Scripture. It is the absorption of its teaching so that its truth is infused in our lives and its teaching becomes the means of our holding communion with God, receiving his promises and expressing our gratitude by obeying his commands.

Reflection or *meditatio* does not naturally recommend itself to us; as a matter of fact, since most of us are energetic "doers" and high pragmatists, reflection seems like a most unproductive pastime. The only kind of thinking we are really interested in is that kind which either solves problems or gets something started. Reflection by its very nature is neither outwardly directed at a problem nor does it seek immediate effects such as getting some project going. Why, then, should we imagine that reflection has anything to be said for it?

The answer is that the things of God are only partly involved with solving problems and launching projects, as much as we might like to think that the whole of spirituality is involved with these activities! God is our Eternal Contemporary standing in relationship to us through Christ not merely when we are solving problems or launching projects, but at every moment of our lives. God is not closer to us in our moments of activity than at other times; and the other times are not worthless because they are not spent in activity!

Reflection is, in fact, the soil in which our loves, hopes, and fears all grow. If we never took thought, we would never fear anything, love anyone, or hope for anything. Reflection is how the truth of God first takes root in us, how it is first to be "owned" by us as its interpreters, and how it owns us as we interpret it.

Oratio obviously includes praying as requesting but it is by no means limited to this, for prayer is a many-sided expression of a God-centered life. Being God-centered in one's life is essential to being God-centered in one's thoughts. This God-centeredness is the *sine qua non* of good theology, for, without it, it is impossible to think our thoughts after God, which is what defines good theology. Prayer and theology, therefore, require the total orientation of the person—of heart, mind, and will—to God. Theology without trusting, submissive prayer is no longer good theology; it is merely an academic exercise which may itself pose as a substitute for the process of knowing God. Where this happens, the means has become the end in a kind of perverse idolatry.[8]

Reflection and prayer are matters in which we engage; *tentatio* is something which occurs to us and, for that reason, I wish to say little about it. I merely observe that most of us slip easily into a loose godlessness—however well hidden it is beneath religious language and the outward expressions of piety—unless we are kept in a state of spiritual tension by life's disconcerting experiences. The adversity which is encompassed by *tentatio* is what disciplines the spirit and, difficult as this may be, it is an essential ingredient in the writing of all profound Christian thought.

The construction of doctrine, then, is a complex matter in which there must be a constant and intense interplay between the authoritative Word through which the interpreter is addressed and the interpreter who hears this Word. It requires that we learn syntax, verbal forms, and conjugations and that we sustain a personal relationship to the God of that Word.[9] The divine address is verbal communication by which and through which God makes self-disclosures and, in that disclosure and address, elicits our "wonder, love, and praise." Doctrine, correspondingly, must not only capture and clarify what it is that has been communicated in Scripture but it must also bring us face-to-face with the Communicator. It, too, must elicit from us "wonder, love, and praise."

Aberrations to Be Avoided

There are, I believe, two major aberrations which have gained popularity amongst evangelicals in the last decade and which, in my judgment, seriously vitiate the process of constructing doctrine in a way that is in faithful conformity to Scripture. These are, first, the toying with Catholic and Anglo-Catholic notions of tradition and, second, the imposition on Scripture of systems that are alien to it.

The new concern with tradition is in part justifiable. There is no question that in much fundamentalism and evangelicalism, the Word of God is held captive to the parochialisms of this age, not to mention the personal eccentricities of domineering, authoritative preachers. The Word of God is often what *they* say it is, and unbelief is defined as disagreeing with *their* interpretations! These authoritarian figures often function as an *ad hoc* magisterium. How Scripture has been interpreted in the past is often dismissed as irrelevant. By a strange quirk of logic we have, therefore, come to repeat the errors we chastised the liberals and Roman Catholics for committing. On the one hand, by our historical amnesia we break our continuity with historic Christian faith as did the liberals and, on the other, we accord to some preachers a magisterial authority in interpreting Scripture not unlike Roman Catholics do!

The argument that tradition should have a major role in the interpretation of Scripture, however, usually carries with it a concealed assumption as to what authority is, where it is located, and how it should operate. The traditional Roman Catholic position on tradition[10] involved two distinct arguments. First, it was argued that the way in which Scripture has been understood in the church must prescribe for us what Scripture is understood to declare because it is the Holy Spirit who has provided this interpretation. It is perfectly clear, though, that the Spirit has never given a uniform sense on what Scripture teaches, not even in the patristic period. Vincent of Lérins' *Commonitorium* in the fifth century sought to address the fact that there was a welter of opinions within extra-biblical tradition. This effort was in a measure successful but it is interesting to note that in the Middle Ages Peter Abelard was nevertheless driven to write his *Liber Sententiarum sic et non* citing over one hundred and fifty subjects on which the early Fathers were in considerable disagreement with one another! It is this fact which, as in the early church so now, has been a powerful force in moving people toward the acceptance of the second part of the argument, namely, that there must be an authoritative church which will adjudicate finally, absolutely, and even infallibly on which interpretations should be seen as resulting from the Spirit's illumination and which should not. The argument for tradition as authoritative teacher becomes, almost inevitably, an argument for an authoritative church.

The Protestant Reformation is often perceived as having pitted the biblical Word of God against ecclesiastical tradition. It is true that sometimes the Reformers complained about the way in which tradition nullified the teaching of God's Word.[11] The real argument, however, was not so much with tradition as with a church which used tradition authoritatively. The Reformers opposed God's authoritative Word to this church which, in their view, had arrogated to itself an authority which was entirely illicit. They accepted tradition in the role of guide and counselor; they denied it could act as authoritative teacher.

In taking this view the Protestant Reformers believed that they were merely recovering the essence of patristic Christianity which needed to be affirmed against the later medieval development with which the church of Rome had become identified. Luther, Calvin, and Cranmer, not to mention a multitude of their successors, expressed the view that the Christianity of the first five centuries coincided with their theology and was at odds with that of Rome.[12]

Their confidence was not ill-founded, especially in their attitude toward tradition. In the early patristic period it was common to draw a distinction between the apostolic *paradosis* (tradition) and the church's *didaskalia* (teaching). The former, it was asserted by Irenaeus, Tertullian, and others, was authoritative and the latter was not. And even *didaskalia* was distinguished from *theologia*.[13] The individual views of a teacher should not be considered the teaching of the church and the teaching of the church should not necessarily and automatically be considered the teaching of Scripture. Thus did Origen, for example, speak of *theologia* as the effort of the individual to "make sense" out of Scripture but he immediately asserted the tentative nature of any such interpretation.[14] In Gregory of Nazianzus the element of indirectness, of being one step removed from the original data, is identified with the word *theologia* and Pseudo-Dionysius employed it as a synonym for mysticism![15]

Two important changes occurred in this situation, however. First, with the passage of time the apostolic tradition, which had been the sum and substance of (the Apostles') teaching on the life, death, and resurrection of Christ, became broadened to include extra-biblical, oral teaching which was supposed to have come from the Apostles. This was a deleterious development because canonical and non-canonical, biblical and non-biblical material was being indiscriminately blended. Second, as the church was troubled by heresy and schism from within and by the State from without, uniformity of belief and practice became a necessity. The means adopted to arrive at this end was to place great authority in the hands of powerful bishops and then, in the fourth and fifth centuries, in the hands of a central, authoritative church in Rome under whose leadership the others were expected to be subject. These two developments drastically changed the meaning of tradition. It now became a category broad enough to include extra-biblical beliefs and practices and then, as it was employed within an authoritative church, it became the means of achieving uniformity, oftentimes without reference to Scripture itself. It was at that point that the early church lost the power to reform itself in the light of God's Word, because at that point it had dislodged the Word of God from its functional authority and replaced it by pseudo-ecclesiastical authorities.

The longing for a tradition that will make sense out of our evangelical tower of Babel, the recoil from self-serving exegesis, and the dissatisfaction with the miserable and stultifying parochialism of much evangelicalism are entirely understandable. Our longing for order and security, made all the more intense by our involvement in a chaotic and changing world, should not, however, be followed naively down the road of tradition. The siren voice of authoritative tradition is really a beckoning call into an authoritative church. And once we arrive there, as the overwhelming majority of contemporary Catholics has discovered, we find that few problems have actually been resolved and many more have been created. The truth of the matter is that there are no infallible interpreters of God's Word in this world, not even in Rome. It is this fact which creates the space in our inner life to develop our own trust in God. In the midst of each exigency, we must learn to trust that the one who gave us this Word will also give us a sufficient understanding of it, despite all of our sins and prejudices, so that we can live in his world on his terms as his faithful children.

The second aberration has come in a multitude of forms but common to them all is a search for a key which will unlock the "real" meaning of Scripture, a meaning which, it is assumed, is presently obscure or hidden. This search has commonly taken mystical, rational, and literary forms, but it is the rational and the literary which are most common in contemporary evangelicalism.

The search for a rational key, in fact, often results in an imposition on Scripture of a system not arising naturally from it and is really a perversion of the truth of Scripture's unity. Examples of it are numerous but perhaps one of the most widespread and, I dare say, blatant is in some of the footnoted Bibles that litter the shelves of our bookstores.

If the purpose of these various footnoted Bibles, the most influential of which is no doubt Scofield's, was merely to provide background information so that the text might be understood better, then substantial objections would be hard to make. The truth of the matter, however, is that these footnotes invariably provide "the system" without which, we are forced to conclude, Scripture would be forever blurry.

If the Scofield "system" and others like it are plausible, they are plausible only at the level of hypothesis. As such, the system itself must always be exposed to the correction of the Word it is seeking to explain. The problem is, however, that the hypothesis has often become as fixed and unchangeable as the Bibles to which it is appended. There are a large number of lay Christians, for example, who, despite the far-reaching changes which some of Scofield's more learned disciples have worked into his scheme, still see his original, footnoted "system" as being as infallible as the Bible which it seeks to explain. The facts and the hypothesis have become identical. Once the hypothesis found its way into footnotes at the bottom of each page, the "system" became a way of understanding the Word, which understanding, in practice, is not itself really subject to correction by that Word as long as those Bibles are in existence.

It is one of the curious ironies of our time, however, that New Testament scholars who rail most loudly at the imposition of theological systems on the text are themselves often proponents of their own type of system. They merely substitute a literary system for a rational one.

This is nowhere more evident than in the current infatuation with redaction criticism. It has always been recognized, of course, that the authors of the Gospels each had a viewpoint in the light of which each made his paraphrastic selection of material.[16] The argument now, however, is that the sayings of Jesus had three contexts.[17] The first was the original context in which the words were uttered; the second was provided by the believing community which adapted his words to their lives; the third was provided by the redactor who adapted the saying, as heard from the community, for his own work which came to represent his "theology." What we should understand the Gospels to say, therefore, is not to be found primarily through an exegetical consideration of the text, but rather from a history which lies behind the text. The meaning of Christian faith is bound up in discovering what this history was rather than in what the text itself says.

There are two significant problems created by this approach. First, it holds the meaning of the text captive to the meaning of a history so shadowy that it cannot be said with any assurance what it was. The facts, in this instance, have been inverted. This history is at best only a clue to what the text says; the text is not supposed to be used as a clue to this history, for then the text would only be indirectly related to the meaning of the Christian faith. Second, it holds the meaning of Christian faith captive to the workings of the scholarly elite. The ecclesiastical magisterium is now replaced by a scholarly magisterium, for only they have the knowledge to uncover this history and it is only in this history that the meaning of faith can be found![18]

We need to conclude, therefore, that it is dangerous to assert that God the Holy Spirit inspired the Scriptures but somehow omitted to give us the key to understand them! Systems of understanding are legitimate and proper only to the extent that they arise from the biblical Word and are themselves disciplined by it. No one can legitimately impose a system on the Word. This applies both to rational systems, such as Scofield's, and to literary systems, such as those advanced by some advocates of redaction criticism. The issue the Protestant Reformers faced is quite as much ours as it was theirs: if we do not assert the right of Scripture to stand in authoritative relationship to every presupposition, custom, and tradition, every teaching, practice, and ecclesiastical organization, then that authority will be co-opted either by an ecclesiastical magisterium or by a scholarly one. Magisterii of this type may imagine that they are invested with some form of infallibility but time will reveal how mistaken this assumption is. The Word of God must be freed to form our doctrine for us without the interference of these pseudo-authorities. It was for this that the Reformers argued and it is for this that we must argue. It is this contention that is heralded by *sola scriptura*, and without the *sola scriptura* principle an evangelical theology is no longer evangelical.

Theology and the Pole of Culture

In the model which I have proposed, using electronic media as an example, it will be seen that theology is related to doctrine as the second step ("encoding") is to the first ("decoding") in the same process. Theology is that effort by which what has been crystallized into doctrine becomes anchored in a subsequent age and culture. It is the work of making doctrine incarnate. God's Word is "enfleshed" in a society as its significance is stated in terms of that cultural situation.

If doctrine might be represented by an object such as a chair, then theology would be the use to which that object is put, its effect on its surroundings and the perspective it gives on its environment. Theology differs from doctrine as what is unrevealed does from what is revealed, fallible from what is infallible, derived from what is original, relative from what is certain, culturally determined from what is divinely given. Doctrine cannot change from generation to generation, otherwise Christianity itself would be changing. Theology must change in each succeeding generation, otherwise it will fail to become a part of the thinking processes and life-style of that generation. The attempt to change doctrine imperils Christian faith; the unwillingness to incarnate doctrine in each age by theology imperils the Christian's credibility. In the one case Christianity can no longer be believed; in the other, it is no longer believable.

This is, to be sure, a somewhat selective understanding of what is entailed in doing theology. In addition to the role which has been described briefly, it has been customary to see theology also functioning within doctrine in both a protective and a constructive capacity.[19] These tasks are not in any way denied, although they are not presently being discussed. The church, it is true, has always had to find ways of protecting its doctrine. Simple reassertions of biblical language by themselves have often proved inadequate. The Fathers who sought to ward off Arianism in the early fourth century discovered this to their chagrin. Arius agreed to all of the biblical titles and expressions used of Christ's divinity because each one could be interpreted in such a way as to ascribe to him a diminished divinity (which, in biblical terms, could not be a divinity at all). The Fathers at Nicea therefore reluctantly resorted to the use of *homoousios* which was not altogether felicitous but at least it was an effective discouragement to Arianism.

The use of *homoousios* and all other such protective terms are provisional and should not be seen to participate in that infallibility which attaches to the Word they are protecting. The Nicene Creed and the Chalcedonian Definition are statements of extraordinary clarity and have been of immeasurable benefit in the life of the church. However, they are not divinely revealed and they, too, along with all other confessions, creeds, and statements of faith, must be subject to the correction of the biblical Word.

Theologians have likewise always found it beneficial to develop terms, concepts, and organizing principles for the work of construction. Proponents of dispensationalism and of covenant theology, for example, have alike argued that Scripture itself provides a concept in the light of which its variety all makes sense. In the one case it is the principle that, in each of a series of succeeding ages, God has tested his people in terms of their obedience to a particular form of his revelation; in the other, it is the proposition that God's salvation is divinely initiated and established, that it is the same salvation throughout the Bible, and that it is the notion of covenant which articulates this. The first keys on the differences between the testaments and the second keys on their unity. These are large and ambitious forms of construction and there are many lesser examples of it in and out of evangelicalism. Gustav Aulén's contention, for example, that the New Testament teaching on Christ's death is teaching simply about his conquest of the devil—the "classic motif"— falls into this category as does Karl Barth's understanding of evil conveyed in his term *das Nichtige* or Karl Rahner's "supernatural existential." These constructive devices are in principle legitimate and need to be accorded legitimacy. But they, too, must be subject to the correction of God's written Word. Constructive devices of either an organizational or a conceptual kind cannot be allowed to impose an understanding on Scripture which is not supported by it and which does not faithfully commend biblical teaching.

It is the relational role of theology which is, however, at the focus of this essay—the way in which theology relates doctrine to each age in a vernacular which is native to that age. In this connection I wish to speak briefly again of the positive principles entailed and then of certain aberrations which need to be avoided.

Principles of Construction

What, then, is the basis on which this incarnating work should take place and how should it be done? In the nature of the case, answers to these questions can only be sketched out in a rudimentary way.

First, with respect to the basis it should be observed that, while it is true that there is a soteriological discontinuity between God and human nature, there nevertheless remains a revelational *continuity*.[20] There is a structure to reality, which is both moral and epistemological in nature and which, by God's own design and providential operation, is unaltered by human rebellion. This revelation is natural, in the sense that it is part and parcel of both the creation and human nature, and it is general, inasmuch as it is a functional component in all human perception and cognition. It is the common thread linking vastly different cultural and social situations. It is what makes Christian discourse possible within the diversity of languages, social customs, and cultural values prevalent on the earth. It is prevenient to the gospel and it is the *sine qua non* for communicating the nature of the Christian world-view.

With respect to method, it is worth pondering whether or not a legitimate distinction might be drawn between the content of evangelical theology and its form or between what Paul Lehman calls its "referential" and its "phenomenological" aspects. The latter, of course, is provided by the concrete situation which is being addressed, while the former is the biblical norm in accordance with which an evangelical theology shapes itself and before the God of which it stands accountable. In earlier evangelical theologies content and form were identical; the content of biblical revelation was crystallized into doctrinal form and this doctrine, it was assumed, would be self-evident to reasonable people. It may be increasingly necessary, however, to allow the concrete situation, rather than the biblical revelation, to propose the "doctrinal" loci or the organizing forms in terms of which biblical faith needs to speak, because the secularism of our time has so transformed the way people think that Christian faith is now in a cross-cultural situation. Such a proposal in no way invalidates the search for doctrinal forms that are consistent with the substance of the biblical revelation; it merely means that their discovery will constitute but a halfway house rather than the journey's destination itself. These doctrinal forms will then have to be adapted to and translated in terms of the assumptions and norms of the American situation in such a way that the Word of God is preserved in its integrity but affirmed in its contemporaneity.

The situation that we face today is one in which the moral norms and cognitive expectations of the culture have also invaded the church. They form the foundation on which much doctrine is unwittingly built. The doctrine produces outward Christian activity—an informal code on what is "Christian" life-style (the agreed points of which are nevertheless being whittled down with each passing year), Christian activity in and out of church, and a Christian empire with organs of entertainment, education, and political influence—but it does not necessarily produce Christians who are, at the roots of their being, Christian. It does not necessarily produce men and women who have the capacity or the desire to contest the worldliness of our time or to flesh out an alternative to it. This doctrine, even in its most orthodox forms, can become nothing more than a mask which conceals the real operating principles in a person's life which may be worldly and secular. It is, then, the task of theology to expose these principles in the interest of securing a real adherence to the doctrine which is being given outward assent.[21]

An orthodox veneer is, I suspect, something that happens to

us almost unknowingly since we often do not understand how our culture has shaped us in the very depths of our being. This is especially the case in the way that technology operates in our culture.

Emil Brunner has asserted that we in the West are living in a unique moment.[22] Never before has a major civilization attempted to build deliberately and self-consciously without religious foundations. Beneath other civilizations there were always religious assumptions—whether these came from Islam, Buddhism, Hinduism, or Christianity—and it was these assumptions which gave both legitimacy and stability to the social order. Beneath ours there are none. In their absence we have technology. Technology is the metaphysic of twentieth-century America.

This, of course, is the theme that has been developed at some length by Jacques Ellul.[23] Technology, he argues, is a metaphysic because it prescribes a world-view, it has its own ethic—what is right is what is *efficient*—and it is its own justification. That being the case, it controls by right those who live in a society organized to cater for its needs educationally, industrially, and politically. It forms them into people of narrow vision and diminished humanity. They become small functionaries in a larger scheme of things, technicians who view all of life in a mechanical fashion. Life poses problems. Problems demand solutions. The solutions adopted are those that *work*, with little regard being given for what the long-range consequences might be, whether the means being chosen are best suited to the ends being sought or whether they are intrinsically moral or not. This mentality has become ubiquitous in our society.

Peter Berger has gone on to argue that it produces its own way of knowing.[24] It requires a quantifying habit of mind, the kind which reduces all knowledge to mathematical formulae and statistics. This is perfectly appropriate when divorce rates or demographic changes are being plotted, but it is peculiarly inappropriate when matters of intimacy are under discussion, such as the praxis of the bedroom or matters of complexity such as human motivation and the makeup of religious conviction.

The truth is, however, that once we allow ourselves to become technicians in our society we are thereafter required always to act and think like technicians in all circumstances.

The technological society in turn destroyed "natural groupings." A "natural grouping" is a small social unit made up of people whose lives are in some measure interlaced and who provide for each other a stable context in which the orderly transmission of values can take place from parents to children. The most important of these is the conjugal family, but in ethnic environments the extended family and the neighborhood are also included. There is a wholeness to the group, a sharing of lives at many different points.

These social groupings are being destroyed. Industrial development has brought workers into the great urban organizing centers and in the process has driven a wedge between a person's worklife and his or her homelife. It has produced extraordinary mobility which in turn has destroyed most functioning neighborhoods because their residents are so transient. It has reduced the family, in many cases, to being a passing convenience for its members. Its function is simply to meet the most minimal needs of shelter and procreation.

In place of the former importance of these natural groupings there has emerged a greater stress both upon the individual and upon the mass collective. The individual, increasingly emancipated psychologically from the binding family context and social matrix of a neighborhood, imagines that he or she is floating somewhat indeterminately in society, blessed by a "freedom" unparalleled in previous ages. This, counters Ellul, is an illusion. The place of personal responsibility within and accountability to a natural grouping is filled by the demands of the mass collective. Its process—the life of technology—is operating merely on the flat plane of what works and it asserts its total authority over the individual; it asks for its price.

That price is not only a loss of real freedom and responsibility but also the willingness to define what is of value in life in terms of what technology can deliver. In this connection, Daniel Yankelovich has argued, for example, that an astonishing number of Americans have accepted Abraham Maslow's distinction between "lower order" and "higher order" needs. Lower order needs, however, are not seen as being met merely by sufficient food and adequate shelter. They will only be met when affluence liberates us more or less completely from concerns of this type in order that we might experience more leisure and give ourselves more fully to discretionary and recreational pursuits. Thus has a view of human development been married to a psychology of affluence.[25]

It is in this framework, it is with these presuppositions, with these mental habits, and with these functional values and spiritual expectations that evangelical theology must wrestle. It is not enough to argue that people, according to biblical teaching, are made up of a mortable body and an immortable soul. The spiritual dimension to life has also to be seen as it is being shaped within contemporary culture.

It may be asserted, for example, that rationality is a part of the image of God. Rationality, however, is but a capacity. It is a capacity whose specific form and operations are, in some measure, a reflection of the socio-psychological environment in which it functions. The capacity is God-given but the content is culturally informed and shaped. The presence of this capacity provides Christian theology with its *entrée*, but the particular cultural orientation which it has demands of the theologian that his or her proclamation be angled in such a way as to take account of these presuppositions.

Christian theology declares, then, that in Christ we are called to receive not only God's forgiveness but also the healing of our own mind as well as that of our humanity. This is nevertheless a meaningless affirmation if it is not cognizant of the fact that family life is under assault, that as a result many people feel alienated from their families and have never found viable substitutes, that their experience within our technological society has left them feeling a profound sense of dissatisfaction with themselves from which they urgently seek escape through drugs, sex, or recreation. They are people who feel as if they have been cut loose on a sea of relativity where absolute norms and enduring values have disappeared forever. It is people like these who need to rediscover their humanity through Christ; the human beings who are defined and described in our theological abstractions exist only as idealized, abstract specimens of humanity.

Contextualization, then, is but another name for describing the servant role of theology. The Son of God assumed the form of a servant to seek and save the lost and theology must do likewise, incarnating itself in the cultural forms of its time without ever losing its identity as Christian theology. God, after all, did not assume the guise of a remote Rabbi who simply declared the principles of eternal truth, but in the Son he compassionately entered into the life of ordinary people and declared to them what God's Word meant to them. But in so doing, the Son never lost his identity as divine. Christian thought is called to do likewise, to retain its identity (doctrine) within its role as servant (theology) within a particular culture.

Aberrations to Be Avoided

The contextualization of which this essay speaks is quite different from that in vogue in WCC circles and occasionally on the fringes of evangelical thought. "Contextualization" is here used of the process whereby biblical doctrine is asserted within the context of modernity. It recognizes that there is a twofold relevance to be presented, to the text as well as to the context, but it insists that the relevance to the modern context will collapse as soon as the relevance to the biblical text is lost. It is this insistence which is often lost in WCC discussions on contextualization. These discussions assume a disjuncture between doctrine and theology. The meaning of faith is cut loose from many biblical controls. Its substance becomes an amalgam derived as much from political ideologies (with which God is said to be identified) as from the Scriptures (with which God is thought to be loosely associated). In the one understanding of contextualization, the revelatory trajectory moves only from authoritative Word into contemporary culture; in the other, the trajectory moves both from text to context and from context to text, and in the midst of this traffic the interpreter, rather like a police officer at a busy intersection, emerges as the sovereign arbiter as to what God's Word for our time actually is.

This development is actually part of a much more complex movement whose roots reach back into the eighteenth and nineteenth centuries. The evolution of this movement has been analyzed well by Hans Frei.[26] What he shows is how under idealist, romanticist, or rationalistic impulses the meaning of the biblical narrative was no longer seen to be identical with the meaning of the text of the biblical narrative. The words, sentences, and configurations of the narrative were seen merely to exhibit a consciousness whose continuity with the modern consciousness was assumed but whose actual expression differed vastly from the modern expression of it. The continuity of Christian faith was therefore seen to lie in the continuity of this consciousness rather than in preservation and affirmation of the same doctrinal content.[27]

This was, of course, the central proposition in both European and American liberalism and it has been affirmed in much recent Protestantism, even by those who, in other respects, are opposed to liberalism. A case in point is Rudolf Bultmann. It is, of course, his contention that the early Christians employed "myth" to formulate their experience of the post-resurrection Christ. The way they explained their experience was to employ the cosmology at hand which, in the first century, was one in which reality was seen to be natural and supernatural, in which there was a heaven and a hell, and in which miracles could occur. They had no option but to employ these conceptions. No person, Bultmann argues, can simply choose his or her world-view. World-views are given to us, prescribed for us by the circumstances, culture, and times in which we live.[28] New Testament Christians, therefore, were *obliged* to see Christ as a world-transcending, cosmic being replete with pre-existence, miraculous powers, and divine status. We who live in the twentieth century with its radical desacralization, its staggering redefinition of reality wrought by science and technology, cannot believe in the same figure or the same cosmology. What is important is not how this mysterious Galilean might have thought of himself or how the early church conceived of him but how his openness to the divine can be replicated in our own experience.

South American and Asian liberation theology has been fiercely critical of most existential theology, Bultmann's included. What seems most offensive about it is that faith is made identical with insight. Existential theologies are intensely private and inward Liberation theologians have charged that God becomes the alibi for not engaging with the world. And engagement with the world is precisely what liberation theologies are about.

It is ironical to note, however, that these theologies which have made an anti-Western attitude their watchword continue to echo the approach of much modern, Western theology![29] What Protestant liberalism, Bultmannianism and liberation theology all have in common is the supposition that the modern context *determines* how we should or how we can read the biblical narrative. They all assume—although Bultmann is unusually and refreshingly candid in this respect—that the interpreter's cognitive horizon limits or determines the cognitive horizon of the text.

What this means in practice is that the Bible is unable to deliver to us its cargo because the twentieth century has made us incapable of receiving it. As a description, this may be correct; as a theological prescription, it is disastrous. The interpreter is now no longer subject to the Word being interpreted but, in his or her own name and in the name of enlightened twentieth-century consciousness, he or she redefines its content! This inverts the proper relationship between text and interpreter, committing the same kind of blunder as did the schoolboy who was startled out of an illicit slumber by his teacher's question and blurted out that science had indubitably proved all monkeys are descended from Darwin! It leads us in some cases to think that given our understanding of reality—and the assumption is that this understanding is well in advance of any that has pertained in previous ages—Scripture must be demythologized since it is clear that Scripture cannot be believed at face value in the twentieth century. It leads us in other cases into equating the substance of faith with a variety of ideological and political positions with which we (and it is assumed God) are aligned. To act in faith is to act politically.

The truth of the matter is that it is not Scripture which needs to be demythologized but the twentieth century! To take twentieth-century experience (in the case of the existential theologians) or political reality (in the case of liberation theologies) as an absolute in the light of which the meaning of faith must be redefined is to capitulate to the *Zeitgeist* at the very points where the *Zeitgeist* often needs most to be challenged. Accommodation of this kind is worldliness.

It is indisputable that the modern context affects the interpreter of Scripture psychologically and epistemologically. The context in practice often limits or distorts what Scripture is heard to say. Bultmann believes this is inevitable; that must be challenged. Liberation theologies see this context—especially in its political makeup—as providing the foundation on which the truth of the biblical Word can build, but all too often in practice this means that the political context yields the agenda for theology and that prevailing political ideologies determine how that agenda will be followed. And that, too, must be challenged!

The issue today, it needs to be said in conclusion, is no different in principle from what it was in the sixteenth century. The Protestant Reformers insisted that the Word of God must be free to speak unhampered by tradition or by the limitations of experience. In the case of the Roman Church, tradition had come to exercise a restraining role on biblical revelation; it was, Luther asserted, gagging Scripture. By the same token, some Anabaptists allowed Scripture (the *externum Verbum*) to be authoritative in practice only insofar as its teaching was authenticated by inner experience (the *internum Verbum*). The Reformers countered that both the church and our experience must alike be subject to Scripture, for it is through our willingness to hear the Word of God that we exercise our accountability before the God of the Word.

In a fallen world, authorities in competition with God and his

Christ and his Word are precisely what one would expect to find. What one would not expect to find is these pseudo-authorities being given aid and comfort within the structures of evangelical theology, but that is precisely what we have today. It underscores the contention of the Reformers, however, that reformation should not be seen merely as a past event but should always be a contemporary experience. In every generation the Word of God must be heard afresh and obeyed afresh if the God of that Word is to be accorded our obedience at the places where it really counts.

11   The Use of Scripture in My Work in Systematics

GABRIEL FACKRE

Andover-Newton Theological School
Newton Centre, Massachusetts

The answer to the question—Well, how do you do
it?—will be given by stopping the action in mid-
course and examining its features. That means looking at a current inquiry on the soteriological
singularity of Christian faith.[1]

Jesus Christ, the Life of the World

Increasing religious pluralism in modern societies poses sharp
questions for Christians about their claim that Christ is *the* way,
truth, and life. This contemporary "plural shock" has caused
more than a few cases of christological heart failure. I have
sought to identify that kind of response and other reactions in a
typology that runs from views which eliminate or significantly
alter Christian assertions of finality (parallel pluralism, synthetic
pluralism, degree pluralism) through the qualified particularist
themes of Rahner and Barth (centripetal singularity and centrifugal singularity) to positions of radical exclusiveness (imperial
singularity). Do these current types exhaust the possible alter-
natives? A quest for an answer takes me to the biblical texts.

My starting point is the *locus classicus* for "the scandal of particularity," John 14:6. Making use of both traditional and contemporary methods and interpretation[2] and employing

"theological exegesis" as well,[3] the inquirer seeks to discern the meaning of this awesome affirmation of the Johannine Christ: "I am the way, and the truth, and the life; no one comes to the Father, but by me." Three major motifs emerge as constitutive of assertions about the decisiveness of Jesus Christ. (1) God's saving *way* into the world was by the singular route of the birth, life, death, and resurrection of Jesus Christ. (2) The definitive *truth* of revelation is manifested in these events. (3) The decisive *life* of redemption is made available to human beings through these events. Thus in Jesus Christ a *deed* is done, a *disclosure* is given, and a *deliverance* is effected. Any response to pluralism faithful to biblical warrants must cohere with these awesome claims to particularity.

Has the way this text and its auxiliaries been read by the tradition of imperial singularity done justice to the depth of their meanings? In the field of systematics there have been some twentieth-century theologies that have sought to be faithful to the scandalous particularity but have claimed to discover aspects of universality neglected by imperial views. Thus both Barth and Rahner, each in his own very different way, assert a deed and disclosure of finality in Jesus Christ, yet they go on to declare for a universality in the soteriological effects and/or relationships of the singular action to all humanity. However, the conception of "anonymous Christianity" in Rahner and mission as "vocation" in Barth compromises the singularity of deliverance in Christ—that in him alone is to be found *life* and salvation for the believer by grace through faith.[4] The issue of Christian response to pluralism seems to be joined most critically here around the meaning of life and salvation or, more technically, around the application of the benefits of Christ's saving work, "redemption applied."[5]

A survey of texts that deal with the New Testament assumptions about the appropriation of the benefits of Christ's work makes an overwhelming case for the inextricable unity of the faith response to the good news of saving grace, however any of these terms are conceived, whoever the writer, whatever the community, wherever the layer of tradition. In each case we hear the refrain as it is formulated in a key Johannine "life" text: "God so loved the world that he gave his only begotten Son, that whoever believes in him should not perish but have eternal life" (John 3:16). A systematics rooted in Scripture and responding to pluralism must think within the framework of the claim to singularity found in these passages.

Matt.	8:10–13; 9:1–8, 19–22, 28–38; 10:32–33, 37–40; 11:27–30; 12:36–37; 17:19–20.
Mark	2:5–12, 34; 8:34–38; 9:23–25; 10:52; 11:22–26.
Luke	5:20–25; 7:9–10, 50; 8:48–50; 10:25–28; 15:7; 18:29–30.
John	1:12–13, 16–18; 3:3–8, 16–18, 28, 36; 4:10–14, 22, 42; 5:24; 6:29, 33–40, 47–51, 53–58, 68–69; 10:10; 11:25–26; 12:25–26, 50; 14:1–7, 23–24; 15:1–11; 17:1–5, 25–26; 20:30–31.
Acts	2:36–39, 47; 3:17–19; 4:11–12; 8:21–22; 10:43; 11:13–18; 13:38–39, 48; 15:6–11; 16:30–34; 20:21, 32; 26:16–18.
Rom.	1:16–17; 3:21–22, 25–31; 4:3–17; 5:1–2, 8–11; 6:23; 8:28–30; 10:9–13; 11:1–6, 11, 13–14, 21–22.
1 Cor.	1:9, 18–29, 21–24; 3:15; 5:5; 6:9–11; 15:1.
2 Cor.	2:14–16; 4:4, 14; 5:18–21; 6:2; 7:9–10; 8:7–9; 10:7; 13:4–5.
Gal.	1:4; 2:15–16, 19–21; 3:6–14, 22–29; 4:4–7; 5:4–6; 6:8–9, 15.
Eph.	1:4–7; 2:3–5, 8–9, 13, 16, 18–19; 3:10–12, 17–19; 4:30–32; 5:8.
Phil.	2:12–13, 15–16; 3:8–11.
Col.	1:12–14, 20–23, 26–28; 2:2, 6, 12–13; 3:1–4, 12–13.
1 Thess.	1:9–10; 2:11–12, 16; 4:12, 14, 16; 5:5, 23–24.
2 Thess.	1:3–10; 2:10, 12; 3:1–2.
1 Tim.	1:16, 19; 2:3–6; 4:1, 16; 5:8; 6:12.
2 Tim.	1:5–10, 18; 2:11–13, 15.
Titus	1:1–3; 3:5–8.
Heb.	4:2–3; 5:9–10, 12; 6:5–6; 7:24–25; 9:14–15; 10:32–36, 39; 13:20–21.

James	1:17–18, 21; 2:5, 20–26; 5:20.
1 Peter	1:5–9, 19–23; 2:23; 4:17–19; 5:10.
2 Peter	1:3–4, 10–11.
1 John	1:1–7; 2:1–3; 3:1–4, 23–24; 4:9–10, 13–15; 5:4–5, 11–33.
2 John	1:9.
Jude	1:20–23.
Rev.	14:12.

The overwhelming New Testament evidence for the union of confession of faith with salvation converges with the testimony of the traditions of Christian piety that stress decision and personal engagement. Thus the two major features of evangelicalism, commitment to the authority of the Bible and centrality of the act of faith, are integral to any "evangelical option" in soteriology.[6]

One significant attempt to respond to questions posed by pluralism is precluded by the foregoing consideration. A mention of it here helps to clarify the methodological issues with which this essay struggles. A minority opinion in the Reformed tradition, expressed by such men as Charles Hodge and Benjamin Warfield, holds that *all* humans who die in infancy are thereby redeemed by the transfer to them of the benefits of Christ's saving work.[7] The development and influence of this charitable *theologoumenon* correspond to the heightening awareness in Western theology of both global reality with its teeming populations, unreached and unreachable, and the magnitude of disease, desolation, and infant mortality, an expanded horizon akin to what we have called plural shock. The meeting between this cultural sensibility and a Reformed theology which blends the mercy work of Christ with the *Grundmotif* of divine sovereignty helped to shape this view in which the role of decision/ faith, underscored in the foregoing plethora of passages, is adjudged "for adults only." The same nineteenth-century Christian problematic had other responses which stayed closer to both the textual warrants and evangelical experience, and to them we shall refer shortly. Points here to be noted from the

Hodge-Warfield experiment are, on the one hand, the readiness within a rigorously biblical tradition to *develop doctrine* beyond older formulations, and that readiness in apparent response to an era's perceptions and questions, and, on the other, the too easy accommodation to culture when speculatively shaped doctrinal presuppositions bypass the biblical evidence.

Pluralism does not exhaust the meaning in which the issue of soteriological singularity is currently cast. Modernity brings with it the focus on the *humanum*. In our own time two aspects of human reality claim us with special force. On the one hand, peoples long marginalized have begun to demand access to the essentials of human life—from food, clothing, and shelter to the right to participate in the decisions that affect their destiny—in other words, to justice and freedom for all. On the other hand, peril to the whole human enterprise has mounted because of the steady proliferation of planet-threatening nuclear weaponry. This latter quantum leap in destructive capability in combination with the revolution of rising expectations constitutes a new angle of vision for viewing the biblical testimony to redemption. Already we have had the first nervous responses to it both in secular theologies that reduce the meaning of salvation to social or personal change in the horizontal dimension and in apocalyptic theologies which reduce it to a catastrophic verticality. These predictable, first encounters of the Christian community with new cultural fact (similar to the accommodationist and imperialist first encounters with pluralism) put this question: Can a commitment to Christ as "the life of the world" find a place for the *rudiments* of life as health of the body and historical relationships, as well as for the *fundaments* of life as health of the soul and its transhistorical relationships?

A scriptural search for an answer gives us an overwhelming *Yes*. Ronald Sider, in *Cry Justice*, has done a significant piece of this investigative work. There the red thread of a two-testament witness is traced in which God wills life, hope, and wholeness for human beings in their physical and historical being. A sampling of these passages includes:

Exod.	3:7–10; 6:2–9; 20:1–3, 13, 15, 17; 22:25–27; 23:6–8, 10.
Lev.	5:7–11; 12:6–8; 14:1–22; 19:9–10, 11–18, 32–34, 35–36; 23:22; 25:8–17, 35–55.
Deut.	1:16–17; 8:1–20; 10:17–19; 15:1–11; 16:18–20; 23:19–20; 24:10–11, 17–22; 25:13–16; 26:1–11; 27:19; 32:4.
1 Sam.	2:8.
2 Sam.	11:1–4, 6, 14–15; 12:1–7
1 Kings	21:1–19.
Neh.	10:31.
Job	5:11–16; 22:5–9; 24:1–12, 19–22· 29:1–17.
Pss.	9:7–12, 8; 10:2–4, 15–18; 12:5 15:1–5; 35:19; 37:22–26; 41:1–2; 68:5–6; 69:30–33; 72:1–4, 12–14; 82:1–5; 89:14; 94:1–15, 20–23; 96:10–13; 103:6–7; 109:30–31; 113:5–9; 140:12; 146:1–10.
Prov.	14:21, 31; 15:25; 16:11–12; 17:5; 19:17; 21:13; 22:9, 16, 22–23; 23:10–11; 28:3, 8, 27; 29:4–7, 14, 26; 31:8–9.
Eccles.	4:1.
Isa.	1:10–17, 21–26; 3:13–25; 5:8–13, 15–16, 22–24; 9:6–7; 10:13–19; 11:1–4; 25:6–8; 26:5–6; 29:17–21; 32:1–3, 6–8, 15–17; 33:14–16; 42:1–7; 58:1–10; 61:1.
Jer.	7:1–15; 12:1–2, 5, 7; 22:1–5, 11–12.
Lam.	3:34–46.
Ezek.	18:5–9; 22:1–3, 6–12, 15–16, 23–31; 45:9–10.
Amos	2:6–8; 4:1–3; 5:6–15, 21–24; 6:4–7; 7:10–17; 8:4–8.
Mic.	2:1–10; 3:1–4, 9–12; 4:1–4; 6:6–8, 9–15.
Hab.	2:5–12.
Zeph.	3:1.
Zech.	7:8–10; 8:14–17.
Mal.	3:5
Matt.	5:17–20; 6:1–4, 11, 24–33; 7:12; 10:42; 12:1–8, 15–21; 19:16–30; 23:23; 25:31–46.
Mark	8:1–9; 10:41–45.
Luke	1:46–55; 3:7–11; 4:16–21; 6:20–25; 7:18–23; 11:42; 12:32–34; 14:12–14, 15–23; 16:19–31; 19:1–10; 20:45–47.

John	2:13–16; 13:1–17, 34–35.
Acts	2:41–47; 4:32–37; 6:1–7; 9:36–41; 11:27–30; 20:32–35.
Eph.	4:28.
1 Tim.	4:4–7.
James	2:1–9, 14–17; 5:1–6.
1 John	3:11–18; 4:7–12.
Rev.	7:13–17; 21:4–5, 22–27.

Decisive for the interpretation of these texts is the christological lens. How can Christians speak of redemption in any less terms than Christ spoke and acted? As in the texts cited and in the pattern of his activity and preaching, as detected by either a historical-critical or grammatical-historical reading of the New Testament, there can be no doubt that he was a healer of and carer for body as well as soul. He brought good news to the poor as well as to the poor in spirit. He brings peace to a broken world as well as to a broken heart. Further, all the rudimentary healings that have to do with the life of bodies in societies happen by a christic grace that works in those who do not know its source, as such, as well as in those that do (Matt. 25:31–46; John 1:3–5, 9–10). By the presence of the Word, Jesus Christ, light and hope happen where the name is not named in the common venture of "life."

The texts and their christological guide press us to honor a soteriological work done by the Savior wherever life is rendered livable in its most elemental sense. Using the distinction, made in Cruden's *Concordance*, between two biblical usages of the concept and word *salvation*, we can ascertain deliverance from *evil* as well as deliverance from *sin* and *guilt* throughout the Scriptures—salvation from war, oppression, sickness, destruction, enemies, poverty, hunger. To believe that Jesus Christ is Savior is to understand the release from this bondage as his saving work. For the eye of faith, Christ is present incognito wherever human life is made and kept human in its rudimentary sense, including the work of that grace in those aspects of the teaching and practice of other religions or people of no religion. An imperial singularity, which does not acknowledge this universal activity of salvation by grace through love *from the powers of evil*, obscures a basic biblical refrain.

The *fullness* of salvation cannot be encompassed by the grace aforementioned, the one that assures bread and breath. We do not live by them *alone*. There is a dimension of life *coram Deo*, eternal life, for which we are destined, another kind of hunger and hope. This life with God is *liberation from sin and guilt* and, thus, reconciliation with the One with whom we finally have to do. To one community the good news of this salvation in Jesus Christ is given. Herein lies the evangelical mandate to tell the story, through the hearing of which saving faith is born.

If these fundaments of salvation, salvation in its verticality, are promised to those who hear and accept the good news, are we then driven ineluctably to the position of imperial singularity? Already we have differed from this view in discerning in Scripture the two dimensions of salvation. There is another distinction. In the same century that the theory of infant universalism had been propounded by Hodge, others wrestled with the questions posed by pluralism, especially as it rose from the missionary situation. As ones for whom the evangelical decision was crucial, yet whose knowledge of the unreached and unreachable millions weighed upon them, a different dynamic was put in motion.[8] A thread of texts came into focus: 1 Peter 3:19–20; 4:6; Ephesians 4:8–9; John 5:25–29; Matthew 8:11; 12:40; Luke 13:28–30; Hebrews 9:15; Romans 10:7; Revelation 21:25. In one way or another these passages indicate the *postmortem* possibilities of grace. The Petrine centerpiece, which had to deal with a question raised by the lengthening eschatological horizon (our question here), formulates its response with christological firmness. The overall New Testament picture of the implacable love of a just Savior is described in these texts as reaching the unreached dead in eschatological proclamation. Thus the glorified Christ as well as his Body on earth is the organ of the good news, the Hound of Heaven whose pursuit cannot be confined to calendars and timetables of our own making. A patristic tradition that put to the fore "the descent into hades"—the place of the dead—in the developing rule of faith was an early strand of doctrinal exposition of the texts in question along just these lines. Thus tradition, ancient and modern, constitutes a resource for understanding our biblical source.

Working out of these various textual strands, in dialogue with primary and secondary traditions, and guided by a christological vision, this theologian tries to confront a fundamental question posed by culture. The response is grounded in a firm commitment to the claims of christological and soteriological particularity and in the consequent rejection of various accommodationist views. At the same time, the fresh cultural context opens up aspects of biblical universality heretofore obscured by earlier formulations. Thus the trajectory of received interpretation is followed, its direction revised (not reversed) to do justice to *both* the scandal of particularity and that of universality. Let us now turn to the assumptions about the use of Scripture that lie underneath this inquiry in systematics.

The Role of the Christian Community in the Interpretation of Scripture

I had not brought to full awareness the extent to which the Christian community functions in my use of Scripture until this exercise in methodological self-examination. There are tracks in the snow of the following companions.

(1) While there is no identifiable doctrine as such, a composite of traditional assertions about the person and work of Christ and about the nature of revelation and salvation constitutes the claim to particularity that we have characterized as "reconciliation, revelation, and redemption." This inherited pattern of thought functions in the theological exegesis of John 14:6 and its counterparts. Here then is doctrinal sedimentation, discoverable in wide ranges of the life, thought, worship, and witness of the Christian community (its catholicity) and, thus, "tradition" in the sense in which that word is often used.

(2) The community appears in another way, as does its doctrinal distillation, in the more focused assumptions of the Reformation tradition.[9] Thus the personal response of faith plays a

critical role in the dynamics of redemption. The texts assembled are read in the light of (a) the importance of hearing and responding, (b) the cruciality of justification by grace through faith, (c) the explicit belief element in faith (necessary albeit not sufficient), and (d) the inseparability of "applied redemption" from faith (a premise overturned by the divine sovereignty emphasis of Hodge, incidentally).[10]

(3) The Reformation perspective is underscored at the points of personal appropriation and depth of decision by the evangelical tradition as contributory to the interpretation of the redemption texts. Evangelical experience cannot require all believers to replicate the cataclysmic nature of choice, but neither can it conceive of salvation as being without an explicit "Yes" to Jesus Christ. "Tradition" here refers not only to doctrinal deposits but also to the more encompassing environment of life, worship, and mission.[11]

(4) While it is not often recognized as such, the phenomenon of "critical scholarship" is in fact a community of critical scholars and one which develops from time to time its consensus points or relative consensus points.[12] Critical scholarship in the more restricted sense of the use of the historical-critical method is invited into the textual discussion above at various points. In a wider sense, one that would include a range from the new literary criticism and canon criticism to grammatical-historical and word studies, this sub-community of biblical reflection plays its role in our work here on soteriology. But more about the specifics of textual inquiry in a moment.

The acknowledgement of the role of tradition in these various senses is captured in an observation from a Faith and Order Study of the WCC. After twenty-five years of research and colloquy on the authority of the Bible in the churches, a participant noted, "The biblical texts can never be interpreted *ab ovo*; interpretation is always conditioned by the tradition in which the interpreter stands."[13] An important step forward could be taken in the exploration of the use of the Bible in Christian theology if this kind of recognition was more widespread.[14]

How tradition functions vis-à-vis Scripture is another matter.

Two convictions are at work in our soteriological investigations (a) The discernment of the riches of the text is in direct relationship to the depth and width of ecclesial vision. Narrow perceptions of biblical meaning come predictably from slit-eyed exegesis. This is a powerful argument for ecumenical tradition. (b) The function of tradition in relation to Scripture is heuristic. Tradition is *ministerial* and Scripture is *magisterial*.[15]

The church and its post-biblical tradition(s) constitute the *resource* for understanding the scriptural *source*. But the source is just that, the ultimate authority in systematic theology. Hence the distinction between Scripture as "the rule that rules" (*norma normans*) and tradition as the rule that is ruled (*norma normata*) functions in the author's systematic proposals.[16] With these observations we are on our way to the role of the text itself.

Canon, Common Sense, and Continuity

Final recourse to the text for the systematic theology done in our soteriological inquiry means answers to three kinds of questions: Wherefore? What? Why?

"*Wherefore* text," when one has said the text cannot be detached from ecclesial context?[17] The answer is twofold. (1) To acknowledge the influence of ecclesial perspective does not require a historical-relativist ideology, ecclesial or cultural, one which would deny the possibility of cross-cultural and transtemporal communication, one which is less rather than more (and strives to be less rather than more) controlled by perspectival commitments and thus able to discern the intended meaning of Scripture. The belief that human beings, rather than treat the common life as a battlefield where raw power decides policy, can emerge sufficiently from their commitments and conditionings to enter into conversation on matters of importance is the basis for civil discourse and rational decision making in the human community. Also, contextual orthodoxies are being challenged today by proposals addressed to both the time and the space gap, as in the "merging of horizons,"[18] and by theories about the relative rates of change in ephemeral, conjunctural, and structural history.[19] Accessibility of the text's meaning is assumed in the use made of Scripture in our soteriological inquiry, given the meeting of the hermeneutical conditions here developed. We are not so locked into our ecclesial or cultural positions that its truth cannot make itself known to us—the Word addresses the hearer—even to the extent that a contemporary perspective from which a text is viewed can be challenged, modified, and even overturned by the text. (2) Cultural and ecclesial relativisms deny in fact what they assert in theory. The orthodoxy that there is no historical truth claim allowable is itself exempt from the rule of relativity. What's sauce for the goose is sauce for the gander.[20]

"*What*" does the text as last court of appeal entail? Here a configuration of themes comes into play: perspicuity, intentionality, honesty, analogy, unity, continuity, propositionality.

Perspicuity refers to the accessibility of Scripture. The plain meaning of the text is its controlling significance. As such, its understanding is not confined to a privileged few, i.e., ecclesiastical or academic *cognoscenti*. We have noted that both the ecclesial and critical communities do make their contributions, but they do not hold the keys that unlock the mysteries. The Bible is an open book. Here the priesthood of all believers (and thus the availability of the Scriptures to all with the will, mind, and heart to encounter them) is a crucial hermeneutical presupposition.

Intentionality has to do with the purposed meaning of the text. What the author intends, in the context and way that purpose is executed, is normative for exegesis. Indeed, a text may have both *implications* and *applications* far beyond the authorial purpose (the former has to do with the *sensus plenior* about which we shall speak subsequently, and the latter is the homiletical challenge every Sunday morning), but original textual intention must adjudicate these proposals.[21]

For clarification of intention the best tools of scholarship are welcome. The honest study of genre, grammar, word usage, historical context, and textual form and development are resources in this process. A responsible encounter with the text will be marked by integrity of inquiry, using the tested instruments of historical and literary analysis.

Given the singular nature of the Scriptures, the warrants for which we shall discuss in the next section, the final word on textual intention cannot be said by the aforementioned disciplines. Influenced as these inquiries in their present state are by value frameworks of their own and in consideration of the divergent opinions in the present state of the art, the decisive interpretive framework for a text is the whole canonical context. Scripture, thus, is its own best interpreter. Key to this is the principle of analogy in which the more elusive texts are read in the light of clearer ones.[22]

Assumed in the canonical environment for a given text is the unity of Scripture. That is, there is an overall coherence and directionality in the Bible which constitutes the horizon against which the biblical drama and declarations are to be viewed. This unity is established by the divine action itself as it moves through events in the great narrative of salvation—the deeds, centering in Christ's liberating and reconciling work, as they are presented and interpreted in prophetic-apostolic testimony. In speaking about this big picture in which the textual microcosm is situated we have, of necessity, anticipated some of the "Why" questions and will return to them.

Texts make truth claims. That is the point of those who declare for the propositional status of Scripture, which bears particularly on systematic theology. As "expression[s] in language or signs of something that can be believed, doubted, or denied or is [are] either true or false" (*Webster's New Collegiate Dictionary*, 2a), propositions do occur in the Bible and are derivable from biblical materials in the form of doctrinal assertions. We shall argue in the next section that the evocative and expressive nature of biblical truth claims are better described as "affirmations," but here our point is simply that this systematic theology cannot do without statements with the referents of human and divine reality to which the terms "Yes" and "No" are appropriate, without "expression in language or signs of something that . . . is either true or false."

The presence of each of these foregoing themes can be seen in the use of Scripture in our soteriological inquiry. The plain meaning of the texts is at work in the passages dealing with salvation in both microcosmic and macrocosmic dimensions, as is the canonical resonance. Central features of the drama of continuity were presupposed in the unpacking of the paradigmatic text. The canonical range of authority functions in the uncovering of surprises in the Scriptures as in the eschatological soteriology texts obscured by inherited patterns of exegesis and doctrine. In all the investigation the propositional status of textual evidence is assumed.

"*Why*" must we be responsible to the intended meaning of texts with theological import? The answer lies in the doctrine of revelation presupposed in one's view of biblical theology. The former is the underside of the latter.[23] A brief exploration of revelatory assumptions is therefore appropriate.

Revelation happens along the timeline of the biblical narrative. What God *does* in that drama to reconcile the parties alienated from the divine purpose is inextricably bound up with what God *discloses*; the deeds of God are foundational to the knowledge of God. While revelation cannot be *reduced* to the acts of reconciliation, as was the tendency in some recent versions of *heilsgeschichte* conceptuality, "biblical theology," etc., neither can it be severed from them.[24]

In the history of Christian theology—both its catechetical/confessional and its systematic/speculative expressions—doctrinal affirmation follows the timeline of the biblical drama. From the first rules of faith and the early economic Trinity, through the creedal formulations and their interpreters (viz., Athanasius), to later confessional symbols and traditional dogmatics, the great saga constitutes the outline of statements of Christian faith: the missions of the triune God in creation, fall, covenant; in Christ's life, death, and resurrection; in the church, salvation, and consummation. Here we are drawing on the resource of tradition to make our point. But while tradition instructs, Scripture must confirm (The Scots Confession, chap. 20). It does so in setting before us the movement from creation to consummation. In all this we learn that the power that patterns revelation is constituted by the deeds of reconciliation.

Revelation is grounded in, but not exhausted by, the history of the reconciling acts of God. The events of this narrative are witnessed to, and/or interpreted by, "seers" whose eyes are opened to their inner meaning. Thus a doctrine of inspiration is a necessary part of a doctrine of revelation, a point regularly ignored by proponents of "revelation as event" in their eagerness to avoid fundamentalist views of the Bible.[25] The process of revelation includes, therefore, a reliable account of the definitive events in the biblical narrative, including the trustworthy interpretation of those events. The Holy Spirit, whose power brings the events to be, also grants insight into them by the biblical envisioner and is present in that mysterious pilgrimage in which insight, affect, idea, and word make their journey together toward us. Thus the inspired prophetic-apostolic testimony is part and parcel of the revelatory process.

Because of the inseparability of the partners in this pilgrimage, the words and imagery in their canonical appearance are under the custodianship of the Spirit. We have to do here in this sense with verbal inspiration. The Spirit working in the community grants this charter with its special fusion of deed, interpretation, and word. We return always to this language of Canaan as the font of systematic theology. The inspiration is "plenary" in that no decision of ours, doctrinal or methodological, can restrict the range of words and insights to selected preserves within the full canon and thereby restrict the full range of the Spirit's work and the surprises of the Spirit that may await us in what appear to be the most unpromising—"uninspiring" by human reckoning—stretches of Scripture.

The verbal nature of inspiration is associated with the kind of writing the Bible is and that, in turn, with the character of revelation itself. A faith whose substance is what God does and discloses in a historical drama, one with a view to engaging the reader personally in the action, will be cast in the genre of story with its plot developing in characters and events moving over time and space through conflict toward resolution. As such, its language is critical to its purpose, featuring tensive symbols that, on the one hand, express the tone of the action and, on the other, evoke the response of the whole person, addressing the affective as well as the cognitive self. Austin Farrer has described inspiration in somewhat the same terms, viewing it as the gift of insight in images.[26] Long before him John Bunyan wrote:

> Solidity indeed becomes the Pen
> Of him that writeth things Divine to men;
> But must I needs want solidness, because
> By Metaphors I speak? Were not God's Laws,
> His Gospel-Laws, in olden time held forth
> By Types, Shadows, and Metaphors? Yet loth
> Will any sober man be to find fault
> With them, lest he be found for to assault
> The highest Wisdom. No, he rather stoops,
> And seeks to find out what by Pins and Loops,
> By Calves, and Sheep, by Heifers, and by Rams,
> By Birds, and Herbs, and by the blood of Lambs,
> God speaketh to him. And happy is he
> That finds the light and grace that in them be.
> ...
>
> Dark Figures, Allegories? Yet there springs
> From that same Book that lustre, and those rays
> Of light, that turns our darkest nights to days.[27]

The function of story and symbol in biblical interpretation has been brought to the fore by the use of tools from the new literary criticism.[28] This perspective has given to the role of imagination in Scripture the attention which it deserves but which it has not always gotten in biblical studies and rarely receives in the world of systematic theology. However, enthusiasm for this dimension has obscured and even denied, in some quarters, the cognitive weight and transcendent referents of biblical narrative and symbol. The biblical story is "true to life," (human and divine) objectively, as well as "true for me," subjectively. It makes assertions about the way things are, identifiable by "affirmation," as well as brings us into relationship to the way things are by the power of symbol. Wilbur Urban's defense of the complementarity of "the truth of the symbol" (the reliability of its objective reference) and "symbolic truth" (the power of its subjective impact) in religious language is a helpful way of honoring the dual dimensions of biblical imagery and saga.[29] By insisting upon the former, the concern of the propositionalist is honored. Yet the way truth claims are made in the biblical setting is an *affirmation* from the world of life and death, drama and commitment, not by a proposition from the spectator world of formal logic.[30]

Substance: the Biblical Narrative

What is really at stake in the determination to hold the affirmational/propositional status of scriptural language are the truth claims of the biblical meta-story, the great drama that moves from creation to consummation. It is no accident that modern partisans of inerrancy are also passionate defenders of "the fundamentals."[31] And for others who support inerrancy, but for whom the term "fundamentalist" would be inappropriate (i.e., Carl Henry), the heart of the biblical witness is clearly the narrative of God's purposes and deeds of deliverance from beginning to end.[32] What these events were, are, and will be and their valid interpretation constitute the refrains of classical Christian belief.

Functionally, the inerrantist stress on the fundamentals (the non-negotiables of Christian conviction, historic faith) converges with the emphasis of the "infallibilists" on the Bible as authoritative in soteric knowledge, although the former believe that the doctrinal assertions and assumptions of the Bible can only be protected by the inerrancy of the text in its entirety.[33] As inerrantists do make a contribution to the use of Scripture in systematic theology in the various emphases, we have noted, so too do the infallibilists, especially so at this point where the purpose of Scripture for faith and life is brought to the fore.[34]

In fact the soteric use of Scripture is a natural correlate of evangelical piety. Evangelicalism at the Reformation—with justification by faith as its material principle and scriptural authority as its formal principle—employed Scripture as a source of saving knowledge, as juxtaposed to a textbook for scholastic speculation. As "evangelical" came to be understood more and more in terms of intensification of justification in personal experience and the rigor of obedience, the Bible continued to be instrumental to that end. When advance in the natural and social sciences and the importance of scholarly apparatus in the study of Scripture raised questions about the reliability of biblical cosmology and chronology, that tradition, based as it was on the evangelical use of Scripture for saving knowledge, did not deem its source of authority imperiled, and in fact today it finds its earlier focus on the evangelical core confirmed. This Evangel—the good news of God's saving deeds done over the timeline of the Christian narrative—constitutes the *substance* of the scriptural *source*. As such the gospel story is the principle of interpretation of the rich and variegated materials of the Bible. The canon in its entirety is viewed through the lens of the divine saga with Jesus Christ as its center. To return to our earlier discussion of symbol, the macro-story is the horizon against which all micro-stories and their expositions are to be viewed. Thus Scripture is used in this systematic work as it has been regularly used in classical theology over the centuries, not as an encyclopedia of varied information but as "the sacred writings which are able to instruct you for salvation through faith in Christ Jesus. . . . profitable for teaching, for reproof, for correction, and for training in righteousness, that the man of God may be complete, equipped for every good work" (2 Tim. 3:15–17). And it is to that end that "all scripture is inspired by God" (2 Tim. 3:16a).

Discussion of the soteric use of Scripture is not complete without reference to the "internal testimony of the Holy Spirit." Because there is an Author of this Book who works in, with, and under the authors of these books, neither source nor substance comes home until the truth of the affirmations met here convicts and converts. Illumination in its deepest sense includes hearing the Word within the words, and thus being transformed by this confrontation with God. God can only be encountered in a way commensurate with who God is and how God comes to us—in suffering struggle and personal commitment.[35] "Readiness to learn" from this Book, therefore, means a posture befitting the gift, a meeting with the text in hope and fear, whetted expectation and trembling. Thus a double subjectivity is bound up with the soteric use of Scripture: God the subject by the power of the Holy Spirit present in the believer's subjectivity of encounter. When this happens, the doctrine of sin becomes the confession of it, and the doctrine of grace becomes a cry of exultation.

The Setting for Source and Substance

Another element involved in the use made of Scripture in the above exercise has been variously described and justified in terms of "reason," "context," "contemporary experience," "historical method," "cultural and/or sociological analysis." The warrants for its use have been associated traditionally with such concepts as general revelation, common grace, the hidden Christ, and the image or likeness of God in humans. Here we choose to speak of the first concept as the "what"—as *human experience* in its richness and variety with special reference to its rational, moral, and affective dimensions.[36] Its legitimacy or "why" is grounded in the presence of a universal grace, one already pointed to in our soteriological inquiry. Christ's healing work in creation includes a grace that renders our general experience reliable enough at critical junctures to allow the great saga to move forward. Our experience is indeed so corrupted by a will in bondage that human thoughts, moral perceptions, and intuitions, as such, can neither discern the divine purpose nor power us toward it. But the Son of God has not left this world so bereft that intimations of our destiny are denied to us. This universal grace enables us to go ahead, literally, with the day-to-day business of making and keeping life livable toward the future.

The role of human experience so conceived is apparent at these points in scriptural interpretation. (1) First there is the reliance upon the canons of logic. Ordinary discourse and argument presuppose elemental rules such as the law of non-contradiction, and these are assumed here also.[37] (2) Next comes the use of biblical scholarship in all of its traditions, pre-critical, critical, and post-critical. The influence of culture and doctrine on these arts, and their offering as sub-communities of "tradition" in the conversation about a text (see earlier comments on tradition) means that they are resources, not *the* source of authority. They are tools for a "faith seeking understanding." (3) Then there is the help from the moral perceptions of a time, place, or constituency. God raises up from stones children of Abraham (Matt. 3:9; Luke 3:8) and uses Assyria as the rod of the divine anger (Isa. 10:5). Movements that seek justice, freedom, and peace in times of forgetfulness, including the amnesia of the Christian community, bring to our awareness visions and commitments within our own biblical charter. We are able to read texts with a sensitivity to the meaning intended in them by their Author when our eyes are opened to them by forces outside of the communities of biblical faith. Perceptions of both a cognitive and a spiritual sort, as well as moral ones, may enrich our capacity to see what Scripture has to say to us in our time and place. (4) Finally, there are the questions put to us by an era. At the level of affect, but not excluding discursive elements, human experience at a given time and place sensitizes us to issues of high moment, often best expressed in the art and literature of a period. In such a *kairos*, a special Word is spoken to us from the Scripture.[38] In sum, human experience as conceived above constitutes the *setting* in which the scriptural *source* and gospel *substance* is read.

What effect does this have on systematic theology? The consequence is twofold: (1) the translation of biblical substance into language that connects with the settings, perceptions, and questions and is coherent according to the laws of logic; (2) the development of doctrine along the trajectory established by earlier resource tradition and in conformity with the biblical source. In the first case, systematic theology perceives *applications* to this time and place in the idiom of this time and place in modes different from other times and places. In the second case, systematic theology draws out *implications* of the substance of the Bible not seen in earlier formulations of doctrine. In this sense there can be a *sensus plenior* to key texts used in systematic inquiry. Thus the intention of the text as a faithful expression of the divine purpose holds a meaning not grasped in its fuller implications by earlier exegetes because the necessary setting of human experience was not present, and the exegete was not therefore positioned at the angle of vision to see that signification. Human experience in the sense of ever new contexts of question and perception performs a catalytic function in the use of Scripture. This function is at work in the historical and eschatological aspects of soteriology developed in our inquiry.

Jesus Christ

One of the ironies of the modern hermeneutical discussion is the way the name of Jesus Christ has come into dispute and even into disrepute. Whereas classical Christianity maintained that he is the eternal Word to which all of Scripture testifies and Reformation Christianity used christological language to interpret the meaning and force of the Bible ("*was Christum treibt*"), today the use of similar categories evokes suspicion.[39] Indeed, there are reasons for some of this. In the struggle against fundamentalism and a speculative biblicism, both "neo-orthodox" and "liberal" protagonists have sought to validate Scripture by an appeal either to themes within it believed to be out of range of critical scholarship or to a way of encountering the Bible faithful to its invitation to personal engagement. Thus "Christ" as the Word heard "within" the biblical words or Scripture as "witness to the Word" has become a familiar counter-interpretation of the Bible's authority. Within many of these proposals other dynamics were often at work. One was the denial of the cognitive weight of biblical assertions, a judgment influenced by existentialist fears that claims to "objective knowledge" would deflect the believer from subjective encounter.[40] Revelatory significance was then transferred either to the encounter itself or to events, the chief of which was the figure of Jesus. From here it was a short step to interpreting "Christ" to be the historical Jesus as recovered by the scholarship of the New Quest. Indeed a very influential use of this latter historical Jesus view is to be found in the work of Edward Schillebeeckx and Hans Küng and also in the increasing use of a critical reconstruction of the Jesus of history by various liberation and process theologies.[41]

By appeal to the Jesus of history as recovered in modest form by new-quest scholarship, the post-Easter apostolic testimony to the significance of Jesus is moved from its classical place as authoritative canonical teaching to that of first contextual interpretation, with the respect indeed due to its proximity to origins but similar *in kind* to our own subsequent efforts at appropriating Jesus for our time and place.[42] Thus fundamental teaching about the person and work of Christ disappears from the "Christ" distilled from the Scripture. Further, in many cases the content poured into the word "Christ"—where critical scholarship sketches its picture of Jesus, and where it does not—is supplied by a philosophical conceptuality, sociopolitical program, psychological construct, or cultural agenda. There are good reasons, therefore, for scrutinizing carefully any proposal to incorporate a christological norm into the interpretation of Scripture.

With these risks in mind I will seek to show how Jesus Christ can be understood as the final standard in the use of the Bible in systematic theology. The christological norm is constituted by the following. (1) Theology begins in prayer and ends in praise (Aquinas, et al.). The Christian theologian lives and works out of prayer in the name of Jesus and looks to the eternal Word for illumination. Christ is the Alpha and Omega of all that is thought and said. A prayer always close to this theologian in study and writing is: "Speak to us the Word that we need, and let that Word abide in us until it has wrought in us your holy will. . . ." (2) With the authority of canonical Scripture here affirmed in conjunction with the narrative framework for interpreting it, one is driven to ask how Scripture is construed at the very center of that saga. How does Jesus Christ himself use Scripture? The answer is found in the following passages:

Matt.   4:4, 6, 7, 10; 5:21, 27, 31, 33, 38, 43; 7:12; 8:17; 9:13;
         11:10, 13, 17, 22–24; 12:3–7, 18–21, 39–42; 13:14–15,

35; 15:4–9; 16:4; 19:5, 7, 18–19; 21:13, 16, 42; 22:29–30, 31–32, 35–40, 44; 24:15, 24, 31; 27:46

Mark 2:25–26; 4:12; 7:6–7, 9–10; 9:12; 10:3–6; 11:17; 12:10–11, 24–27, 29–31, 35–37; 14:21, 27, 49; 15:34.

Luke 4:4, 8, 10–12, 17–19, 25–28; 6:3–4; 7:22–23, 27, 32; 10:13–15, 26–28; 11:29–32, 49; 13:4, 28–29, 34; 16:16, 29–31; 17:26–30; 18:20; 19:46; 20:17–18, 28, 37–38, 41–44; 22:37; 23:46; 24:25–27, 44–47.

John 5:39–40; 9:2–3; 13:18; 14:6; 15:25.

The clear message of these texts is that Jesus used the Scriptures to witness to his person and work. The passages from the Hebrew Bible cited by the Christ of the New Testament were read by him in the light of a christological norm. And the Apostles followed their teacher in that same usage of Old Testament texts. As Scripture's own record of its Lord's practices, the christological norm becomes decisive for this systematic theologian. Thus, Scripture in its entirety is the source of Christian teaching, but Jesus Christ in his particularity is the norm. What this means we must now unpack with a view to the "perils of modernizing" mentioned earlier.

Christ is the Word who speaks to us through the Bible in two senses that must be clearly distinguished. (1) As the Light of the divine Life, Jesus Christ does the work of convincing the believer of biblical truth. The truth of the text "comes home," it persuades, because Christ speaks through the words by the power of the Holy Spirit. The Spirit of God the Son attests by internal movement (*testimonium Spiritus Sancti internum*) that what is said is so. As such, truth *for all* becomes truth *for me*, a general declaration becomes a personal conviction. Here is the presence and power of Christ in the subject, hence the "subjectivity" of the christological norm. (2) Subjectivity is not subjectivism, for the complementary work of Jesus Christ is the act of *testing* objectively as well as *attesting* subjectively.[43] Statements in theology, which are claimed as biblical warrants for positions held, must pass muster before the norm of Jesus Christ. This works in two ways in the writer's systematic theology. The questions are asked: Do *traditional* claims stand up under the scrutiny of what the Bible declares about Jesus Christ? Are there *new* dimensions to inherited Christian doctrine not perceived in earlier formulations? As noted before, the setting of a given time and place re-situates the theologian and provides a fresh vantage point for viewing the great narrative of faith. In this new historical location, delimited understandings of faith are exposable and enriched understandings may be discernible. The figures of reduction and enrichment are purposely used here because they suggest the ongoing character of Christian teaching—a journey in faith. That is, Christian doctrine is revisable but not reversible; it develops along the line of the trajectory that comes from its origins. That is why ever new truth and light do really break forth from God's Word. Underneath this conviction is the trust that the Holy Spirit is present in the church in the ministerial work of the tradition, in this sense of rightness of direction. Thus the central tradition of the Christian community as resource is undergirded by the noetic work of the Spirit in *illumination*, just as Scripture the source is made possible by the noetic work of the Spirit in *inspiration*.

In the soteriological question, important use was made of the norm of Jesus Christ. Proposals for enriching traditional understandings of salvation by recovering the biblical duality of redemption from sin and guilt, on the one hand, and of redemption from evil, on the other, were catalyzed by the questions and perceptions of life on an imperiled planet and movements to sustain life in the face of its varied threats. Then the proposals were finally tested by the words and works of Jesus Christ who struggled against the forces of evil and sin and who overcame death in its most rudimentary and fullest meaning. Also, questions posed by the heightened awareness of religious pluralism uncovered veins of biblical ore waiting to be mined further, namely, those on the theme of eschatological confrontation. Here again, christological discernment was decisive, for both the implacable love of Christ in his historical career searching for the lost and the last (a commitment also present in the infant salvation scenarios of Hodge and Warfield) and the specific textual warrants for speaking about the love of Christ that pursues the unreached into eternity lead this systematician to seek to hold together particularity and universality in a different and, it is hoped, more biblically developed fashion.

Conclusion

The way Scripture is used in this exercise in self-understanding reflects a fundamental premise of the writer's work: the richness of faith requires a full-orbed approach to it. In the foregoing analysis there are a variety of perspectives at work: the contributions of inerrantists as well as infallibilists, the insights of both event-oriented and propositionalist hermeneutics, the use of historical-critical as well as grammatical-historical methods, attention to the "truth of the symbol" as well as "symbolic truth," the role of tradition as well as of Scripture, the cultural setting

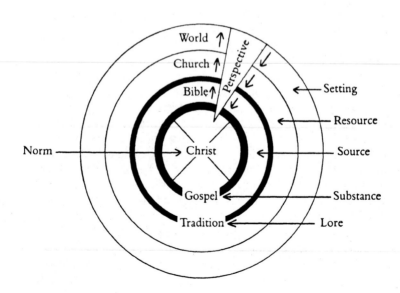

as well as the christological norm. Efforts at inclusive thinking in this as in other theological matters can be, finally, an irenic but muddleheaded eclecticism. What preserves the quest for a full-orbed faith from this kind of ersatz holism is the clear understanding of the role each partner plays, and the warrants thereof, as set forth throughout this essay. We conclude with a visual presentation of the components and their inter-relationships

The *world* leaves its imprint on all systematics, with a self-critical theology seeking to deal with the formative questions and perceptions of a given time and place. A *perspective* shaped by the special peril and promise of modern life and by the fact of religious pluralism sets the stage for our encounter with the soteriological affirmations of Scripture. Our way into the biblical center is traversed with the assistance of the *church's* two thousand years of struggle with these themes, especially as it has crystallized its lore in the inner ecclesial orb of *tradition*, a thickened line yet one open to development as indicated by its brokenness but always along the arc formed by its original direction. This reach in toward the truth is met by the *biblical source*, the texts that address the question in the context of the canon, as both participate in the *substance* of the *gospel* story. Theological affirmations that rise from this encounter are put to the final test by the *christological norm*, even as their truth comes home to us personally by the internal attestation of the Spirit of the Son. (Turning our circles to profile position would indicate the revelatory work of the Spirit that underlies and shapes the cone of authority.) Doctrinal assertions emerging from this pilgrimage return by the same route to address the *setting* of theological discourse, there both to challenge culture and to communicate with it. This hermeneutical "circulation" does not entail the adjudication of christologically warranted affirmations by the cultural setting—the experiential context is *not* the arbiter of the biblical text—as in too much uncritical usage of the circle metaphor in hermeneutics. Here we think of an arrow-like movement to a destination, yet a journey with its dynamic movement in and out.

This effort to honor the contribution of a variety of constituencies is a special kind of evangelical option. Its Corinthian modality is an expression of ecumenical evangelicalism. Standing in a long tradition of commitment to the universality of faith and to the faith community, yet grounded unambiguously in the gospel distinctives, it is a decision for evangelical catholicity. [44]

Notes

Foreword
ROBERT K. JOHNSTON

1. M. J. L. Abercrombie, *The Anatomy of Judgment* (New York: Basic Books, 1960), p. 11, quoted in Eric Osborn, "Exegesis and Theology," *Australian Biblical Review*, 29 (October 1981), 32–33.
2. Robert McNair Price, "The Crisis of Biblical Authority: The Setting and Range of the Current Evangelical Controversy," doctoral dissertation, Drew University, 1981, p. 144. Cf. Robert M. Price, "Inerrant the Wind: The Troubled House of North American Evangelicals," *The Evangelical Quarterly*, 55, No. 3 (July 1983), 129–144.
3. Cf. Carl F. H. Henry, *The Uneasy Conscience of Modern Fundamentalism* (Grand Rapids: Eerdmans, 1947).
4. Igor Stravinsky, *Poetics of Music in the Form of Six Lessons* (New York: Vintage, 1947), pp. 66–67.

1. Introduction: Unity and Diversity in Evangelical Theology
ROBERT K. JOHNSTON

1. Ninian Smart, *The Science of Religion and the Sociology of Knowledge* (Princeton: Princeton University Press, 1973), pp. 6–7.
2. David Kelsey, *The Uses of Scripture in Recent Theology* (Philadelphia: Fortress Press, 1975).
3. Billy Graham, quoted in Kenneth L. Woodward, "The Split-up Evangelicals," *Newsweek*, 99 (April 26, 1982) 89.
4. Martin Marty, quoted in ibid.
5. Robert Schuller, quoted in ibid.

6. John R. W. Stott, "The Evangelical View of Authority," *Bulletin of Wheaton College*, 45 (February 1968) 1.

7. Robert McAfee Brown, "Theology in a New Key," *Union Seminary Quarterly Review*, 33, No. 1 (Fall 1977), 24.

8. Ibid.

9. Harvie M. Conn, "Contextualization: Where Do We Begin?" in *Evangelicals and Liberation*, ed. Carl E. Armerding (Grand Rapids: Baker Book House, 1977), pp. 97–98.

10. Cf. Charles H. Kraft, *Christianity in Culture: A Study in Dynamic Biblical Theologizing in Cross-Cultural Perspective* (Maryknoll, NY: Orbis, 1979); C. René Padilla, "Hermeneutics and Culture—A Theological Perspective," in *Down to Earth: Studies in Christianity and Culture*, ed. John R. W. Stott and Robert Coote (Grand Rapids: Eerdmans, 1980), pp. 63–78; Harvie M. Conn, "Contextualization."

11. Conn, "Contextualization," p. 101; Charles H. Kraft, quoted in Conn, "Contextualization," p. 100.

12. Conn, "Contextualization," p. 100.

13. Geoffrey Wainwright, "Towards God," *Union Seminary Quarterly Review*, 36, supplementary issue (1981), 21.

14. "The Chicago Call: An Appeal to Evangelicals," in *The Orthodox Evangelicals: Who They Are and What They Are Saying*, ed. Robert E. Webber and Donald Bloesch (Nashville: Thomas Nelson, 1978), p. 12.

15. Ibid.

16. Cf. Peter W. Macky's comments regarding the use of C. S. Lewis by evangelicals, "Living in the Great Story," *Theology, News and Notes*, 28, No. 4 (December 1981), 24–25.

17. Michael O'Laughlin, "Scripture and Tradition," *Again*, 2 (July–September 1979), 14.

18. Robert E. Webber, *Common Roots: A Call to Evangelical Maturity* (Grand Rapids: Zondervan, 1978), pp. 125, 127.

19. See David F. Wells' essay in this volume, "The Nature and Function of Theology."

20. Cf. David F. Wells, "Reservations about Catholic Renewal in Evangelicalism," in *The Orthodox Evangelicals*, ed. Webber and Bloesch, pp. 216–217.

21. James D. G. Dunn, *Unity and Diversity in the New Testament* (Philadelphia: Westminster Press, 1977), p. 380.

22. James D. G. Dunn, "The Authority of Scripture According to Scripture, Part One," *Churchman*, 96, No. 2 (1982), 112.

23. Robert McNair Price, "The Crisis of Biblical Authority: The Setting and Range of the Current Evangelical Controversy," doctoral dissertation, Drew University, 1981, p. 247.

24. Karl Barth, "How My Mind Has Changed in This Decade, Part Two," *The Christian Century*, 56, No. 38 (September 20, 1939), 1132.

25. Karl Barth, letter to Rudolf Bultmann, December 24, 1952, in *Karl Barth—Rudolf Bultmann Letters, 1922 to 1966*, ed. Bernd Jaspert and Geoffrey Bromiley (Grand Rapids: Eerdmans, 1981), p. 107. Cf. Jan M. Lochman, "Toward a Theology of Christological Concentration," in *The Context of Contemporary Theology: Essays in Honor of Paul Lehmann*, ed. Alexander J. McKelway and E. David Willis (Atlanta: John Knox Press, 1974).

26. Jack B. Rogers, *Confessions of a Conservative Evangelical* (Philadelphia: Westminster Press, 1974), p. 62.

27. G. C. Berkouwer, *Holy Scripture* (Grand Rapids: Eerdmans, 1975), p. 166.

28. From Matthew Arnold's "Dover Beach," quoted in Nicholas Lash, *Doing Theology on Dover Beach* (Cambridge: Cambridge University Press, 1978), p. 26.

29. Cf. Robert M. Price, "The Crisis of Biblical Authority."

30. Cf. Geoffrey Wainwright, *Doxology: The Praise of God in Worship, Doctrine, and Life* (Oxford: Oxford University Press, 1980).

31. Helmut Thielicke, *The Evangelical Faith*, 3 volumes (Grand Rapids: Eerdmans, 1974–1982).

32. For a further discussion of Thielicke's *The Evangelical Faith*, see Robert K. Johnston, "Thielicke's Theology," *Christianity Today*, 21 (June 3, 1977), 26–28.

33. Robert K. Johnston, *Evangelicals at an Impasse: Biblical Authority in Practice* (Atlanta: John Knox Press, 1979), p. 151.

34. Claude Welch and John Dillenberger, *Protestant Christianity* (New York: Scribner's, 1954), p. 179.

35. Donald Bloesch, *Essentials of Evangelical Theology*. Volume 1. *God, Authority and Salvation* (San Francisco: Harper and Row, 1978). Cf. Donald Bloesch, *The Future of Evangelical Christianity* (Garden City: Doubleday, 1983).

36. Jack Rogers, "The Search for System: Theology in the 1980s," *The Journal of Religious Thought*, 37 (Spring–Summer 1980), 12–13.

2. How I Use the Bible in Doing Theology

CLARK H. PINNOCK

1. E. J. Carnell, *The Case for Orthodox Theology* (Philadelphia: Westminster Press, 1959), p. 13.

2. B. B. Warfield, *The Inspiration and Authority of the Bible* (Nutley, NJ: Presbyterian and Reformed, 1948), p. 210.

3. These issues are well discussed both by Grant Wacker in "The Demise of Biblical Civilization," in *The Bible in America*, ed. Nathan O. Hatch and Mark A. Noll (New York: Oxford University Press, 1982) and by the volume explaining the shift from the people bringing it to us,

Christian Theology: An Introduction to Its Traditions and Tasks, ed. Peter C. Hodgson and Robert H. King (Philadelphia: Fortress Press, 1982).

4. James Dunn's point in *Christology in the Making* (Philadelphia: Westminster Press, 1980).

5. J. A. T. Robinson, "Dunn on John," *Theology,* 85 (September 1982), 332–338.

6. Leon Morris, "The Emergence of the Doctrine of the Incarnation," *Themelios,* 8 (September 1982), 15–19.

7. Gordon D. Kaufman, *Systematic Theology: A Historicist Perspective* (New York: Scribner's, 1968), p. 154.

8. J. Christiaan Beker, *Paul the Apostle: The Triumph of God in Life and Thought* (Philadelphia: Fortress Press, 1980).

9. Werner G. Kümmel, *The New Testament: The History of the Investigation of Its Problems* (Nashville: Abingdon, 1972), p. 13.

10. John Warwick Montgomery, *The Suicide of Christian Theology* (Minneapolis: Bethany, 1970), p. 287.

11. Peter Toon, *The Development of Doctrine in the Church* (Grand Rapids: Eerdmans, 1979), pp. 106–113.

12. Millard Erickson, *Man's Need and God's Gift* (Grand Rapids: Baker Book House, 1976), p. 334.

13. Marvin Anderson, *The Battle for the Gospel: The Bible and the Reformation, 1444–1589* (Grand Rapids: Baker Book House, 1978), chap. 2.

14. Cf. D. A. Carson, *Divine Sovereignty and Human Responsibility* (Atlanta: John Knox Press, 1981).

15. Bernard Ramm, *Protestant Biblical Interpretation* (Boston: Wilde, 1956), p. 161.

16. Cf. William J. Abraham, *Divine Revelation and the Limits of Historical Criticism* (New York: Oxford University Press, 1982).

17. By far the most important book a position like mine will have to face is Edward Farley, *Ecclesial Reflection: An Anatomy of Theological Method* (Philadelphia: Fortress Press, 1982). It represents a devastating critique of the Scripture principle which I try to use and will have to be answered by conservatives. Among other things, I have attempted an answer myself in *The Scripture Principle* (San Francisco: Harper & Row, 1984).

3. In Quest of Canonical Interpretation
JAMES I. PACKER

1. Jesus' acceptance of the truth and authority of his Bible (our Old Testament) has often been demonstrated. See, for instance, John W. Wenham, *Christ and the Bible* (London: Tyndale Press, 1972), pp. 11–37, and "Christ's View of Scripture," in *Inerrancy,* ed. Norman L. Geisler (Grand Rapids: Zondervan, 1980), pp. 3–37; J. I. Packer, *"Fundamen-*

talism" and the Word of God (London: IVF; Grand Rapids: Eerdmans, 1958), pp. 54–62.

2. Calvin, *Institutes*, I.vii.5: "Enlightened by him (the Spirit), no longer do we believe that Scripture is from God on the basis of either our judgment or that of others; but, in a way that surpasses human judgment, we are made absolutely certain, just as if we beheld there the majesty (*numen*) of God himself, that it has come to us by the ministry of men from God's very mouth. . . . I speak of nothing but what every believer experiences personally (*apud se*), only my words fall far short of an adequate (*justam*) account of the reality" (author's translation).

3. The Westminster Confession speaks of "the consent of all the parts" as one argument whereby the Bible "doth abundantly evidence itself to be the Word of God." (I.v.) Demonstrations of the Bible's thematic coherence were made by various writers of the British Biblical Theology school: e.g., A. M. Hunter, *The Message of the New Testament* (Philadelphia: Westminster Press, 1944); A. G. Hebert, *The Bible from Within* (London: Oxford University Press, 1950); H. H. Rowley, *The Unity of the Bible* (Philadelphia: Westminster Press, 1955).

4. The phrase "analogy of Scripture" or "of (the) faith" goes back to Calvin, who took Rom. 12:6 to mean that what is preached must accord with revealed truth, and spoke of "the analogy of faith, to which Paul requires all interpretation of Scripture to conform." (*Institutes*, IV.xvii.32) The principle covered interpreting what is peripheral by what is central, what is obscure by what is clear, and what is ambiguous by what is orthodox in the sense of firmly established by thorough exegetical and theological testing.

5. See Martin Luther, *The Bondage of the Will*, tr. J. I. Packer and O. R. Johnston (London: James Clarke; Old Tappan: Fleming H. Revell, 1957), *passim*.

6. Examples are *Knowing God* (London: Hodder and Stoughton; Downers Grove, IL: InterVarsity Press, 1973); *Knowing Man* (Westchester: Cornerstone, 1979); *God's Words* (Leicester: InterVarsity Press; Downers Grove, IL: InterVarsity Press, 1981); *Evangelism and the Sovereignty of God* (London: IVF; Downers Grove, IL: InterVarsity Press, 1961); *Keep in Step with the Spirit* (Old Tappan: Fleming H. Revell, 1984); *I Want to Be a Christian* (Wheaton, IL: Tyndale House, 1977), a contribution to catechetics: "Steps to the Renewal of the Christian People" and "An Agenda for Theology," in *Summons to Faith and Renewal*, ed. Peter S. Williamson and Kevin Perrotta (Ann Arbor: Servant, 1983), pp. 107–127, 151–155.

7. Cf. *"Fundamentalism" and the Word of God*; *God Has Spoken*, 2nd ed. (London: Hodder and Stoughton; Downers Grove, IL: InterVarsity Press, 1979); *Freedom and Authority* (Oakland: International Council on

Biblical Inerrancy, 1981) = *Freedom, Authority and Scripture* (Leicester: InterVarsity Press, 1982).

8. Cf. *Beyond the Battle for the Bible* (Westchester: Cornerstone, 1980), esp. chap. 2, "Inerrancy in Current Debate"; *God Has Spoken*, pp. 110–114 and pp. 138–153 (the Chicago Statement of Biblical Inerrancy); *Summit II, Hermeneutics; Explaining Hermeneutics: A Commentary* (Oakland: International Council on Biblical Inerrancy, 1983).

9. My own tentative thoughts on this subject are in "Thoughts on the Role and Function of Women in the Church," in *Evangelicals and the Ordination of Women*, ed. Colin Craston (Bramcote: Grove Books, 1973), pp. 22–26; and "Postscript: I Believe in Women's Ministry," in *Why Not?*, 2nd ed., ed. Michael Bruce and G. E. Duffield (Appliford: Marcham Manor Press, 1976), pp. 160–174. Among advocates of relational subordination of women, with more or less fixed roles, see esp. Stephen B. Clark, *Man and Woman in Christ* (Ann Arbor: Servant, 1980); James B. Hurley, *Man and Woman in Biblical Perspective* (Leicester: InterVarsity Press; Grand Rapids: Zondervan, 1981); George W. Knight III, *The New Testament Teaching on the Role Relationship of Men and Women* (Grand Rapids: Baker Book House, 1977); Fritz Zerbst, *The Office of Woman in the Church* (St. Louis: Concordia Publishing House, 1955); Karl Barth, *Church Dogmatics* (Edinburgh: T. & T. Clark), III 1, pp. 288–329, section 41 (1958); III 2, pp. 285–316, section 45 (1960); III 4, pp. 116–240, section 54 (1961). Among advocates of relational egalitarianism, free from role restriction upon women, see esp. Paul King Jewett, *Man as Male and Female* and *The Ordination of Women* (Grand Rapids: Eerdmans, 1975, 1980); Don Williams, *The Apostle Paul and Women in the Church* (Van Nuys: BIM Publishing Co., 1977); Letha Scanzoni and Nancy Hardesty, *All We're Meant to Be: A Biblical Approach to Women's Liberation* (Waco: Word, 1977); Virginia Ramey Mollenkott, *Women, Men and the Bible* (Nashville: Abingdon, 1977). For analyses of the biblical interpretation on both sides, see Willard M. Swartley, *Slavery, Sabbath, War, and Women: Case Issues in Biblical Interpretation* (Scottdale, PA: Herald Press, 1983), pp. 152–191; Robert K. Johnston, *Evangelicals at an Impasse: Biblical Authority in Practice* (Atlanta: John Knox Press, 1979), pp. 48–76.

10. Jewett, *Man as Male and Female*, pp. 119, 134, 138.

11. I use this image as Anthony C. Thiselton does in "Understanding God's Word Today," in *Obeying Christ in a Changing World I*, ed. John R. W. Stott (London: Collins, 1977), pp. 90–122, esp. pp. 101–105, and in his book, *The Two Horizons: New Testament Hermeneutics and Philosophical Description* (Grand Rapids: Eerdmans, 1980), esp. pp. 15–17, 307–310. I do not suggest that Gadamer views Scripture as the Word of God in the way that I do.

4. Scripture and the Theological Enterprise: View from a Big Canoe
RUSSELL P. SPITTLER

1. For a compact but very able exposition of the classical Pentecostal churches in the United States, no better source can be named than Grant Wacker, "A Profile of American Pentecostalism," to appear in a forthcoming volume to be edited by Timothy L. Smith et al., tentatively entitled *The American Evangelical Mosaic*. This interpretive essay sets the emergence of American Pentecostalism in its historical context and outranks the numerous clichéd histories by providing a penetrating analysis of the essence of Pentecostal piety—an aspect often overlooked or distorted.

2. Myer Pearlman, *Knowing the Doctrines of the Bible* (Springfield, MO: Gospel Publishing House, 1937). Though he is careful to credit by name the few quotations used, Myer Pearlman uses no footnotes. Nor does there appear any bibliography or list of books for further reading.

3. Donald Gelpi, *Experiencing God: A Theology of Human Experience* (New York: Paulist Press, 1978).

4. There are several more recent doctrinal writings by classical Pentecostals. Ray Pruitt of the Church of God of Prophecy provided *The Fundamentals of Faith* (Cleveland, TN: White Wing Publishing House, 1981). For the Pentecostal Free Will Baptists, Ned Sauls wrote *Pentecostal Doctrines: A Wesleyan Approach* (Dunn, NC: Heritage Press, 1979). These are denominationally focused doctrinal handbooks. The name of a former general superintendent of the Assemblies of God, Ernest S. Williams, appears on a three-volume set titled *Systematic Theology* (Springfield, MO: Gospel Publishing House, 1953). The contents in fact were edited by a fellow teacher, Frank Boyd, from class lecture notes used by Mr. Williams in a course of that title offered at Central Bible Institute (name changed to Central Bible College in the mid-1960s) during the early and middle 1950s. Basic theological studies, from which are likely to emerge less parochial theological statements, have come from younger scholars associated with the Society for Pentecostal Studies (135 North Oakland Avenue, Pasadena, CA, 91101). These include Harold D. Hunter's 1979 Fuller Seminary Ph. D. thesis now revised and published as *Spirit-Baptism: A Pentecostal Alternative* (Lanham, MD: University Press of America, 1983).

5. Details *passim* in Richard Quebedeaux's three volumes (all New York: Harper and Row): *The Young Evangelicals* (1974), *The Worldly Evangelicals* (1978), and *The New Charismatics II* (1983 [1976]). James DeForest Munch's history of the NAE, *Cooperation Without Compromise* (Grand Rapids: Eerdmans, 1956), carries the story only through the mid-1950s.

6. It was this same period when, in 1961, AG minister David J. du Plessis was asked to cease his developing ministries among churches aligned with the NCC and WCC—no doubt an embarrassment to the NAE at a time when du Plessis' denominational chief executive was serving as the NAE's elected head. Because he declined to discontinue such associations, du Plessis was divested of his AG ministerial credentials in 1961, an action reversed twenty years later.

7. Two articles by Gerald T. Sheppard provide greater detail: "Biblical Hermeneutics: The Academic Language of Evangelical Identity," *Union Seminary Quarterly Review*, 32 (Winter 1977), 81–94; "Word and Spirit: Scripture in the Pentecostal Tradition: Part One," *Agora: A Magazine of Opinion within the Assemblies of God* [no longer published], 1, No. 4 (Spring 1978), 4–22; and ". . . Part Two," 2, No. 1 (Summer 1978), 14–19. Gordon Fee reminds me that the same 1961 change in the doctrinal statement deleted "entire" from the point treating sanctification—evangelicalization at the expense of distancing from holiness roots.

8. In fact, the original 1916 form of the Statement of Fundamental Truths contained seventeen points. What was then listed as item thirteen, "The Essentials as to the Godhead," was by 1933 placed under point two, "The One True God"—resulting in the sixteen-point Statement which has been usual ever since. Between 1917 and 1925 "combined" copies of the Minutes with those reaching back to 1914 were published. The identification and publication of the actual *Minutes* as produced at the successive early General Council is a complicated but urgent task.

9. Harold Lindsell, *The Battle for the Bible* (Grand Rapids: Zondervan, 1976).

10. *The Pentecostal Evangel*, No. 2932 (July 19, 1970), 6–9. Through years of mutual involvement in the NAE, Thomas Zimmerman and Harold Lindsell have long been acquainted.

11. The literature on the recent phase (1970 onward) of evangelical thought on Scripture is abundant and increasing. The issues are delineated in Robert K. Johnston's volume *Evangelicals at an Impasse: Biblical Authority in Practice* (Atlanta: John Knox Press, 1979), esp. chap. 2, "The Debate over Inspiration: Scripture as Reliable, Inerrant, or Infallible?" pp. 15–47. Publication in 1979 of Jack Rogers' and Donald McKim's volume, *The Authority and Interpretation of the Bible: An Historical Approach* (San Francisco: Harper and Row), awakened renewed discussion, evoking a critique by John D. Woodbridge, *Biblical Authority: A Critique of the Rogers/McKim Proposal* (Grand Rapids: Zondervan, 1982).

12. Originally South-Eastern [*sic*] Bible Institute—"SEBI" in my day—the school has exemplified a predictable development pattern, becoming South-Eastern Bible College (four-year) in 1957 and shifting to a

now regionally accredited Southeastern College ("of the Assemblies of God") in 1977. The school is located in Lakeland, Florida. I entered in September 1950 and graduated in June 1953. Enrollment in my day never exceeded one hundred and eighty.

13. To this day I have not yet had a course in "Western Civilization," or the like, though I think it and English composition are the most important undergraduate courses.

14. Grant Wacker, "A Profile of American Pentecostalism" (cf. note 1 above).

15. I will limit sharply the elaborate notes usual to formal exegesis in view of the essay format used here. Whether I am capable (some would say, guilty) of such conventional accoutrements of scholarship readers could judge from my thesis ("The Testament of Job: Introduction, Translation, and Notes," Harvard Ph. D. thesis, 1971) or from an article in the Merrill C. Tenney *festschrift*, "The Limits of Ecstasy: An Exegesis of 2 Corinthians 12:1–10," in *Current Issues in Biblical and Patristic Interpretation*, ed. Gerald F. Hawthorne (Grand Rapids: Eerdmans, 1975), pp. 259–266.

16. F. F. Bruce, *1 and 2 Corinthians*, New Century Bible (Greenwood, SC: Attic Press, 1971), p. 24.

17. Interpreters will be helped to consult Linda Mercadante's history of interpretation of the passage to 1978, *From Hierarchy to Equality: A Comparison of Past and Present Interpretation of 1 Cor. 11:2–16 in Relation to the Changing Status of Women in Society* (Vancouver, BC: G-M-H Books/Regent College, 1978). Three later and worthy though unconventional interpretations of 1 Cor. 11:1–16 deserve mention. Jerome Murphy-O'Connor, *1 Corinthians*, NT Message, 10 (Wilmington, DE: Michael Glazier, 1979), thinks that Paul is not addressing the subordination of women but the distinction of sexes: "Women should be women, and men should be men, and the difference should be obvious" (p. 106). James B. Hurley, in *Man and Woman in Biblical Perspective* (Grand Rapids: Zondervan, 1981), suggests Paul cautions against letting the hair down and loose (rather than keeping it done up). Alan Padgett, in *Journal for the Study of the New Testament* No. 20 (February 1984), 69–86 ("Paul on Women in the Church: The Contradictions of Coiffure in 1 Corinthians 11:2–16"), sees 11:3–7b as a reflection of the Corinthians' own viewpoint, not that of Paul whose own view, lauding woman, appears in 11:7c–16. None of these views affects my interpretation of 11:2–16.

18. A very helpful treatment of the topic and its implications is F. F. Bruce, *Tradition Old and New* (Exeter: Paternoster Press, 1970). This work deserves to be better known and used.

19. James Packer, *"Fundamentalism" and the Word of God* (Grand Rapids: Eerdmans, 1958).

20. James Packer, *God Speaks to Man: Revelation and the Bible*, Christian

Foundations, 6 (Philadelphia: Westminster Press, 1965), p. 81.

21. Even sortilege, radically dehistoricized random use of Scripture for personal or group guidance, is practiced in some Pentecostal and charismatic circles. A balanced and resourceful pastoral counsel on the practice is provided by John F. Maxwell, "Charismatic Renewal and Common Moral Teaching on Divination," *Theological Renewal*, No. 23 (March 1983), 19–29. It would be grossly distorted to characterize the Pentecostal churches generally as given to sortilege.

22. *Constitution*, Article X, d; *Bylaws*, Article VII, section 2, h (1981 edition of both).

23. I serve, gratefully, at just such a place—Fuller Theological Seminary in Pasadena, California.

24. My professional interest as a *Neutestamentler* lies at least as much in critiquing the commonly adopted critical methodology as in applying it. I should like to tinker with the adequacy of assumptions behind its use. These days, such an enterprise suggests forays into the writings of such persons as Michael Polanyi, Peter Stuhlmacher, and Walter Wink—maybe even the poetry of William Blake.

25. In revising this paper I had the benefit of written comments from the following colleagues: Isaac Canales (Fuller); Gordon Fee (Gordon-Conwell); William MacDonald (Gordon College); and Robert Meye (Fuller). I did not follow all their suggestions, so I take responsibility for the outcome.

5. A Christological Hermeneutic:
Crisis and Conflict in Hermeneutics

DONALD G. BLOESCH

1. In later Israelite history it came to be believed that Yahweh would complete his work of redemption through a Messiah figure whom Christians naturally associated with Jesus Christ.

2. See Jaroslav Pelikan, *From Luther to Kierkegaard* (St. Louis: Concordia Publishing House, 1950), pp. 24–75.

3. Wilhelm Vischer, *The Witness of the Old Testament to Christ*, trans. A. B. Crabtree (London: Lutterworth Press, 1949), pp. 68–81. Vischer is adamant that the story of Cain and Abel refers not to the Kenites of the days of David but to "an event of primeval times—the original event which prepares the way for the special history of God's revelation within fallen humanity and for the election of one race of mankind to be the bearer of the special revelation of God" (pp. 79–80). For Vischer this is an event in *Urgeschichte* (pre-history) and not *Historie* (the area of world occurrence accessible to historical investigation). It is a poetic elaboration of that which is hidden from the purview of historical research but which is kept alive in the memory of the race through the illumination of the Spirit of God.

4. One might argue (as does Vischer) that the more specific intent of the text is to point out how the original fall or original sin gives rise to a primal murder, though it is impossible to ascertain what is genuinely historical in this saga, nor should this even be attempted if we are to remain true to the central thrust of this passage.

5. To question the direct Pauline authorship of the pastoral epistles does not take away their divine inspiration, but it means that they have to be treated in a different manner. I believe that there are genuine Pauline fragments in these epistles, though they were probably written by a disciple or disciples of Paul.

6. Quoted from Harry Escott (ed.), *The Cure of Souls: An Anthology of P. T. Forsyth's Practical Writings* (Grand Rapids: Eerdmans, 1971), p. 70.

9. How Does the Bible Function in the Christian Life?

WILLIAM A. DYRNESS

1. I am grateful to Professor Patricia Benner of the University of California Medical School (San Francisco) for calling my attention to the model proposed by Stuart E. Dreyfus in "Formal Models versus Human Situational Understanding: Inherent Limitations on the Modeling of Business Expertise," Air Force Office of Scientific Research (Contract: F 49620–79–C–0063), National Technical Information Service, February 1981, AD–A097468/3. Report no. ORC–81–3. Cf. H. L. Dreyfus, *What Computers Can't Do: The Limits of Artificial Intelligence* (New York: Harper and Row, 1979).

2. Bernard Lonergan, *Method in Theology* (New York: Herder and Herder, 1973), p. xi.

3. Rudolf Bultmann, *Jesus Christ and Mythology* (New York: Scribner's, 1958), pp. 37–38.

4. As he admits: "It is, of course, true that de-mythologizing takes the modern world-view as a criterion." Ibid., p. 35.

5. Peter Berger, *A Rumor of Angels: Modern Society and the Rediscovery of the Supernatural* (Garden City, NY: Doubleday, 1969), p. 94.

6. Peter Berger, *The Social Reality of Religion* (Middlesex: Penguin Books, 1967), p. 170.

7. Cf. L. Malevez, S. J., *Histoire du Salue et Philosophie: Barth, Bultmann, Cullmann* (Paris: Cerf, 1971), pp. 40ff. "Pour ne pas être assez attentif à l'homme, il peut arriver qu'on ne comprenne pas la Parole de Dieu" (p. 42).

8. Robert L. Saucy, "Doing Theology for the Church," *Journal of the Evangelical Theological Society*, 16, No. 1 (Winter 1973), 1–9.

9. Conrad Boerma, *The Rich, the Poor, and the Bible* (Philadelphia: Westminster Press, 1979), p. 29.

10. Bernard Ramm, *Special Revelation and the Word of God* (Grand Rapids: Eerdmans, 1961), pp. 154–155.

11. M. Eugene Osterhaven, *The Faith of the Church: A Reformed Perspective on Its Historical Development* (Grand Rapids: Eerdmans, 1982), p. 64.
12. Martin Luther, *Works*, volume 26 (St. Louis: Concordia Publishing House, 1983), p. 387, quoted in Donald Bloesch, *Essentials of Evangelical Theology*, volume 1, (San Francisco: Harper and Row, 1978), p. 61.
13. H. Jackson Forstman, *Word and Spirit: Calvin's Doctrine of Biblical Authority* (Stanford, CA: Stanford University Press, 1962), pp. 19, 36. Cf. G. C. Berkouwer, *Holy Scripture* (Grand Rapids: Eerdmans, 1975), p. 306, who notes that the "sola" can only be perceived along the way. Cf. Abraham Kuyper, *Principles of Sacred Theology* (Grand Rapids: Eerdmans, 1968), p. 575: "At the end of the way, all these factors are made to disappear, so that finally our well-balanced conviction rests *upon nothing but the Holy Scripture.*"
14. Quoted in Osterhaven, *The Faith of the Church*, p. 65.
15. We are not in any way agreeing with David Kelsey who, in a recent book, seems to argue that inspiration is defined by its function. Rather, it is the reverse: its function is seen in the end to rest on the fact of its inspiration. Cf. David Kelsey, *The Uses of Scripture in Recent Theology* (Philadelphia: Fortress Press, 1975).
16. Karl Barth, *Church Dogmatics*, I, 2 (Edinburgh: T. & T. Clark, 1956), p. 682.
17. I have outlined how Scripture may be read in this way in *Let the Earth Rejoice! A Biblical Theology of Holistic Mission* (Westchester, IL: Crossway Books, 1983).
18. See Patricia Benner, "From Novice to Expert," *American Journal of Nursing* (March 1982), 402–407. She argues that becoming an expert (mature in our terminology) involves processes that can only be partially explained: "It is frustrating to try to capture verbal descriptions of expert performance because the expert operates from a deep understanding of the situation"; "Maxims are used to guide the proficient performer, but a deep understanding of the situation is required before a maxim can be used" (p. 405).
19. Donald Bloesch, *Essentials of Evangelical Theology*, volume 1, p. 69.
20. Karl Barth, *Church Dogmatics*, II, 2 (Edinburgh: T. & T. Clark, 1957), p. 647.

10. The Nature and Function of Theology
DAVID F. WELLS

1. On the question of biblical authority in Reformation theology much has been written but especial note should be taken on A. Skevington Wood, *Captive to the Word: Martin Luther, Doctor of Sacred Scripture* (Grand Rapids: Eerdmans, 1969); Kenneth Kantzer, "Calvin and the Holy Scripture," in *Inspiration and Interpretation*, ed. John F. Walvoord

(Grand Rapids: Eerdmans, 1957), pp. 115–155; Roger Nicole, "John Calvin and Inerrancy," *Journal of the Evangelical Theological Society* 25, No. 4 (December 1982), 425–442; and Philip E. Hughes, *Theology of the English Reformers* (Grand Rapids: Eerdmans, 1965), pp. 9–44.

2. Krister Stendahl, "Biblical Theology, Contemporary," *Interpreter's Dictionary of the Bible*, I, (New York: Abingdon, 1962), pp. 419–420.

3. The original idea was borrowed from Claude E. Shannon and Warren Weaver's *The Mathematical Theory of Communication* (Urbana, IL: University of Illinois, 1949) and used in David Hesselgrave's *Communicating Christ Cross-Culturally* (Grand Rapids: Zondervan, 1978), pp. 28–37. From its context in missions, it was appropriated for theology.

4. This distinction was first suggested but not at all developed in my *Search for Salvation* (Downers Grove: InterVarsity press, 1978), pp. 39–40.

5. See John Warwick Montgomery, "The Theologian's Craft," *Concordia Theological Monthly* 37, No. 2 (February 1966), 67–98.

6. See, i.e., Charles Hodge, *Systematic Theology*, I, 21 (Grand Rapids: Eerdmans, 1960); L. S. Chafer, *Systematic Theology*, I, 5 (Dallas: Dallas Seminary Press, 1947); and H. O. Wiley, *Christian Theology*, I, 16 (Kansas City: Beacon Hill, 1940).

7. On the significance of *oratio*, *meditatio*, and *tentatio*, I am indebted to comments made by Paul Holmer at Yale, the essence of which were developed later into his study *The Grammar of Faith* (New York: Harper and Row, 1978).

8. A similar perspective is presented in Helmut Thielicke, *A Little Exercise for Young Theologians*, trans. Charles Taylor (Grand Rapids: Eerdmans, 1962), pp. 6–41.

9. It was, of course, the contention of the neo-orthodox theologians in particular that if revelation is personal—and they insisted it was—then it could not be propositional. The price which they paid to secure its personal aspect (which was the denial of its propositional nature) was both unnecessary and unwise. This particular issue is reviewed helpfully in the essays by Gordon H. Clark, "Special Revelation as Rational"; Paul K. Jewett, "Special Revelation as Historical and Personal"; and William J. Martin, "Special Revelation as Objective"; in *Revelation and the Bible*, ed. Carl F. H. Henry (Grand Rapids: Baker Book House, 1958), pp. 25–72. It is powerfully developed, negatively and positively, throughout the first three volumes of Carl F. H. Henry's *God, Revelation and Authority* (Waco: Word, 1976–1979).

10. The essential elements in the traditional understanding of tradition were left intact by the Second Vatican Council but it was made a more fluid reality to be defined as much by the people of God as by the magisterium. See G. C. Berkouwer, *The Second Vatican Council and the New Catholicism*, trans. Lewis B. Smedes (Grand Rapids: Eerdmans,

1965), pp. 89–111; and David F. Wells, "Tradition: A Meeting Place for Catholic and Evangelical Theology?" *Christian Scholar's Review*, 5, No. 1 (1975), 50–61.

11. See, i.e., Martin Luther, *Works*, volumes 26; 52, ed. Jaroslav Pelikan (St. Louis: Concordia Publishing House, 1955–1963); and John Calvin, *Institutes of the Christian Religion*, Library of Christian Classics, volumes 20–21, ed. John T. McNeill, (Philadelphia: Westminster Press, 1960), III.xviii–xix; IV.xx, xxiii.

12. "If the contest," Calvin declared, "were to be determined by patristic authority, the tide of victory—to put it very modestly—would turn to our side" volume 20, "Prefatory Address to King Francis," 4 (p. 18).

13. Occasionally *didaskalia* and *theologia* are equated or used interchangeably as in Ammon., *Jo.*I, 8; Dion., *Ar, d.n.*, III, 3; Max., *Prol Dion.* These are, however, the exceptions. Cf. Just., *Dial.*, xxxv, 8.

14. Or., *De Princ.*, I, 2–8, 10.

15. Greg. Naz., *Or.*, xxviii, 2.

16. This position was advanced even in the "pre-critical" period by Calvin. This general approach is well represented by Ned Stonehouse's *The Witness of Luke to Christ* (Grand Rapids: Eerdmans, 1951) and *The Witness of Matthew and Mark to Christ* (Grand Rapids: Eerdmans, 1958).

17. This argument and the reasons for it are clearly explained by Norman Perrin, *What Is Redaction Criticism?* (Philadelphia: Fortress Press, 1969).

18. See further the fine essay by D. A. Carson, "Redaction Criticism: On the Legitimacy and Illegitimacy of a Literary Tool," in *Scripture and Truth*, ed. D. A. Carson and John D. Woodbridge (Grand Rapids: Zondervan, 1983), pp. 119–146.

19. James I. Packer, "What Did the Cross Achieve? The Logic of Penal Substitution," *Tyndale Bulletin*, 25 (1974), 3–45, esp. 3–16.

20. The most illuminating discussion of the issues at stake is probably to be found in the exchanges between Emil Brunner and Karl Barth. Brunner's position, in my judgment, has much to be said for it at this point. See Emil Brunner, *Natural Theology: Comprising "Nature and Grace" by Emil Brunner and the Reply "No!" by Karl Barth*, trans. Peter Fraenkel (London: G. Bles, 1946). On the question in general see G. C. Berkouwer, *General Revelation*. Studies in Dogmatics (Grand Rapids: Eerdmans, 1955).

21. Cf. Harry Blamires, *The Christian Mind: How Should a Christian Think?* (Ann Arbor: Servant Books, 1963), pp. 3–4.

22. Emil Brunner, *Christianity and Civilisation*, I, 1–14; II, 1–15 (New York: Scribner's, 1948–1949).

23. Ellul's principal work is his *The Technological Society*, trans. John Wilkinson (New York: Vintage Books, 1964), but see also his *The Technological System*, trans. Joachim Neugroschel (New York: Continuum,

1980). Ellul's thought is helpfully analyzed in C. George Benello's essay, "Technology and Power: Technique as a Mode of Understanding Modernity," in *Jacques Ellul: Interpretive Essays*, ed. Clifford G. Christians and Jay M. Van Hook (Urbana, IL: University of Illinois Press, 1981), pp. 91–107 and Michael R. Real's essay, "Mass Communications and Propaganda in Technological Societies," in the same volume pp. 108–127.

24. Peter Berger, *Facing Up to Modernity: Excursions in Society, Politics and Religion* (New York: Basic Books, 1977).

25. Daniel Yankelovich, *New Rules: Searching for Self-Fulfillment in a World Turned Upside Down* (New York: Random House, 1981).

26. Hans W. Frei, *The Eclipse of Biblical Narrative: A Study in Eighteenth and Nineteenth Century Hermeneutics* (New Haven: Yale University Press, 1974). Some of the same points are echoed, albeit more stringently, in Gerhard Maier, *The End of the Historical-Critical Method*, trans. Edwin W. Leverenz and Rudolph F. Norden (St. Louis: Concordia Publishing House, 1977).

27. The present employment of Scripture in theological discourse is analyzed by David Kelsey, *The Uses of Scripture in Recent Theology* (Philadelphia: Fortress Press, 1975).

28. Rudolf Bultmann and Karl Jaspers, *Myth and Christianity: An Inquiry into the Possibility of Religion Without Myth* (New York: Noonday Press, 1958), pp. 3–10.

29. Jürgen Moltmann, "An Open Letter to José Miguez Bonino," in *Mission Trends No. 4: Liberation Theologies in North America and Europe*, ed. Gerald H. Anderson and Thomas F. Stransky (New York: Paulist Press, 1979), pp. 59–62.

11. The Use of Scripture in My Work in Systematics
GABRIEL FACKRE

1. Formulation of these theses appears in the January 1983 issue (volume 22, No. 1) of *Mid-Stream*. More extensive development of the material found there and in this chapter will be found in a forthcoming systematics volume, *The Christian Story: Authority and Revelation*.

2. We follow Raymond Brown here in the interpretation of "the way" as primary predicate and one read against the background of its Old Testament usage (as in the parallelism of Ps. 86:11) with modifications by Qumran tradition, rather than as shaped by Mandean and Hermetic sources. However, the linkages of the Johannine "way" with God's making of a way through the desert argued by de la Potterie underscore the feature of action that is assumed in Brown but is somewhat muted by his noetic preoccupation. With Schnackenburg the writer believes that truth and life are to be read as expression and clarification

of way, rather than as the rationale for it. (The epexegetical "truth" and "life" can be construed in either sense.) Indeed, Christ as revealer is a dominant note in John and is seen as the giver of life to those who know the truth. But the subjective soteriological assertion is the issue of the unity of Father and Son, one rendered possible by the way made by the Son into the world. We may have life because it comes from the Source through the Stream as it breaks forth in our midst. As Johannine texts like this are read in the context of the canon (according to the hermeneutical procedure to be described), the kind of incarnational singularity stressed in the Johannine "way" is complementary to other New Testament perspectives on the decisive action of Christ, as its portrayal in the Pauline corpus in terms of his vicarious work or the synoptic delineations of the eschatological prophet and the resurrection.

3. On the validity of theological exegesis see T. F. Torrance, *Reality and Evangelical Theology* (Philadelphia: Westminster Press, 1982), pp. 42, 48–51, 68–71. My own use of this method relates a text to Scripture in its entirety as interpreted by evangelical substance and christological norm, on the one hand, and to "tradition" on the other. More about this subsequently.

4. Waldron Scott has astutely identified this point in Barth's soteriology. See his *Karl Barth's Theology of Mission* (Downers Grove, IL: Inter-Varsity Press, 1978).

5. John Murray, *Redemption: Accomplished and Applied* (Grand Rapids: Eerdmans, 1955, 1978).

6. For elaboration see the author's article, "Evangelical" in *Dictionary of Christian Theology*, revised edition ed. Alan Richardson (Philadelphia: Westminster Press, 1969).

7. Charles Hodge, *Systematic Theology*, I (New York: Scribner, Armstrong, and Co., 1871), pp. 26–27; and Benjamin B. Warfield, *Two Studies in the History of Doctrine* (New York: The Christian Literature Co., 1897), p. 230.

8. Egbert C. Smyth, "Probation After Death," *The Homiletical Review*, 11, No. 4 (April 1886) 281–291; and Thomas Field, "The 'Andover Theory' of Future Probation," *The Andover Review*, 7, No. 41 (May 1887), 461–475. As in Paul's struggle with the place of Israel in God's saving purposes (Rom. 9–11), so here too there is a unique soteriological and eschatological relationship of those who are heirs to Abraham, the father of faith, one more complex than can be treated in these pages.

9. This tradition is a gift to the church universal, an offering assimilable by a genuinely catholic understanding of Christian belief. The same is true about the special gifts to the wholeness of faith by Roman Catholic and Eastern Orthodox traditions in other areas of faith. On this

complementarity see Peter Toon, *The Development of Doctrine in the Church* (Grand Rapids: Eerdmans, 1977), pp. 105–126.

10. In an excellent study of Paul Althaus' theology, with particular reference to the question of Christian faith and world religions, Paul Knitter has discovered the import of the Reformation theme. His rejection of this and his pursuit of another course along the lines of Rahner's anonymous Christianity dissolve the classic claims to both epistemological and soteriological singularity, a fact which alerted the writer to the importance of the faith act in each of these dimensions. See Paul Knitter, "Jesus—Buddha—Krishna: Still Present?" *Journal of Ecumenical Studies*, 16, No. 4 (Fall 1979), 650–671; and "Christianity as Religion: True and Absolute? A Roman Catholic Perspective," *Concilium*, 136 (1980), 12–21.

11. For some illuminating observations on this wider view of tradition see Avery Dulles, "Tradition and Theology: A Roman Catholic Response to Clark Pinnock," *TSF Bulletin*, 6, No. 3 (January–February 1983), 6–8.

12. Kierkegaard makes this point forcefully in his struggle to turn the abstractions, "the press" and "the public," into their human constituents. See *The Present Age* (New York: Harper and Row, 1962), and *Attack Upon Christendom* (Princeton, NJ: Princeton University Press, 1968).

13. Ellen Flesseman-van Leer (ed.), "Introduction," Faith and Order Paper No. 99, in *The Bible: Its Authority and Interpretation in the Ecumenical Movement* (Geneva: World Council of Churches, 1980), p. 2.

14. The evidence of its use even by the most rigorous inerrantist is: (a) the consistently selective use of texts and their derivative doctrinal formulations; and (b) the tacit assumption that acceptable received versions of the Bible, while guarded by a grace of preservation, have come to us over the centuries through the instrumental cause of the Christian community, a convergence of divine and human similar to that of the process of canonization. Not to affirm this conjunction of grace and church would be to fall into an ecclesiastical docetism or monophysitism.

15. See Clark Pinnock's exposition of this in his American Theological Society paper, "How I Use Tradition in Doing Theology," *TSF Bulletin*, 6, No. 1 (September–October 1982), 2–5.

16. The reworking of terminology, as in the WCC Faith and Order rendering of tradition as the encompassing category in the sense of "the Gospel," and the Bible and post-biblical lore as deposits thereof, are intriguing, related as they are both to New Testament scholarship on the development of traditions and to ecumenical dialogue. We retain the older usage here to assure criteriological clarity: post-biblical tradition as always ministerial to the prophetic-apostolic testimony of canonical Scripture.

17. The same kind of question would be put by a secular historical relativism holding that access to it as such is denied by cultural contextualization.

18. Hans-Georg Gadamer, *Truth and Method* (New York: Seabury Press, 1975). For a penetrating exposition of Gadamer's thought and its relationship to other perspectives in New Testament hermeneutic and philosophical inquiry, see Anthony C. Thiselton, *The Two Horizons: New Testament Hermeneutics and Philosophical Description* (Grand Rapids: Eerdmans, 1980).

19. As developed by cultural historians F. Braudel and P. Chaunu.

20. Carl F. H. Henry underscores this regularly in his volumes on *God, Revelation and Authority* (Waco: Word, 1976–1979).

21. Current talk of the polyvalence of texts by exegetes making use of the new literary criticism and Jungian categories fails to take adequate account of the controls of intentionality. That the richness of textual meaning can be honored within the bounds set by the author's purpose is illustrated by David Steinmetz in a provocative essay on the continuing relevance of medieval exegesis (fourfold meaning: literal, allegorical, tropological, anagogical). See David C. Steinmetz, "The Superiority of Pre-critical Exegesis," *Theology Today*, 37, No. 1 (April 1980), 27–38.

22. See the discussion of the analogy of faith by R. C. Sproul in *Inerrancy and Common Sense*, ed. Roger R. Nicole and J. Ramsey Michaels (Grand Rapids: Baker Book House, 1980), pp. 119–136.

23. For both exposition and visualization see Gabriel Fackre, *The Christian Story* (Grand Rapids: Eerdmans, 1978), pp. 20–21.

24. In some quarters Langdon Gilkey's 1961 essay on the incoherence of the concept "acts of God" (in "Cosmology, Ontology, and the Travail of Biblical Language," *Journal of Religion*, 41 [1961], 194–205) is thought to have given the coup de grace to this theme. On closer inspection, Gilkey's argument shows itself to be a variation on the Ebionite refrain that has appeared in every doctrinal debate since the early christological controversies. The paradox of divine-human coterminality is found not only in the person of Christ but also in the doctrines of salvation, the church, the sacraments, etc., and is always challenged by reductionists of either a humanizing or divinizing stamp.

25. Attempts to change this have begun as in Paul Achtemeier's book, *The Inspiration of Scripture: Problems and Proposals* (Philadelphia: Westminster Press, 1980). From the evangelical side, see the effort of William Abraham to reconceptualize inspiration by blending an acts theology with divine speech themes, in *The Divine Inspiration of Holy Scripture* (Oxford: Oxford University Press, 1981).

26. Austin Farrer, *The Glass of Vision* (Westminster: Dacre Press, 1948),

pp. 38–56. On the unity of biblical language and thought, see also Bernhard W. Anderson, *The Living World of the Bible* (Philadelphia: Westminster Press, 1979).

27. John Bunyan, *The Pilgrim's Progress*, Harvard Classics, volume 15, ed. Charles W. Eliot (New York: P. F. Collier & Son, 1909), pp. 7–8.

28. The considerable interest in "narrative theology" is related both to the recovery of imagination and the recognition of the limits of discursive thought in matters of ultimate commitment and to the narrative structure of biblical faith itself as a plot with characters moving over time and space through conflict toward resolution. Storytelling theology comes in various forms, often overlapping.

(1) A literary-esthetic view of narrative influenced by such critics as Erich Auerbach and Northrop Frye and shaped significantly by the work of Amos Wilder and Stephen Crites. Biblical texts, especially the parables, are the focal point of inquiry with classic and contemporary literature providing reference points. Contributing significantly to the current discussion are Sallie McFague, Dominic Crossan, Dan Via, Robert Funk, Robert Roth, and Robert Detweiler.

(2) An interpretation of story in terms of personal formation and expression influenced in some cases by learning from psychology, frequently that of Carl Jung, in others by pedagogical issues, in others by social-ethical concerns, and in still others by some aspects of Karl Barth's theology. The story in psychological context finds expression in the work of such figures as James Hillman and Sam Keen, and in Catholic idiom in Thomas Cooper, John Navonne, and John Dunne. Its social-ethical dimensions are explored by Johannes Metz, James McClendon, Robert McAfee Brown, and Michael Goldberg. Thomas Groome has developed its catechetical possibilities and Richard Jensen its homiletical implications. George Stroup explores its meaning at the point of collision between personal and community stories. David Stuart has investigated its role in personal testimonies.

(3) A theological employment of narrative in which the macro-story of redemption is the focal point. Drawing on a tradition with roots in the biblical saga itself, expressed in the primitive kerygma and more systematically in the economic Trinity and the classical creeds, nineteenth- and twentieth-century "salvation history" perspectives lifted up the drama that stretched from creation to consummation with its critical historical trajectory running from exodus to Easter. Oscar Cullmann, G. Ernest Wright, and Bernhard Anderson are among its better known interpreters and Karl Barth is its profoundest twentieth-century expositor. Current narrative theologians who work with these categories in one way or another are Hans Frei, Ulrich Simon, Robert Roth, and Amos Wilder. For an exploration of these varying uses of

story and a case made for an encompassing reformulation of the third view, see "Narrative Theology: An Overview," in *Interpretation*, 37, No. 4 (Fall 1983), 340–352.

29. Wilbur Urban, *Language and Reality* (New York: Macmillan, 1939).

30. There is a distinction to be made between weighing biblical assertions as propositions in Webster's second sense and "propositionalism," a theory that goes beyond the biblical usage of them. Propositionalism as we construe it here does not take into account adequately:

(1) The analogical character of all biblical statements and doctrinal assertions as they touch upon transcendent reality. In reaction to subjectivism, legitimate as that reaction is, propositionalists insist upon the univocity of theological language. But this flies in the face of Scripture's own testimony to the nature of its seer's perceptions as "seen through a glass darkly." A venerable tradition of analogy which asserts uncompromisingly the truth of theological declarations acknowledges the finitude of our language: theological language is necessary but not sufficient access to the divine glory.

(2) The exfoliation possibilities inherent in biblical language and thus the developability of Christian doctrine is not sufficiently recognized by propositionalism. The assumption that specific doctrinal assertions are found laying on the surface of Scripture and are appropriable in unchangeable form in the work of theology does not take into account the catholic nature of revelation. If the truth claims of Christian faith are to be true for all times and places, then the inspired original language and ideas of the Bible must be subject to unfolding over these times and places, dealing with the issue and in the idiom of them. That process to which we shall give attention in a subsequent section does not overturn doctrinal perceptions grounded firmly in Scripture, but it does enlarge their scope in meaning. Doctrine develops. In our soteriological exposition there is an enrichment rather than an overturning of the received tradition.

(3) The word "proposition" does not adequately convey the character of biblical truth claims. Its association with formal logic ("a theorem or problem to be demonstrated or performed"—*Webster's* 1 c) conveys the meaning of discursive reasoning. But biblical assertions call for decisions and entail life and death commitments. Truth claims in Christian teaching therefore are best denominated *affirmations* not propositions. The claims cannot be made without the association of them with acts of engagement and the import of ultimacy. To say that Christ is the way, the truth, and the life is to make such an affirmation, an act eminently more than the setting forth of a proposition. An unambiguous truth claim is operative in my use of Scripture, one wit-

nessed to by the accent of proposition in current discussion of biblical authority, but better expressed in affirmational and analogical fashion.

31. See the treatment of these in essays by Kenneth Kantzer and John Gerstner in *The Evangelicals*, ed. David F. Wells and John D. Woodbridge (Nashville: Abingdon, 1975). Also consult George Marsden, *Fundamentalism and American Culture* (New York: Oxford University Press, 1980); and Ed Dobson and Ed Hinson in *The Fundamentalist Phenomenon*, ed. Jerry Falwell (Garden City: Doubleday, 1981).

32. Carl F. H. Henry, *God, Revelation and Authority*, volume 4, p. 465.

33. As we do not have the autographs and thus the total errorlessness which they guarantee, but only derivative copies for which no comparable claims can be made, the inerrantist argument against the infalliblist view proves to be logically flawed: the reliability of the biblical teaching of the inerrantist is also associated with a theoretically errant received text. If God can use a theoretically errant received text in the hands of the believing Christian to convey sound doctrine to the inerrantist, there is no warrant for denying the same claim made by the defenders of a soteric view of biblical authority.

34. That is the way the Bible functions in most Christian theology including, as we have noted, those who insist that scriptural authority extends to matters in the areas of the natural and social sciences.

35. "The speculative philosopher . . . proposes to contemplate Christianity from the philosophical standpoint. It is a matter of indifference to him whether anyone accepts it or not; such anxieties are left to theologues and laymen—and also surely to those who really are Christians, and who are by no means indifferent as to whether they are Christians or not. . . . Only the like is understood by the like . . . *quidquid cognoscitur, per modum cognoscentis cognoscitur.* . . ." Søren Kierkegaard, *Concluding Unscientific Postscript*, trans. David F. Swenson and Walter Lowrie (Princeton: Princeton University Press, 1941), p. 51.

36. With rough correspondence to the distinctions of thinking, doing, and feeling in Schleiermacher's, *The Christian Faith* (New York: Harper and Row, 1963) and to the classical categories of truth, goodness, and beauty.

37. On the law of non-contradiction see Henry, *God, Revelation and Authority*, volume 4, pp. 49, 59, 114, 227; and E. L. Mascall in his defense of the "Intellectual Principle," in *Whatever Happened to the Human Mind?* (London: SPCK, 1980), pp. 1–27.

38. Tillich's "method of correlation" expresses this formally, but other agenda take over his execution of the method. The formulations of "the question" of the modern era is influenced to such a degree by his philosophical presuppositions that significant features of the classical "Christian answer" disappear from view.

39. As in Affirmation 1 of the 1982 Declaration of the International Council on Biblical Inerrancy. See Tom Minnery, "What the Bible Means," *Christianity Today*, 26, No. 20 (December 17, 1982), 45–47.

40. A commitment traceable to Kierkegaard's defense of "subjectivity" in his critique of Hegelian speculation, on the one hand, and "the Christian crowd," on the other. See *Concluding Unscientific Postscript*, pp. 115–224.

41. Edward Schillebeeckx's *Jesus* (New York: Seabury Press, 1978) and *Christ* (New York: Sheed and Ward, 1963); and Hans Küng's *On Being a Christian* (Garden City, NY: Doubleday, 1976).

42. For a monumental effort to make this category change and attempt to argue its consonance with traditional understandings of apostolic authority see Schillebeeckx's *Jesus, passim*, and the critique of same in the writer's study, "Bones Strong and Weak in the Skeletal Structure of Schillebeeckx's Christology," *Journal of Ecumenical Studies* 21, No. 2 (Spring 1984), 248–277.

43. As suggested by Robert Johnson's discussion of the same in *Authority in Protestant Theology* (Philadelphia: Westminster Press, 1959), pp. 15ff.

44. The commitment to catholicity in the use of Scripture is kindred in spirit to Avery Dulles' effort to honor the truth in various conceptions of revelation in his important work, *Models of Revelation* (Garden City, NY: Doubleday, 1983), although different in focus (Scripture in one, revelation in the other), in the status accorded the Roman Catholic magisterium, and in questions the writer would raise about using the symbolic model as the organizing principle for restatement. Again, while I do not employ here David Kelsey's specific distinctions of how Scripture is used in contemporary theology and am unpersuaded by his functionalist proposals, many of the positions he examines appear in the foregoing discussion. The normative work here goes beyond Kelsey's project by drawing on elements from one or another usage, identifying the respective roles they play, and seeking to integrate them. See David H. Kelsey, *The Uses of Scripture in Recent Theology* (Philadelphia: Fortress Press, 1975).

Notes on Contributors

Donald G. Bloesch

Bloesch is professor of theology at Dubuque Theological Seminary, Dubuque, Iowa, and a past president of the American Theological Society, Midwest Division. A minister in the United Church of Christ, he received his Ph. D. from the University of Chicago. Among his most significant publications are:

Crumbling Foundations, Zondervan, 1984.
The Future of Evangelical Christianity, Doubleday, 1983.
The Struggle of Prayer, Harper & Row, 1980.
Essentials of Evangelical Theology, 2 vols., Harper & Row, 1978–1979.
Jesus Is Victor!, Abingdon, 1976.
The Ground of Certainty, Eerdmans, 1971.
The Reform of the Church, Eerdmans, 1970.

Donald W. Dayton

Dayton is associate professor of historical theology at Northern Baptist Theological Seminary in Lombard, Illinois, and chairman of the steering committee of the evangelical theology section of the American Academy of Religion. A layman in the Wesleyan Church of America, he received his Ph.D. from the University of Chicago. Among his writings are:

Theological Roots of Pentecostalism, Scarecrow Press, 1984.
(editor) "The Higher Christian Life: Sources for the Study of the Holiness, Pentecostal and Keswick Movements, 1830–1920," a forty-eight volume reprint series, Garland Publishing Co., 1984.
Discovering an Evangelical Heritage, Harper & Row, 1976; 2nd ed. with new epilogue, 1985.
(editor) Charles Grandison Finney, *Reflections on Revivals*, Bethany Fellowship, 1979.
(editor) *Contemporary Perspectives on Pietism*, Covenant Press, 1976.
(editor and with an introduction) *Five Sermons and a Tract by Luther Lee*, Holrad House, 1975.

William A. Dyrness

Dyrness is president and professor of theology at New College for Advanced Christian Studies, Berkeley, California. A layman in the Presbyterian Church, he completed his D. Theol. at the University of Strasbourg. Among his writings are the following:

Christian Apologetics in a World Community, InterVarsity Press, 1983.
Let the Earth Rejoice: A Biblical Theology of Holistic Mission, Crossway, 1983.
Christian Art in Asia, Rodop (Amsterdam), 1979, (distributed by Humanities Press).
Themes in Old Testament Theology, InterVarsity Press, 1979.
Daniel in the Television Den: A Christian Approach to American Culture, Western Baptist Press, 1975.
Rouault: A Vision of Suffering and Salvation, Eerdmans, 1971.

Gabriel Fackre

Fackre is Abbot Professor of Christian Theology at Andover-Newton Theological School, Newton Centre, Massachusetts. An ordained member of the United Church of Christ, he completed his Ph. D. at the University of Chicago. Among his selected publications are:

The Christian Story: A Narrative Interpretation of Basic Christian Doctrine, Eerdmans, 1978, revised and enlarged edition, 1984.

The Religious Right and Christian Faith, Eerdmans, 1982, 1983.
Word in Deed: Theological Themes in Evangelism, Eerdmans, 1975.
Do and Tell: Engagement Evangelism in the '70s, Eerdmans, 1973.
Liberation in Middle America, Pilgrim, 1971.
The Promise of Reinhold Niebuhr, Lippincott, 1970.
Humiliation and Celebration, Sheed and Ward, 1969.

Robert K. Johnston

Johnston is dean and associate professor of theology and culture at North Park Theological Seminary, Chicago, Illinois. An ordained minister in the Evangelical Covenant Church, he received his Ph. D. from Duke University. Among his writings are:

The Christian at Play, Eerdmans, 1983.
Psalms for God's People, Regal, 1982.
Evangelicals at an Impasse: Biblical Authority in Practice, John Knox
    Press, 1979.

James I. Packer

Packer is professor of systematic and historical theology at Regent College, Vancouver, Canada. An Anglican clergyman, he received his D. Phil. from Oxford University. Among his publications are:

Keep in Step with the Spirit, Revell, 1984.
God's Words: Studies of Key Bible Themes, InterVarsity Press, 1981.
Beyond the Battle for the Bible, Cornerstone Books, 1980.
Knowing Man, Cornerstone, 1979.
I Want to Be a Christian, Tyndale House, 1977.
Knowing God, InterVarsity Press, 1973.
Evangelism and the Sovereignty of God, InterVarsity Press, 1961.
"Fundamentalism" and the Word of God: Some Evangelical Principles,
    Eerdmans, 1958.

Clark H. Pinnock

Pinnock is professor of theology at McMaster Divinity College, Hamilton, Ontario, Canada. A clergyman in the Baptist Convention of Ontario and Quebec, he received his Ph. D. from the University of Manchester. Among his publications are:

The Scripture Principle, Harper & Row, 1984.
Reason Enough: A Case for the Christian Faith, InterVarsity Press, 1980.
(editor) *Grace Unlimited,* Bethany Fellowship, 1975.
Truth on Fire, The Message of Galatians, Baker Book House, 1972.
Biblical Revelation, Moody Press, 1971.
Set Forth Your Case, Craig, 1968.
A Defense of Biblical Infallibility, Presbyterian and Reformed, 1967.

Russell P. Spittler

Spittler is associate dean for academic systems, the school of theology, and associate professor of New Testament at Fuller Theological Seminary, Pasadena, California. An ordained minister in the Assemblies of God, he received his Ph.D. from Harvard University. He has written, among other things:

The Church, Gospel Publishing House, 1977.
The Corinthian Correspondence, Gospel Publishing House, 1976.
God the Father, Gospel Publishing House, 1976.
(editor) *Perspectives on the New Pentecostalism,* Baker Book House, 1976.
Cults and Isms: Twenty Alternates to Evangelical Christianity, Baker Book House, 1962.

Robert E. Webber

Webber is professor of theology at Wheaton College, Wheaton, Illinois, and was chairman of the Chicago Call which met in 1977. A layman in the Episcopal Church, he received his Th. D. from Concordia Theological Seminary. Among his published works are:

Evangelicals on the Canterbury Trail, 1985.
Worship Is a Verb, 1985.
Secular Humanism: Threat and Challenge, Zondervan, 1982.
Worship Old and New, Zondervan, 1982.
The Moral Majority: Right or Wrong?, Crossway, 1981.
The Secular Saint, Zondervan, 1979.
Common Roots, Zondervan, 1978.

David F. Wells

Wells is professor of historical and systematic theology at Gordon-Conwell Theological Seminary, South Hamilton, Massachusetts. An ordained Congregational minister, he received his Ph. D. from the University of Manchester. Among his publications are:

The Person of Christ: A Biblical and Historical Analysis of the Incarnation, Marshall Theological Library: Marshall, Morgan and Scott; Crossway, 1984.

(co-editor and part author with Mark Noll, Nathan Hatch, George Marsden, and John Woodbridge) *Eerdmans Handbook to Christianity in America*, Eerdmans, 1983.

The Prophetic Theology of George Tyrrell, American Academy of Religion Studies in Religion, vol. 22, Scholars Press, 1981.

The Search for Salvation, InterVarsity Press, 1978.

(co-editor with Clark Pinnock) *Toward a Theology for the Future*, Creation House, 1977.

(co-editor with John D. Woodbridge) *The Evangelicals: What They Believe, Who They Are, Where They Are Changing*, Abingdon, 1975.

Revolution in Rome, InterVarsity Press, 1972.

John Howard Yoder

Yoder is professor of theology at the University of Notre Dame and, formerly, at the Associated Mennonite Biblical Seminaries. A graduate of the University of Basel (D. Theol.), he has served the Mennonite denomination in both mission administration and overseas relief, as well as at Goshen Biblical Seminary, where he was professor from 1965 to 1984 and president from 1970 to 1973. His publications include:

When War Is Unjust, Augsburg, 1984.
What Would You Do . . . ?, Herald, 1983.
The Legacy of Michael Sattler, Herald, 1973.
The Original Revolution, Herald, 1972.
The Politics of Jesus, Eerdmans, 1972.
Karl Barth and the Problem of War, Abingdon, 1970.

Index of Names

Sandeen, Ernest, 134
Schillebeeckx, Edward, 221
Schleiermacher, Friedrich, 23, 80
Schuller, Robert, 2
Schweitzer, Albert, 80
Semler, J. S., 80
Shedd, W. G. T., 57
Sider, Ronald, 204
Smart, Ninian, 1
Spittler, Russell, ix, 4, 5, 12, 15, 56–77
Stendahl, Krister, 64, 65, 80, 176
Strauss, David Friedrich, 80
Stravinsky, Igor, ix
Strong, A. H., 57
Strugnell, John, 64

Tertullian, 146, 155, 184
Thielicke, Helmut, 14, 15
Thornton, L. S., 2
Tillich, Paul, 2, 82, 158
Torrey, R. A., 57
Tracy, David, 115
Troeltsch, Ernst, 80

Urban, Wilbur, 215

Van Til, Cornelius, 115
Vincent of Lérins, 159
Vischer, Wilhelm, 81, 84, 88
von Rad, Gerhard, 81

Wacker, Grant, 21, 63
Wainwright, Geoffrey, xiii, 7, 8
Warfield, B. B., 2, 21, 74, 79, 131, 203, 224
Watson, Philip, 126
Webber, Robert, ix, 4, 5, 9, 137–158
Welch, Claude, 15
Wells, David, ix, 4, 5, 6, 7, 12, 15, 175–199
Wesley, John, 9, 15, 28, 119, 121, 126, 127, 128, 129, 130, 131, 132, 135, 136, 151, 152
Williams, Colin W., 135
Wright, George E., 2
Wycliffe, John, 119

Yankelovich, Daniel, 193
Yoder, John Howard, viii, ix, 3, 4, 5, 103–120

Zimmerman, Thomas F., 59